FIND OUT WHO YOU ARE WITHOUT PORN

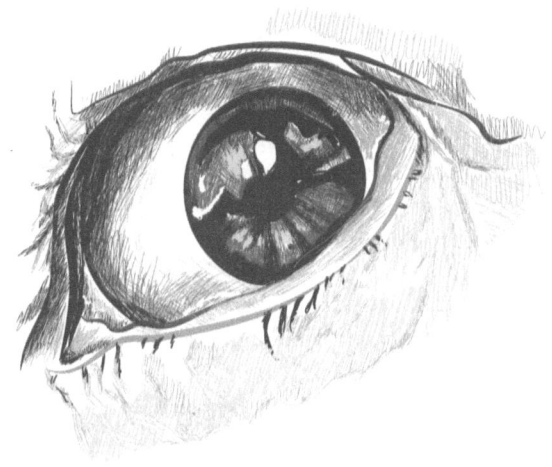

WAEL IBRAHIM

First published by Ultimate World Publishing 2020
Copyright © 2020 Wael Ibrahim

ISBN

Paperback - 978-1-922372-46-8
Ebook - 978-1-922372-47-5

Wael Ibrahim has asserted his right under the Copyright, Designs and Patents Act 1988 to be identified as the author of this work. The information in this book is based on the author's experiences and opinions. The publisher specifically disclaims responsibility for any adverse consequences, which may result from use of the information contained herein. Permission to use information has been sought by the author. Any breaches will be rectified in further editions of the book.

All rights reserved. No part of this publication may be reproduced, stored in or introduced into a retrieval system, or transmitted in any form, or by any means (electronic, mechanical, photocopying, recording or otherwise) without the prior written permission of the author. Any person who does any unauthorised act in relation to this publication may be liable to criminal prosecution and civil claims for damages. Enquiries should be made through the publisher.

Illustration: Jasmine Ghanem
Cover design: Ebony Harper
Layout and typesetting: Ultimate World Publishing
Editor: Marinda Wilkinson

Ultimate World Publishing
Diamond Creek,
Victoria Australia 3089
www.writeabook.com.au

Testimonials

Our world is inundated with porn, yet few people know the impact it is having on individuals, relationships and society. Wael Ibrahim explores the myriad problems that can develop from porn use, then provides practical advice for both recovery and prevention. Full of the latest science, professional experience and personal stories, *AWARE* will leave all who read it informed, equipped and ready to *find out who they are without porn.*

Gabe Deem
Founder of Reboot Nation
Ex-porn addict

Globally, regardless of belief, race or gender, pornography has gripped and upended consumers' thoughts, attitudes, behaviors, safety, sanity, and relationships. Everyone knows someone with a story about how porn has negatively impacted their life—children, teens, young adults, singles, marrieds—our communities everywhere. Slowly, the world is waking up to these harms, looking for help, and banding together to find common connections with others who have similar battle scars. Never before has the need been so great for a book such as this. Wael Ibrahim clearly lays out the problems AND the solutions—Find Out Who You Are Without Porn is an invaluable tool for anyone seeking answers.

Liz Walker, educator, speaker, author, and advocate
Author of Hamish and the Shadow Secret

Wael has written yet another highly informative and beneficial book which breaks down the deep impact and solutions associated with pornography use and addiction in the modern world. With the latest research, real case studies and helpful strategies to navigate and overcome the challenges and harms associated with pornography, this book is a must-have for any individual who owns a smart device or lives in a home with others who do.

This book will serve as a great resource for any parent, educator, spouse, youth worker, counsellor, health worker, or any morally concerned individual. Pornography addiction is truly the impending health catastrophe of the next decade and needs to be tackled head-on and with a proactive approach using resources such as this outstanding book.

Calisha Bennett
Founder of Developing Diamonds

I've always been conscious of what I consume: my food and drink, what I watch and listen to. So, when I inadvertently discovered his porn collection and addiction, I started to listen more closely to his behaviour. Pornography changed him physically, emotionally, and spiritually. As husband and wife, we stopped sharing the same level of accountability

Testimonials

and expectation. Our marriage died a slow, painful, and silent death.

This book unearths the horrors of pornography. It presents a difficult, but necessary read. It inspires healthy dialogue and supports informed decision-making. Addiction disables discernment.

This work offers the addict, enabler, and victim awareness, answers, and hope.

Single mother, South Africa

Wael Ibrahim has brought all the necessary facts about the harms of pornography in this new book; facts that I myself can relate to as a victim of my husband's addiction to porn. I have seen my beloved spouse depending on porn so badly for the sake of temporary pleasure. And as a result, our relationship has come to an end.

I strongly recommend this book to everyone, whether you are an addict yourself, or victim like me or just wanted to educate yourself about the harms of porn and its consequences.

Anonymous

I didn't realize back then what were the consequences of pornography. I have gotten myself into this addiction since I was just thirteen years of age. Some friends who used to shamelessly watch porn had introduced me to it. For them, this was a sign of our manhood. I came from a conservative family, yet still I have fallen into this trap. This massive addiction to porn and masturbation has led to the deterioration of my health, including the weakness of eyesight. It created a massive negative impact on my memory and the level of my concentration and focus.

I believe this book has every answer and all the necessary information you need to know about the harms of pornography and its negative consequences. At the same time, it gives hope to those who want to lead a healthy life.

Dr. Habibullah Habib

This book will truly make you aware of the true color of pornography. As I was reading, I felt that the author knew what had taken place in my life back in the days when I was hooked on porn.

Three chapters in particular resonated with me a lot, namely Chapter 1 (Children without porn), Chapter 11 (Real women without porn), and the last chapter (Faith without porn). I got into pornography at the age of thirteen, even though I grew up in a religious family, I was not spared. A friend of mine passed on to me a CD full of porn, which belonged to her parents. And that was it, since then I would watch pornography whenever I could get the chance to access it. And ever since, my life has become miserable because of pornography. The heavy feelings of shame, anxiety, depression, and a doubled-faced lifestyle were unbearable.

Aware: Find out who you are without porn, undoubtedly will bring about real awareness about the harmful effects of this

Testimonials

dangerous and addictive behavior. It will truly make you understand, that what you used to look at as simple, harmless, and innocent is in fact dangerous, serious, and destructive on all levels.

Single girl, Anonymous

As a successful ex-porn addict of one-and-a-half years so far, I can heavily vouch for the methods endorsed by Wael. I don't vouch only in words to the great cause, but vouch with complete faith as I have personally used the steps recommended here, and can personally say they are the most effective strategies I have found to date.

Porn had affected me directly in so many ways that I had not known of until they were stated to me in Wael's previous book Beat It: 50 plus shades of hope. I realized porn had killed my productivity in my studies and work, had reduced my motivation to achieve my goals and daily targets, led me to a lazy lifestyle and removed my ability to concentrate in my studies. It had also made me into an animal in my thoughts, perceiving the other gender only as a piece of flesh and a form of pleasure. I can also vouch for the numerous benefits of stopping pornography, from the change in my behavior when interacting with women and more natural relationships when communicating with the opposite gender without the sexualized thoughts in the back of my mind. Surprisingly, I also had many more hours in the week to myself instead of to porn and the onset of laziness that porn brings.

Young man, Anonymous

I've been into this cycle of addiction since I was thirteen years old. I found almost all the negative consequences stated by Wael Ibrahim in this book to be absolutely true.

There are two consequences in particular that I found to be relevant to me personally. The first is the weakening of memory and concentration. I used to be an intelligent student with very good memory, but since I got into porn to the point of addiction, I can barely pass any exams now and have a very difficult time remembering what I had memorized.

The other negative consequence that porn had caused me to do is objectification of women. After becoming addicted to porn, I started to compare porn stars with the women that I met everyday, including my family members. I started looking at women's bodies and pointing out faults if they do not resemble the porn stars who became my world of fantasy.

Anonymous

Short testimony from an ex-porn addict, quoted as received

The guilty feeling has always been in the back of my head, each time I watch porn and masturbate, after the climax, I feel like my world is crumbling down. It took me half my life to finally step up and speak to someone about it. I started watching way before I got married, I said to myself once I get engaged I'll stop. It didn't work. Once I get married I'll stop, it didn't work. Once I get a kid I'll stop, still didn't work. I got my second kid and realized when am I going to stop this disgusting habit and snap out of it. I finally met a trustworthy mentor, I became his best friend and after a couple of months I built up the courage to tell him. He straightaway said that he can't help me because I may not take him seriously, then he gave me this number and I gave him a call. I spoke to Wael that night and made a booking for his recovery program. As soon as I spoke to him, I made a promise that I'm going to do my best to stop watching porn. The appointment came and I told him my life story and how it all started until the very end. He was very positive, the first thing he said to me was, *"YOU ARE A GOOD GENUINE PERSON BUT PORNOGRAPHY IS WRAPPED AROUND YOUR HEART"* and that was all he needed to say to me for me to push through the next three months. He gave me some homework to do. I did it and I was like wow so easy and simple I'm ready to conquer the world. Three weeks later I fell and I fell down hard but I wasn't willing to give up without a fight. I used to sit on the couch every Friday afternoon and just daze out for an hour, asking myself should I, or shouldn't I watch porn? Until I force myself to get up and go do something useful. Another three weeks passed and it was the worst three weeks of my life, I went through some hard times when I was alone, battling my inner thoughts and my brain pushing me to do stuff to trigger my addiction and it was driving me crazy. I messaged Wael a couple of times saying I can't take this anymore and he hit me with another line *"It's only going to get worse but you are a good person, don't let it ruin your life, hang in there and I want you to be an example for others to get inspired."* He made me believe in myself. He gave me some more homework to do. It's been eight weeks now and I have just started to get over it, and my thoughts are

Aware

calming down and slowly my life is getting back on track. Don't get me wrong; I've relapsed twice in two months but without watching porn. But hey I can say I've come a long way through Wael's book and his homework.

Anonymous

Dedication

For the entire Aware team all over the world.

Contents

Testimonials	iii
Dedication	xi
About The Author	1
Introduction	3
CHAPTER 1: Children Without Porn	7
CHAPTER 2: Teens Without Porn	23
CHAPTER 3: Relationships Without Porn	35
CHAPTER 4: Sex Without Porn	49
CHAPTER 5: Health Without Porn	61
CHAPTER 6: Productivity Without Porn	71
CHAPTER 7: Career Without Porn	81
CHAPTER 8: Mental Health Without Porn	91
CHAPTER 9: Your Brain Without Porn	103
CHAPTER 10: Real Men Without Porn	115
CHAPTER 11: Women Without Porn	127
CHAPTER 12: Faith Without Porn	139
Final Word	153
References	155
Notes	215

About The Author

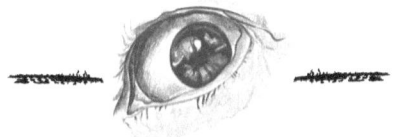

Wael Ibrahim is a certified business and life coach, international speaker, trainer and teacher. He is the author of two previous books on the harmful impacts of pornography, **Change** and **Beat It: 50 plus shades of hope**. His motivational book, **Better Me: 365 ways to transform your everyday life** is also delivered as a training program and workshop to participants in locations all over the world, including the Philippines, Hong Kong, Malaysia, Nigeria, South Africa, Pakistan and Australia.

As a professional trainer, Wael helps people improve and develop in many areas of their life including public speaking, communication, mentoring, leadership, self-development, and life coaching.

While working in Hong Kong City, he was awarded a merit degree in public speaking skills and presentations. Over the past fifteen years, he has delivered hundreds of lectures, workshops, courses, keynote speeches, and training sessions to audiences around the globe.

As well as writing books and presenting workshops, Wael is currently the student counselor at the Australian Islamic College in Western Australia.

Introduction

Just as a professional con artist or coward assassin would "innocently" walk slowly through the crowds, with calm steps and a "peaceful" pace before swiftly and unexpectedly stabbing you from behind, so too does pornography. It may appear as innocent, fun, sexy, artistic, or harmless—yet, just like an assassin, it has the potential to stab you in various areas of your life and literally finish you off.

Talking about the harmful effects of pornography has led me to a lot of funny (formerly embarrassing) situations. The most common question I receive during my seminars, workshop training, and courses is: *"Were you addicted to pornography?"* The answer is no, I am currently not addicted to porn, but yes I was involved in watching this filth early in the 90s. So, you *may* say I was addicted, but not as badly as those who are affected by today's porn. The reason for this is obvious—back in those days, Internet pornography was limited to a few static pictures that will ultimately lead you to the credit card payment page (pay if you wish to see more). And of course, since we were young and broke, paying for anything of that nature was off the table. However, those pictures would cause me to stay up until dawn, until I reached the most irritating moment in the life of any porn addict: the temporary pleasure of orgasm.

You may ask, why orgasm is the most irritating moment in the life of an addict? Isn't that the main reason why they watch porn? Interestingly, NO. Because orgasm hits the person with reality that the life of fantasy that pornography has created is destructive and harmful. That's why their peak of pleasure is not obtained through orgasm. Instead, it comes from the hours spent online searching for the perfect sexual scene, which usually creates the rush of the addictive hormones in their brains.

I have written two books on the subject before. ***Change: A motivational book to break-free from undesirable habits*** (especially pornography), is a 30-day plan on how to give up this compelling addiction and live a free life. Though the book includes some spiritual references, it is suitable for those without faith as well. I then wrote ***Beat It: 50 plus shades of hope***, a step-by-step recovery book for those who are being tortured by pornography in silence and cannot afford to seek help from a personal mentor or professional counselor. Written in a conversational style, it shares the story of an addict as I walk him through the journey of recovery. Finally, this book that you are holding in your hand, ***Aware: Find out who you are without porn***, has been written to open everyone's eyes to the facts about pornography. It shows you the reality of where porn can take you and highlights the many benefits of a life without porn.

This book is simply an invitation for you to learn from the experts, who have conducted countless hours of research to uncover the destructive path of pornography. Take the knowledge seriously and

Introduction

raise awareness about its harms in your circles. Talk to your kids, neighbors, students, spouses, and friends. And if you, yourself have an issue with pornography, then you should immediately seek some professional help.

At the end of this book, you will find an extensive list of references to further your knowledge, as well as my contact details for anyone who wishes to join our recovery programs and retreats. But for now, let us begin the journey of awareness about how pornography can (and does) destroy you—and how you can free yourself and those you love from its harm.

CHAPTER 1

Children Without Porn

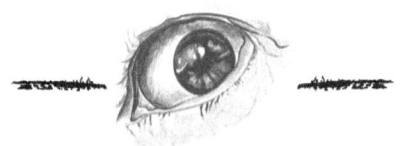

Aware

It was 2:30 a.m. when Sarah, five years old back then, woke up screaming because of a terrifying dream. As she rushed to her parents' room to seek comfort and rest, she was expecting her mom to meet her halfway to check on her and see what was wrong. However, her mom was not in the hallway as expected. Instead, Sarah heard her moaning and "screaming" oddly behind her bedroom door. She pushed the door open, wanting to run into her mom's arms and sleep the rest of the night peacefully. Shockingly, she saw her parents in a position, which later became known to her as sex. Across from her parents' bed, a TV was showing what appeared to little Sarah as a fight between two naked people. There was a violent scene of pornography being played while her parents were having sex. Sarah just had her first encounter with pornography at the tender age of five.

As she sat with me, collecting her breath and sharing her memories, Sarah remembered, *"It was something that shook me so suddenly, I just froze. After being dumbfounded for a few seconds, I then didn't care much about my bad dream. A different nightmare confronted me. It was a nightmare that was too hard for me to bear as a little girl, and it has remained engraved in my memory for as long as I can remember."*

Sipping water during our conversation and repeatedly grabbing tissues to wipe off her tears, Sarah recalled yet another horrifying incident which she had described as the day that snatched her entire childhood away.

She was a few years older by then, and it was summer, which she used to love the most. (Later on, summertime became her least favorite season as a result of this incident.) *"Every summer,"* Sarah proceeded, *"My parents and a few uncles within the family would book for us a huge villa in one of the major North Coast sites where we used to live. All our aunties, cousins and some friends would also join the 10-day annual holiday."*

"These holidays were always fun and happy until one night. It was the night when I lost all respect for one of my uncles and all men in general. It was also the night I became hyperconscious of my body and other people's private areas, especially men's."

"It was just before sunset; we were tired and napping after a long day on the beach. I noticed my mother and a few aunties were getting up to prepare food for dinner. I got up too, excited to eat something delicious as always. All my cousins, who were about the same age as I was, were still asleep. I went to wash up in a private bathroom and it was there that I received the shock of my life. One of my uncles was sitting on the toilet bowl pant-less, reclining with his legs spread apart. He was masturbating. In one of his hands, he was holding what appeared to be a magazine. Again, I didn't know what masturbation was or what exactly my uncle had been doing in there. But I knew instantly that something was wrong as he jumped up so quickly when he saw me and screamed at me to leave."

Her uncle then scolded Sarah for not knocking on the door. *(Although I am unsure why he did not lock the door in the first place.)* He then left the room and went downstairs. But it was not over. Sarah entered the bathroom a few minutes later, *"Perhaps to hide or to wash my face and try to erase the image from my memory. I was standing there wondering. I glanced at the spot where he was sitting. On the floor, next to the toilet bowl, was the magazine he was reading. The colors, the images, and the bodies in the magazine captivated me. I didn't even know why the image of my mom and dad having sex came into my mind, the moaning and the facial expression of my uncle when I caught him jerking off in the toilet. I knew promptly that I wanted to experience the same. I kept browsing the magazine to store as many images as possible into my brain before someone else come in or before my uncle remembered that he had forgotten the porn magazine in the toilet. I was shivering and sweating. My heart was racing. My knees were about to give. I ran back out and fantasized about all those images."*

Sarah is now twenty-nine years of age and addicted to pornography and sex. She abuses drugs occasionally. We had a long initial conversation and several follow-up sessions. She explained how these two incidents had a great negative impact on her entire childhood and life in general. She said, *"When I spotted my parents having sex that night, I knew that I wasn't supposed to see what I had seen. I left quietly because I was worried they might reprimand or ground me. Although my mom looked at me while having sex, she ignored my presence completely. As a result, I left their door open and rushed back to my room and buried myself under the blanket. However, with seeing my uncle masturbating then looking at a pornographic magazine, the case was different. I was about eight or nine. Though I found it hard looking at the images at first, I couldn't resist the excitement and the energetic rush I felt whenever I thought about it, even after a few weeks had gone by. The need to stare at these images became urgent, necessary, and compulsive."*

Sarah grew up overly curious about sexual intimacy without understanding what it was. All she knew was that it was something secret that she wasn't supposed to look at. The opposing emotional pulls of guilt and excitement were enough for Sarah to become an addict for many years of her life.

What the Research Tells Us

Statistics from the nonprofit organization the Center for Parent/Youth Understanding show that Sarah's story is not an isolated case. According to their research, many young people are exposed to pornography before they reach the age of eighteen, with the average age of exposure being just eleven. The researchers noted that the levels of early exposure are much higher for boys (93%) compared to girls (62%).

The organization also found that early exposure often leads to children seeking out pornography for themselves. Of the boys who saw pornography as a child, 70% reported having spent a full thirty minutes or more searching for online pornography at least once afterwards, while 35% had done so on at least ten occasions. For girls, again the number was lower, with almost a quarter saying they had spent a full thirty minutes searching for porn at least once, and 14% reporting they had done so more often.

Early exposure to pornography has also been linked to an increased desire in young children to copy the sexual acts they have seen. In the UK in 2016, the National Society for the Prevention of Cruelty to Children (NSPCC) asked 1,000 children, aged 11–16 about their exposure to porn, and the majority (94%) said they had seen online porn by the age of fourteen. Of the children who had seen porn, 28% saw it by accident, 19% searched for it alone, 19% saw it with friends, 19% were shown it by someone else, and 15% accessed it from another source. Significantly, while at least 75% of the surveyed children said that porn did not help them understand consent, 39% of those aged 13–14, and 21% of those aged 11–12, expressed a desire to copy the porn acts.

In 2018, the NSPCC undertook another survey, this time of 40,000 children aged 7–16 as part of their Wild West Web campaign to protect children from online sexual abuse. The responses revealed that one child in every primary school class has been shown a naked or semi-naked picture on the Internet by an adult, and that one in fifty schoolchildren had sent a nude or semi-nude photo to an adult.

It is important to recognize that children are exposed to pornography from a huge range of sources online. Net Aware, a UK-based organization dedicated to providing parents with information about the apps and websites their kids are using, conducted a survey of 1,725 UK schoolchildren in 2016 to find out about their online habits and exposure to Internet porn. They discovered that 78% of the children admitted to joining social media sites before they reached the specified minimum age and half of the surveyed children reported they had seen adult material on games, apps, and social media.

It is also becoming clear that a surprisingly high number of young children are gaining access to online porn sites. In 2016, cybersecurity and antivirus software company BitDefender conducted research to discover how many children visited porn sites, and they found that around 10% of total porn video site visitors are children. Additionally, of the total visitors aged below eighteen years, 22% of them are under ten years old. While these websites do ask visitors to confirm they are at least eighteen years old before they enter, they lack the capability to check the real age of their users.

How Porn Impacts Children

When children are exposed to sexually explicit materials before they have the maturity to understand consent and consequences it can lead them to make poor and sometimes dangerous choices. As a parent, it is important to be aware that it's not just porn sites or magazines that are a source of exposure – movies, music and social media can also include explicit images and messaging. Below are some of the common negative impacts observed in children who are exposed.

Early Sex
The media frequently provides sex education to minors, however, the lessons tend to be casual and consequence-free. Images that are readily available show unprotected sex, normalized early sexual intercourse, and encouragement of sexual activity, even though children are not yet intellectually, socially, or emotionally ready to understand it.

According to a 2012 study published in *Psychological Science*, movies play a critical role in the sexual behaviors and attitudes of teenagers. It found that teenagers who watched sexual content in movies started having sex earlier in their lives and were also prone to have unprotected and casual sex. Boys who watched sexually explicit media were three times more likely to engage in sexual intercourse and oral sex within two years of first exposure, while young girls are twice as likely to engage in oral sex and one-and-a-half times as likely to engage in intercourse. In addition, a 2009 study published in the *American Journal of Preventative Medicine* found that music laced with degrading sexual references can have the same effect. This is why I am outspoken about irresponsible media who distribute their content without considering the impact it is having on young viewers.

High-Risk Sex
Research tells us that a child exposed to sexual content at an early age is more likely to engage in high-risk behaviors, such as multiple sexual relationships, alcohol or drug use prior to sex, having intercourse frequently, and engaging in unprotected and undesirable sexual activities.

In a study conducted by Dr. Jennings Bryant, at least 66% of boys and 40% of girls who participated said they wanted to engage in sexual behaviors after watching them in the media. This yearning at a young age increases the potential for high-risk sex, which can lead to unwanted pregnancies and sexually transmitted diseases.

Sexual Violence
It is believed that exposure to pornographic and other explicit material before the age of fourteen increases the risk of the child to act out or be a victim of sexual violence. Habitual use of pornographic materials can generate a desire for deviant or violate materials that include depictions of humiliation, torture, or rape.

According to forensic paediatrician doctor Sharon Cooper from the University of North Carolina School of Medicine, unhealthy sexual imagery affects children because it normalises sexual harm by violence and rape, unprotected sexual contact, and a lack of emotional relationship among consensual partners. This is important, because a large part of a child's development and learning happens through the process of observation and imitation of behaviors. The brain's mirror neurons convince them that they are experiencing what they see, so the high degree of sexual explicitness and aggression of porn has a real and damaging effect on children.

Negative Impact on Mental Health
Excessive use of porn, especially if the content is sexually explicit, gender-stereotyped, or violent, can skew the child's worldview and change their capacity to sustain successful human relationships. A child exposed to pornography can experience anxiety, disgust, embarrassment, fear, shock, anger, and sadness after viewing it. He may become depressed, anxious, and be obsessed with acting the sexual acts of adults out. The resulting behavior may also

disturb and disrupt his peers who become victims or witness to his actions.

Pornography Addiction
Research by ChildLine (part of the NSPCC) uncovered that 10% of children aged between twelve and thirteen are worried they may have porn addiction. According to experts, desensitization and mobile accessibility at an early age can be the cause of porn addiction. When online, children can unintentionally stumble across porn, and this has an upsetting and damaging effect on them.

Separation of Sexuality from Love
Pornography tends to separate sexuality from love, but sex should be the consummation of a loving relationship. For boys, porn offers a message that sex is mechanical sans feeling and is an obligation to perform. For girls, pornography creates feelings of anxiety, depression, and suicidal thoughts because they feel depreciated. These girls create a feeling of total disenchantment between sexual practices and loving feelings.

Pornography can interfere with relationships as the child grows, because it breaks the connection between desire, sex, and feelings. Constant exposure to porn makes it difficult for their future selves as adults to build loving relationships, because they assimilate sexuality as an act of alienation and violence. Porn is hostile and sexist to women and teaches children that it is socially desirable and acceptable to demean and behave aggressively towards women. Moreover, it promotes the inaccurate portrayal of sexual relationships and people. These unrealistic expectations among intimate partners may hamper the ability of children to create and maintain healthy relationships.

Negative Attitudes Towards Women
Violent and sexual content teaches children to emulate, accept, and learn from behaviors promoted by the media as attractive, normative, and without risk. A large amount of porn materials shows violence against women and follow the usual script that focuses on the sexual prowess and desires of men. A survey conducted on middle and high school youths between 2001–2004 showed the impact this can have, as 76% of the boys surveyed who used sexually explicit media had also committed some type of sexual harassment.

A 2010 study that analysed fifty famous porn films, illustrated just how much verbal and physical aggression porn contains. All of the fifty films had high levels of verbal and physical aggression and 90% of the porn scenes included an aggressive act. In the films, men committed the majority of the aggression and almost all of it was directed towards women.

How You Can Help Your Children Avoid Porn

Porn is extremely damaging to children and it is essential parents are aware of the dangers. Below I have outlined some strategies that you can use to help your children avoid porn as well as ways to support your child if they have been exposed.

Set Boundaries
With the majority of porn exposure occurring online, setting boundaries around device use can be a helpful strategy to keep your children safe. When it comes to device and media boundaries the whole family must agree on rules and expectations. This means everyone (including the adults) must be accountable for respecting the boundaries and accepting the consequences if the rules are broken. Some examples of boundaries

include not allowing phones in bedrooms, or setting a time when devices must be switched off. In my own home, we use a kitchen timer that is set on the agreed time each child is allowed to use their device. Everyone in the household understands that if they break the rules, they lose access to their phones for an agreed time frame.

Encourage a Healthy Lifestyle
Children who stay physically active with friends, engage in hobbies, or learn new skills can enjoy life without their gadgets—and in the process, they will learn about healthy relationships and dealing with painful emotions too. As a parent, it's important to provide regular opportunities for your children to be active, connect with others, and discover various healthy ways to enjoy and participate in life away from their phones and computers.

Open and Honest Communication
Pornography can damage a child's life if parents do not take an active role in ensuring that their children understand why it is bad for them. Holding open conversations with your children regularly is an important step in protecting them. Instead of interrogating or interviewing your child, provide a relaxed and easy feedback mechanism wherein everyone feels comfortable being open and honest. Keeping the communication lines open is one of the most effective ways you as a parent can keep your children away from the ill effects of porn.

Recognize How Porn Changes the Brain
Porn affects the reward centre of the brain and regular exposure leads to the production of less of the "happy chemicals" like adrenaline, serotonin, and dopamine. It also causes the brain to be less responsive to these chemicals, which means a child who watches porn often will eventually need additional stimulation to feel good.

Once porn is eliminated, his brain will search for other sources of chemical releases. At this time, encourage your child to connect with the positive things in life to support his social, mental, emotional, and physical health. It may start with baby steps, but eventually these positive interactions and activities will replace the worn neural pathways.

As the child creates positive influences and stays away from porn, the pathway he created in his brain for porn starts to shrink. The process will be slow, but he can break free from the bondage of pornography. Chronic overstimulation ceases and neurochemical changes in the brain begin. The child may experience withdrawal symptoms, and this means his brain is changing. The experience may be frustrating, but it is a welcome respite because it means the child is on the road to recovery.

The regular overstimulation of porn causes shrinkage in the frontal lobes, the part of the brain which deals with reasoning, logic, and choice. Scientists believe this change is the main reason why addiction is powerful. However, the frontal lobes can grow back slowly. Each daily victory away from porn can make your child's brain healthier and his recovery easier.

Be a Sex Authority
As a parent, you must teach your children about pornography, sex, and the human body—because if you don't, someone else will. The right time may be when your child hears about sex and starts to ask questions. Take the opportunity to teach your kids about sexual relationships and their private body parts and view it as a privilege. Teach them some ways to recognize and deal with porn. Once you start the conversation about sex, your children are more likely to come to you to ask questions, rather than an unreliable source.

Talk to Children Early

It is common for parents to feel uncomfortable starting the conversation about sex with their children, however, most kids don't feel awkward and treat this conversation just like any other. Many parents put it off because they are embarrassed, then miss the window of opportunity to talk to their children openly about sex and porn. Children then search for answers to their questions elsewhere, from other adults or their peers, and they often end up being misguided.

Conquer Fear

As a parent, you may feel anxious about talking to your children about pornography; but you must not let fear and anxiety rule over you. Talk about your fears with people you trust or write down your feelings in detail so you can understand them yourself. If the fear is causing anxiety, exercise or relaxation can help to calm your mind and body so you can think more clearly.

Use Reflective Listening

Often, parents do not hear what their children are telling them because their mind is busy thinking of the right words to say to fix the problem. Thus, children sense their parents are not listening to them and they may start to hold back their thoughts and feelings. Reflective listening is a technique where you summarize and repeat what the speaker says, and this can be a really helpful way to tune in to what your children are saying.

Seek the Help of a Counselor

If you've discovered your child is into porn, you will likely feel shocked and may not know what to do. Seeking the help of a professional can be very effective, and in some cases it is essential. To assess if your child requires counseling, consider the following issues:

- **Traumatic situations**
  While children are naturally curious about sexuality and their bodies, if they have previously experienced a traumatic event, they may be under internal distress and be looking for ways to cope with emotional pain. Sometimes, children can use porn as one of their coping strategies, so if your child has been through a traumatic event and is turning to pornography regularly, professional counseling will help them address the trauma in a healthier way.

- **Being secretive**
  A secretive child can have high levels of shame or continue the behavior. Counseling may work in confronting the shame, especially if he comes from a "shame-prone family." If that is the case, the entire family will benefit in counseling to confront shame. If the child rejects attempts by the parents to offer structure and support in dealing with porn, counseling can help parents enforce the right boundaries so the child can sustain freedom of choice within the bounds of safe behaviors that meet family expectations and rules.

- **Deviant forms of porn**
  Porn can take various forms of deviant or violent behaviors in videos and other kinds of media and can be confusing and harmful to children. Exposure to these kinds of porn requires counseling to assess their effects on the child and discover if he requires additional professional help.

- **Risk of hurting other children**
  If the risk of experimenting sexually on other children or showing porn to another child is present, the child needs professional help. Children who experience sexual abuse

caused by an adult or another child can do the same to other children.

- **Escalating problem**
  If the child continuously seeks or watches porn, he needs professional help to assess the situation.

Confronting a child's addiction to porn can be overwhelming for any parent, however, you must do something the instant you discover your child is into pornography. Continue to educate yourself so you can deal with the problem effectively, because you hold the key in helping your child overcome it.

CHAPTER 2

Teens Without Porn

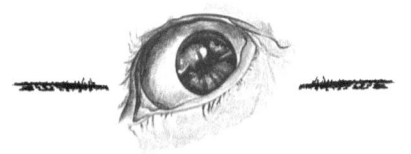

Josh had just turned seventeen when he visited me two years ago. We met during one of my workshops where he showed great interest in taking part in my one-on-one coaching program. I remembered him very well, because he was by far one of the tallest teenagers I've ever seen in my life. He was shockingly good-looking and very muscular to some unnatural degree. But when he entered my coaching office, he appeared to be very weak and broken. Despite his well-structured body and handsome face, he looked very fragile, terrified, and nearly in tears.

After a little chitchat and brief introduction into the session, he was adamant that he is useless and deserves some sort of punishment for what he did to his girlfriend, named here Tina. He then started to cry with heavy breaths as if he's been running for hours. I tried to give him a break and offered him some water to cool him down a bit, but he refused angrily. Josh then told me something that I will never forget. *"Look, I came here to say it all out loud and follow whatever options you may help me with. I am not a religious person and I do not believe in cults, but all I need to do at this point in time is to make it up to my girlfriend, and so I would follow any system to get me where I wanted if it would cost me my life,"* he aggressively stated.

Josh had been in a relationship with his girlfriend for nearly two years and he said it was the best thing. This lovely girl, Tina, was the solace to his heart after his beloved mum was diagnosed with cancer and passed away soon after. Yet, as Josh narrated: *"This night was the worst thing that has ever happened in my entire life, even worse than hearing about my mother's death. It was when we decided to have our very first sexual experience."* Josh then started to vividly remember that night. He had planned the whole night and intended to make it memorable and comfortable, although Tina was reluctant due to some cultural and religious obligations.

However, in the name of love and commitment she was dragged into Josh's demands and desires.

"All was great until I heard her saying, 'I am in pain, please stop.' I didn't know why she wasn't enjoying it. Yes, I was rough at times, but this is what I've learned on porn. I was in control of the moves, but she wasn't moaning like porn stars, which was something I was expecting. Yes I did smack her back, pulled her hair hard, called her dirty names and chocked her several times just like it is shown on porn films, but instead of seeing her enjoying it, which was my intention, she was instead screaming from pain. While my mind was busy as to why she is not happy, my sexual urge went to its peak and I started to ignore her screaming and just kept going. I only stopped when I saw her bleeding like fountains."

Young Tina had suffered from severe cuts in her upper vagina and as a result she was rushed to the hospital. The poor girl left the hospital a few days later, with thirteen stitches and a horrific sexual experience that has traumatized her. She decided to break up with Josh after this, telling him, *"You are selfish, irresponsible and animalistic."*

I asked Josh precisely whether pornography was the primary reason as to how he had acted sexually the way he did with Tina, and his answer was a definite yes. *"What else would it be? I had never learned about sexual interactions from my parents or at school, so pornography was the only way for my generation to get some tips and tricks on how to actually have sex. And unfortunately, in my case this was the type of porn that I thought would make my girl happy."* Josh regrettably stated.

Unfortunately, all interventions by family members and friends have failed to convince Tina that her boyfriend was influenced by his addiction to porn and that he did not intend her any harm.

She decided to move on, and Josh was guided on how to accept this fact.

Pornography, with all its filthy content is the primary educator for many teens today, and the behavior of Josh during his first sexual experience with his girlfriend was inspired by his constant consumption of porn content. He didn't know that smacking or beating during sex or outside of it is hurtful, demeaning, disrespectful, and even illegal. He didn't realize that pulling the hairs backward could injure a person's neck. He didn't understand that during intense moments of sex, chocking could end someone's life. All he did was a copy/paste of what he's been watching for the past eight years (yes, he started watching pornography when he was about nine years old). Seeing the actresses in those films acting happy and pleased with what was going on had made him believe that this is the real way to attain sexual pleasure. He did not know back then that everything on these films is scripted, pre-planned, and those actors and actresses are paid to ACT the way they do. There's no pleasure in slapping or smacking, that is complete nonsense.

What the Research Tells Us

As illustrated in Josh's story above, when teenagers are exposure to sexually violent behavior it can have devastating consequences. A study of sexual violence perpetration published in *Prevention Science* in 2017 found the average age of perpetrators when they committed their first crime was 15–16 years old. Of the teens in the study, all had present exposure to violent pornography, parental/spousal abuse, and aggressive behavior and had shown prior victimization of sexual harassment and present victimization of psychological abuse in relationships.

In 2012, TRU Research conducted online interviews with over 2,000 teenagers and their parents to discover more about their online habits. Of the teenagers surveyed, a third admitted to intentional access of pornographic or nude content online, and 43% of these teens did so weekly. The majority of teens (71%) said they hide what they are doing online from their parents, and this was further highlighted by the fact that only 12% of parents were aware that their teen children had access to porn.

In an Italian study of 1,565 young students aged 18–19 years old, it was reported that 80% of them used porn. Of these, over 20% admitted to habitual use of pornography and almost 10% admitted to porn addiction. Interestingly, 10% of participants also said that using porn lessened their sexual interest to possible real-life partners.

A similar study of Swedish adolescents conducted in 2017 showed that 98% had viewed porn. Of these 11% watched porn at least once every day, 69% watched porn at least once a month and 20% were infrequent users.

How Porn Impacts Teenagers

If they cannot get information from other sources, teenagers often turn to online porn for sex education. However, what they see on porn is far from reality and this provides them with a distorted view of healthy relationships and sexual practices. Below are some of the negative impacts that have been widely observed.

Unsafe Sex Practices and Expectations
Porn promotes unsafe sexual health practices like unprotected sex. Adolescents who use porn regularly, have an increased risk of

engaging in these high-risk sexual practices because they view them as "normal." They are also likely to copy other unsafe or undesirable sexual acts they see in porn including anal intercourse, sex with different partners, facial ejaculation, deep fellatio, and violence directed towards women.

Confusion of Sexual Values

Teens may experience fear, anxiety, and sexual dissatisfaction because of the uncertainties about sexual values and beliefs that porn produces. Moreover, porn content reinforces double standards of a passive female and an active male sexuality receptacle. A male youth who views porn regularly will often regard women as sex objects and will have sexist attitudes towards women and remarkable beliefs in gender stereotypes.

Violence Against Women

Porn strengthens attitudes that support violence against women and sexual violence. When consumed regularly, it increases the risk of teen boys becoming perpetrators of sexual harassment. Instead of seeing women as individuals, male teenagers exposed to porn tend to objectify women and view them as objects. Porn portrays violent or degrading sexual encounters as enjoyable, which makes adolescent men believe that women will enjoy or welcome rape. It creates a culture of men who do not regard rape seriously.

Porn has deeply problematic messages and behaviors about pleasure, power, gender, and sex, particularly in verbal and physical aggression. Porn scenes can include hair pulling, choking, slapping, gagging, and name-calling, which the predominant perpetrators are men.

Rewiring and Changing the Brain
Young people who are frequent porn consumers can have less active, less connected, and smaller brains in some areas. Pornography changes the brain by constantly making new nerve connections and rewiring them. It can overpower the natural ability of the brain to enjoy real sex. According to Columbia University researcher Dr. Norman Doidge, pornography lays down perfect conditions and causes the release of the appropriate chemicals to change the brain permanently.

Problems with Sexual Performance
Doctors have observed that young men can fail to get an erection with a real-life partner due to their porn habits. Porn can cause problems with attraction, arousal, and sexual performance, and there is some evidence of a link between porn and erectile dysfunction, low sex drive, and an inability to reach orgasm.

Frequent porn users often find themselves aroused easily by online porn, but they may have a low sexual desire for real-life partners. Because of their vulnerability to brain rewiring due to frequent porn viewing, teenagers and young adults can experience serious sexual problems.

Distortion of Healthy Views About Sex
Consumers of porn who are below the legal age obtain some (or all) of their education about sex from pornography. Sociologist Dr. Michael Kimmel discovered that porn heavily influences the sexual fantasies of men. If their partners do not want to act out the dangerous or degrading sexual acts, men may turn to prostitutes who can readily live out the porn acts that they want. This was highlighted in a survey of past prostitutes who said 80% of their customers wanted them to perform their favorite porn images and acts.

Distorted Beliefs, Behavior and Values
Porn disorients teenagers during their development phase where they are learning about sexuality and this can lead to confusion and uncertainty about their moral values and sexual beliefs. In a study conducted by University of Saskatchewan psychology professor Todd G. Morrison and his colleagues, exposure to high levels of pornography during adolescence was linked to reduced levels of sexual self-esteem.

High porn consumption among adolescents can also affect their behavior. For young males, this can mean engaging in sexual intercourse with their non-romantic friends or hooking-up with other people. Dr. Rebecca Collins also discovered that adolescents who viewed various sexual content on television had an increased likelihood of initiating sexual intercourse and progressing to advanced non-coital sexual activities over the following year.

Feelings of Loneliness and Shame
Frequent use of porn can increase the occurrence of feelings of loneliness and may even lead to major depression. Its effect on the brain is comparable to the neurological alterations caused by addiction to methamphetamine, alcohol, and cocaine. Moreover, watching porn can incite feelings of shame, but this is not always the case. This could be an indication that some sort of desensitization has already reached society.

Devaluation of Commitment
In general, the exposure of pornography to children and teens results in a hypersexual worldview. Porn promotes the devaluation of marriage, so teens who view it are more likely to see commitment as insignificant. Researchers believe that when children are exposed to parents with multiple partners, it also plays a role in devaluing commitment.

By devaluing and commercializing sex, porn exposes teenagers to having various sex partners prior to marriage and infidelity in a committed relationship. Adopting porn as acceptable and normal, and having sex with anyone, any time, any place, leads to the devaluation of the ideals of extensive and long relationships with a single partner. Porn creates a culture of recreational sex, promotes infidelity, and destroys intimacy.

How You Can Help Teenagers Avoid Porn

Teenagers who watch pornography regularly develop a distorted view of relationships, love, and sex which often results in ongoing emotional and physical issues later in life. To help them avoid the negative effects of pornography, use some of the strategies below to guide your teenagers to make healthy lifestyle choices and good decisions.

Share Stress Management Skills
To thrive in all areas of their life, teens must learn how to effectively manage stress. Otherwise, they will look for alternative ways to escape their worries, which may include unhealthy choices such as viewing porn. Stress can make you tired, desperate, and distracted. If stress is a concern in your home the whole family can benefit from seeking to understand what is triggering it, so it can be minimized. As a parent, be mindful of how you're modelling stress management. Be sure you have excellent self-care habits in the way you balance relationships and seek downtime to replenish your energies.

You should also look for ways to actively support your teenager to manage their stress. This can be as simple as making a list of activities that can renew them, such reading and biking, etc. Another helpful strategy is to list down the relationships that are significant to them and show them how to say "no" to anyone or anything that demands too much of their time.

Limit Technology
Unrestricted use of technology can lead to negative consequences, so if you allow new technology into your house, you must be responsible for it. Even though technology in itself isn't harmful, it can be very damaging to teens if they have free rein. Always set and be clear with limitations on usage, explain why they are in place, and be consistent in enforcing them.

Just to be clear, technology includes video games, movies, phones, computers, television, and music. Even if the new device or technology is common and normal, and all their friends are using it as they please, it doesn't mean that it's risk free. In this case setting limits can be divisive and tiring, but it is essential. You need to communicate clearly and be consistent and graceful in resolving conflicts about the limitations. In particular, keep the focus on teaching your teenager about accountability and trustworthiness, as these are both important skills for them to develop.

Enforce an Open Device Policy
As a parent, we are all looking for ways to teach our teenagers to make excellent decisions. One way you can do so is to create an environment of accountability and openness. Some parents may wish to draw up an "Internet Use Contract" for their children, or to set a household rule to limit the use of electronic devices.

In the Internet Use Contract, you can include the following:

- Sites that your children can visit (include chat rooms, etc.)
- Times of day they can use the Internet

- Length of time they can use it for
- Penalties if the rules are broken
- Privileges for when they follow the rules

Once complete, let everyone sign it, including you. Then, display it somewhere that everyone can see it.

Explain Needs vs. Wants
Take the time to sit down with your teenager to discuss the difference between needs and wants. Sexual gratification falls under the wants list and porn causes a hunger for sex that makes a person anxious until he quenches it. It remains in his thoughts so he can no longer focus on other significant things like hobbies, relationships, and extracurricular activities. However, porn never satisfies.

Thus, you need to teach your teenager to manage wants by casting a vision of the payoff. For instance, you train for a competition through hard work. You may want to give up, but if you persevere, you get the payoff, and you'll do well in the contest. Thus, if your teen wants a healthy sexual and romantic relationship in the future, he must not give in to immediate sexual gratification.

Talk about Mindset, Oxytocin, and Sex
According to researcher J. Dennis Fortenberry, sexuality has four areas: sexual desire, sexual arousal, sexual behaviors and sexual functioning. Sex is the glue in a steadfast and committed loving relationship. Oxytocin is a chemical released during sex that biochemically renews the fidelity in a relationship. Porn distorts the power of this chemical by allowing the brain to think that it is present. The brain produces chemicals to respond to what a person sees to create an experience. If it often occurs with different partners, a person loses attachment over time.

Continuous access to porn creates sexual experiences in a person's mind. The brain releases chemicals to make the person feel the bonding, attachment, and experience of sexual pleasure. Porn releases oxytocin in the brain, so an individual will feel "stuck" to the illusion. He attaches to it, and not to an actual individual. Therefore, porn makes him feel excited now, but it robs him of the ability to bond with an actual individual. You must help your teenager understand the thirst and emptiness that porn creates.

Nurture Wise Decision-Making and Risk-Taking
Teens are naturally impulsive in their decision-making and prone to take risks, so they need guidance in this area of their life. Risk-taking can sometimes be exciting or dangerous, and teens must learn to choose which risks are worth taking. Porn is an exciting risk because it creates an illusion of excitement and novelty among teenagers. For teens, they feel excited about the prospect of doing or looking at something that they aren't supposed to do or watch.

Risk-taking is normal among teens, but normal doesn't mean that it's favorable. It can be damaging if they don't make the right decisions when they are lonely, bored, aroused, angry, or upset. As a parent, teach your child to stop, pause, and think before they let their emotions take them down the wrong path. Teach them to pursue healthy risks, which are fun and not dangerous.

CHAPTER 3

Relationships Without Porn

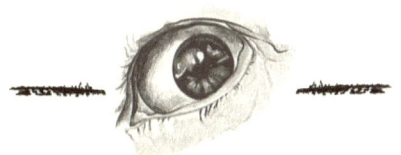

In all my events, I do my best to allocate some time to meet individuals who may require one-on-one assistance. The nature of the topic of discussion forces people in general to shun away from the conversation in public forums, and so I usually place a request with the organizers to arrange a time where I can meet a few people individually to see how I can offer any necessary help in the areas of my expertise.

It was in one of these sessions that I met Rageh. He was from a very conservative background and at that time, was close to forty years of age with three kids. He started the conversation by saying: *"You are the first person I have shared my secret with. I am addicted to pornography and have been for many years."*

This is something I've heard and read in my e-mail inbox literally thousands of times, and is the very reason *why* I've taken the discussion to the public. We are dealing with a massive problem that is seldom discussed. It's often looked at as either a taboo where people usually brush it under the carpet and pretend that everything is fine, or viewed as "normal" and "everyone is doing it anyway" and therefore we shouldn't make a big deal out of it.

Rageh mentioned that he's been addicted for nearly half of his life or even more. He thought that marriage would fix the problem, but he was terribly mistaken. He realized later that marriage could be a major step along the journey of recovery, but it can never be the ultimate solution. So, what did Rageh do after realizing that he is still addicted even though he's married to a beautiful wife and later became a father three times over? He decided to tell his wife, advice that I always give to all addicted men. Your wife might get mad at first, she may think low of herself or feel betrayed, but in the vast majority of cases she will support you and stand by your side in the end because she truly does love you.

Relationships Without Porn

Rageh's wife was shocked at first as to how her beloved husband was able to hide his secret all these years without her noticing anything strange. After a long list of questions posed to her husband, which is something I do not recommend at all, she gave him the worst advice any wife could give to her husband. She said: *"When you are about to watch, call me so we could watch together. In this case you will not be doing anything behind my back."*

And so, it happened. They started the cycle of pornography consumption together for a few years until the wife confessed something to her husband that would change the entire course of their lives forever. She told Rageh: *"I've been watching porn all by myself now, I think I too am addicted."*

"It was the tremor of my life. My head kept spinning and in a split second I was on the ground. When I regained consciousness, I decided to come to you." Rageh confessed.

During another session, a married couple had requested to see me. From the first sight you could tell that the wife is broken, sad, angry, and despaired. Although the man had started the conversation about his porn and sex addiction, she was always interrupting to provide more details into the story that her husband was trying to skip intentionally. In other words, she was willing to pour her heart out in the hope of finding a solution to their misery.

Apparently, their situation was quite complicated and different. Usually when a husband is addicted to pornography, one of the best remedies is for the wife to know and compassionately support her man to recover and live a life of complete freedom from the shackles of his addiction. And one of these remedies is sex itself, which means the wife should assist him whenever she can to provide him with sexual comfort so that he does not resort to prostitution houses and illegal massage parlours. So in the middle of the conversation I asked the wife if she's willing to support him sexually, she said she would, however their physician had advised them to sleep in separate rooms for a minimum time period of 6–8 months. And of course, as a coach I will always ask for the reasons! She said, *"Because my husband and I have developed sexually transmitted diseases."*

You see, pornography falsely promises the consumer a better sex life, different positions and techniques but in the end those same consumers, in many cases would end up having no sex at all because of their bad choices. In the above case the man was heavily addicted to pornography and as a result he was not satisfied with one partner, his wife, and so he started to seek multiple partners through prostitutes. While he was overtaken by his addiction, he didn't see any consequences, he just wanted to get his fix. But now the level of shame that he carries is unbearable.

According to my last conversation with the wife, the physician had extended the period to another five months and the husband is still cheating every now and then under his wife's watch. She had developed a lot of anxiety and depression symptoms and was now being treated and divorce could be the only option that remained for her.

What else can I share with you? The story of a husband who has been forcing his wife to perform a role-play of a little girl while he would carry her powerfully, tie her up and load her in the trunk of their car then drive away to an isolated area and act as if he's raping her all night? Or the man who would ask his wife to insert a cucumber into his anus and force her to do the same to her vagina till both masturbate and eat up their waste? Or maybe the lady who would cheat on her husband every time he would leave for overseas to work because she had discovered his porn collections in one of his wardrobes and later became addicted herself? The stories are plenteous and mostly disgusting but real and deserve our attention. If the very fabric of our society, partners and couples who are supposed to procreate and bring up healthy generations is messed up, then what do you expect from our young ones?

What the Research Tells Us

As mentioned above, pornography consumption is a problem that is far more widespread than most people think. This was shown in 2016, when an American research study reported that 60–70% of men and 30–40% of women below the age of 40 use porn annually—and 45% of men and 15% of women view it weekly. A similar number of users was found in a survey conducted in 2017 by Australian researcher Professor Chris Rissel, who found that 76% of men and 41% of women surveyed had viewed porn. About 50% of the respondents reported that porn had a bad effect on them, with 4% of men and 1% of women admitting they were addicted to it.

In a 2005 survey organized by the American Academy of Matrimonial Lawyers, 56% of divorces that involved one party meeting a new partner on the Internet occurred because the partner showed obsessive interest in porn websites. But interestingly, the National Coalition for the Protection of Children and Families, has found in their research that 40% of people suffering from sex addiction under the age of 35 were women.

The high number of porn users is further illustrated by the porn industry's huge profits. According to an NBC report published in

2015, the porn industry is worth between $10–$20 billion yearly in the US and a massive $97 billion annually around the world.

How Porn Impacts Your Relationships

While it may seem on the surface that porn can spark your marriage and your sex life, the reality is, it generally has the opposite effect. If you or your partner is addicted to porn, it impacts your relationship in a range of negative ways as outlined below.

Loss of Self-Esteem
For women who have male partners who are frequent viewers of porn, loss of self-esteem is common. They often feel that they are in competition with the female actors who star in porn movies and exude bodily perfection and unrealistic intensity. As such, they feel inadequate and not good enough and speculate why their man sticks with them.

Decreased Sexual and Relationship Satisfaction
In marriages where one partner is a heavy porn user, the occurrence of divorce increases significantly. Even marriages that begin as extremely joyful struggle to survive once porn use becomes an issue. For the partner who doesn't view porn, they are emotionally rocked. After the initial shock of discovery is experienced they feel betrayed and it takes work and commitment from both parties to repair the relationship.

A 2017 report titled *Pornography Consumption and Satisfaction: A Meta-Analysis*, concluded that porn use doesn't usually affect women's sexual satisfaction because they mostly watch porn with their partners. However, men who frequently watch porn alone experience sexual dissatisfaction. Why is this so? Partly because body punishing and misogynistic porn doesn't entertain the majority of men. It leaves them estranged from their partners and emotionally unfulfilled. Also, porn makes them dissatisfied with relationships and sex as watching porn alone invades their head space in the bedroom.

Sexual Dysfunction
Men who are heavy porn users often suffer from sexual dysfunction like anorgasmia or failure to reach orgasm, delayed ejaculation, and erectile dysfunction. These types of sexual issues can even affect younger men who are in their sexual prime. Heavy porn use has also been linked to conditioning of the brain to hyper-intensity and novelty so that users find real-world partners less stimulating.

Objectification of the Partner
Porn dehumanizes and objectifies both sexes, but often the scenes hide the men's faces while portraying women as mere objects. When a selection of various famous porn scenes were analyzed, it was discovered that 88% of them depicted violence against women. Porn deceives its viewers by objectifying every person for their pleasure, and not as dignified human beings.

Sex is for the enjoyment of a couple who respect and love each other. Emotional, intellectual, and physical connections cultivate a romantic and healthy relationship; it crumbles without them. A real man respects a woman and her individuality. Porn turns women into objects to satisfy and gratify a man's sexual urge. It eliminates the need for intellectual or emotional connection with a woman.

Setting of Unrealistic Standards
Women who are in a relationship with someone who watches porn, generally feel the need to compete for emotional and sexual

attention with the porn female actors their husbands or partners watch. These female stars are the "fantasy women" who are sexually attractive, unrealistically so due to plastic surgery, digital editing, and stage makeup. Real women feel insecure and inferior because it is impossible for them to match up with these fantasy women.

Porn also shows unrealistic sex scenes. In real life, husbands and wives have sex to show their love, but porn reduces sexual pleasure due to the addict's preference for porn rather than intimacy with their real partner. With porn, men view women as always ready for sex with their perfect airbrushed bodies. They don't need to interact with these women and deal with the issues that affect couples in real life.

A porn addict has a difficult time starting meaningful relationships because women don't measure up to the females he sees in porn magazines and websites. When he finally begins a loving sexual relationship, he sees it through a pornographic filter and fantasizes about porn scenes when he has sex with his partner. He may even force his partner to do things that she's not willing to do like act out some of the pornographic scenes.

Search for Sexual Satisfaction Elsewhere
A person who is addicted to porn is continually searching for new ways to satisfy his sexual fantasy, as tolerance is built easily. Once he is no longer aroused by watching porn, he may try hardcore porn, visit online chat rooms, experiment with what he sees online with other sex partners, or have an affair.

A *Social Science Quarterly* study in 2004 showed that people who admitted to extramarital affairs were at least 300% more likely to admit to viewing porn as compared to people who didn't have an affair. Additionally, it has been found that watching pornography leads to a decreased interest in forming long-term commitments and marriage.

Destruction of Trust
Porn ruins trust that takes time to build due to the defiling of the intimacy of a romantic relationship. A woman who finds out that her partner is into porn can feel that he is cheating on her. She feels that he is bringing other females into the relationship. The extreme hurt that she feels can destroy the relationship. In the US, it is thought that porn use contributes to almost 50% of divorces.

Causes Isolation and Loneliness
Because of the shame and guilt that an addicted person feels, he may feel isolated. Moreover, his use of porn may push him to avoid professional help due to the embarrassment he feels when he admits his addiction. Many people turn to porn as a form of escape from their problems, but oftentimes they feel purposeless, empty, and hollow afterward. Studies have highlighted a close link between porn and feelings of loneliness, anxiety, and depression. Watching porn leads to extreme emptiness, sadness, and darkness.

Promotion of Selfishness
Porn users demand more from their partner. Instead of giving sexual pleasure to their partners, they expect to get more pleasure from them. They often have trouble with their lovemaking, because for them, sex is forced, rushed, and impersonal. They no longer enjoy foreplay and have no desire to arouse their partner because they only focus on getting what they want.

Alteration of the Brain
Research by Cambridge University scientists found that porn triggers the release of dopamine in the brain, in a similar way to addictive

substances. A person who views porn frequently becomes desensitized and his damaged brain makes it difficult for him to break free from it. Unlike the other types of addiction, porn causes an addict to desire different porn. A porn addict will want hardcore porn once soft porn no longer arouses, excites, and satisfies him. He progresses to perverse content, which may in turn lead to crime and violence.

How You Can Repair Your Relationship After Porn

If you discover your partner is addicted to porn, you will likely feel shocked, betrayed, and unsure of what to do next. It can be devastating, but understanding your options in how to repair the relationship and help your addicted partner recover can help you move forward. If you are addicted to porn yourself, being honest with your partner and working together to re-establish trust is an essential step towards saving your relationship. Below are some strategies that you can implement together to leave porn behind and reconnect.

Talk About It
If you want to put an end to your partner's porn addiction, a good place to start is to sit down and have a heart-to-heart talk. Don't be afraid to share how you feel. If you perceive no improvement in your relations after talking to your partner and they continue to watch porn despite having agreed not to, speaking to a counselor together may provide you with additional strategies. Marriage counseling can help you understand the underlying reasons and discover the triggers for his porn use.

Relationships Without Porn

Understand Change Requires Work
If your partner continues to watch porn, even if it might end your marriage, it doesn't mean he has stopped loving you. His desire to watch porn is greater than his desire to commit to your relationship at this moment because he is out of control and literally addicted. In this case, change requires hard work and a long-term commitment. Although you may feel like walking away and giving up on him, in my experience, it is possible for most men to overcome porn addiction with the help of a supportive partner.

Know Your Options
When you are in a relationship with a porn user, you have a range of options. You can choose to ignore it and stay in the marriage as things are. You can enter into compromises or get a divorce. Or you can commit to staying in the relationship and work together to resolve the issue. This last option should always be considered first where possible as I have seen many couples successfully work together to help a partner overcome porn addiction.

Don't Let it Affect Your Self-Confidence
If your partner is using porn, don't let it have a negative impact on you. It is upsetting to discover your partner watches porn, but men are easily aroused by a visual stimulus and it is likely he may have begun using porn early in his life. Watching porn, if it becomes excessive, it can ruin a relationship. Remember, watching porn is his problem, not yours. It has nothing to do with how you look.

Show Empathy but Don't Accept Blame
It's important to realize that your partner's behavior is not your fault, so don't accept guilt or blame for it. They decided to watch porn and allowed it to affect your relationship negatively. The problem is their responsibility, not yours.

However, your husband may have underlying reasons for turning to porn—for example, he might use it as an escape from his problems. If you can show empathy and let him know that you understand and he isn't alone, your love and support can be a catalyst for him to cut down on his porn use.

Don't Be His Porn Police

If your partner is watching porn excessively, you may ask him to choose between you and porn. If he promises not to watch porn anymore, he will either stand firm on his promise or watch it in secret. If he lies about it, eventually, it will compromise your relationship. However, you have no obligation to stop him from watching porn—if wants to stop, he must own it. Resist the urge to create a list of what he does and doesn't need to do because it creates the wrong idea about recovery. He must write his own list and discuss it with you.

Your partner should also be accountable to a person or group other than you. When someone else is involved in the discussions and offering support, you won't feel as hurt if he feels tempted to watch porn again. He may have a counselor or peer group that he meets with weekly or daily. With outside support, you don't need to be traumatized alone every time he struggles or fails.

Set Boundaries

Look for helpful and effective ways to set boundaries if your partner wants to change. For example, you can set up software that blocks porn access and sends a report to his accountability partner every time he goes to pornography sites (Covenant Eyes and FamilyZone are great software that can help in this regard). Importantly, he mustn't have administrator rights on the software. If you're not confident in setting it up, speak to an expert to understand the options available to block use and protect all gadgets against porn.

Redevelop Spiritual and Emotional Intimacy
On its own, regular sex isn't a solution to porn addiction. It can offer some solace and relief, but you and your partner must also rekindle your emotional and spiritual intimacy. He is craving love and acceptance and may be using porn to heal these emotional wounds. Sexual intimacy is a strong and healthy part of marriage. It is a celebration of your union as a couple and ought to be nurtured by spending quality time and being honest and open with one another.

CHAPTER 4

Sex Without Porn

"Never did I imagine that my very manhood would let me down during sex. I've been watching pornography for most of my life to celebrate this moment, yet I was not able to have an erection."

This is how Adam has started his conversation with me. A businessman, aged thirty-one, who is now divorced and reluctant to repeat the marriage experience because, according to him, he is afraid that "it" won't work.

This has become a common problem for young men in the past twenty years or so. It is a condition known as Porn Induced Erectile Dysfunction (PIED). Since the brain has become conditioned to virtual stimulation and screen pleasure instead of real-life partners, when a man is confronted with a real-life sexual experience, his penis may not cooperate. And what is sex really without an erection? This is one major problem that men do not want to experience in their lifetime. In the case of Adam, it became the center of his focus and the misery of his life. He started to resort to casual, unprescribed enhancement medications, which would sometimes do the job, but without any enjoyment—other times, he would fail to maintain an erection.

In 1992, Walker (who is from a very conservative family and religious background) was introduced to pornography. Internet porn back in those days comprised of static nude pictures with a couple of pages that would ultimately lead you to the payment page, if you wish to see more. A few years later, downloading pornographic clips and videos onto your hard disk had become prevalent and increased the level of interest among young guys. Walker was at the top of the porn game; he had a collection of thousands of videos and eighty plus portable hard disks loaded with his favorite films. He was not only pleasuring himself to porn, he would also rent, sell and lend those films that are burned on CDs to customers and close friends. In 1998 Walker finally got married to his sweet pie and girl of his dreams. Walker was well known in his town, very charismatic and loved by so many in his circle. On the wedding night, hundreds of his friends were pouring into the hotel where his wedding party was taking place just to congratulate the couple and see how beautiful they looked together. In his town, it was a tradition for the family members of the couples to drop them up to their house and spend a few hours with them joking about what would take place in the bedroom. Walker believed wholeheartedly that he was the hero and with plenty of pornographic experience would nail the night and please his beloved wife. But he was way, way wrong.

After all the family members were gone, and the couple were left alone ready to celebrate their commitment, the sexual part kicks in and there was a shocking surprise. Walker's manhood didn't move an inch.

"I panicked and perspired like rain. Whatever I tried to get it up failed. My wife tried to calm me down, seeing me all embarrassed, but I was adamant that this is not happening, and all will be all right. I was wrong, there was something definitely wrong." Walker continued his miserable story. *"This has been, by far, the most horrific and hardest night of my life. In my culture, family members visit the married couple in the early hours of the morning, just a couple of hours after the wedding night to check on their hero and how did he handle the night. They shamelessly ask whether the virgin wife has officially become a lady. They would not just believe what you say; they wanted to see evidence. In my town, every virgin wife would keep a small white sheet to soak with her blood when she loses her virginity. This is a sign of manhood, that her husband was capable of handling the first night, and also a sign that she had never given away her chastity to any man before her husband. I was losing my mind, what am I going to tell them?"* Walker exploded with tears at this moment.

Of course, a cycle of lies and excuses have taken place in the life of Walker and his wife. Whenever the elders in the family bring up that question of "evidence" of manhood and chastity, the answer would be. "She's sick, her menses, we lost the sheet, all good, we don't think of children now and so on."

Walker eventually was compelled to relate his agony to one of his close friends who also confessed to him that he had suffered from the same symptoms for years and is now doing great, very confident, with two lovely children and happier than ever. So of course, Walker hits him with the most sensible question in this situation, *"What did you do?"* His friend's answer was, *"I simply quit pornography and masturbation."* And so, Walker did too.

Walker came to see me because he wanted to stop watching porn in order to reverse that condition to his and his wife's favour. His wife was so loyal to him, despite her frustration of not having sex for a complete year. However, all this drama was soon to fade away with the new recovery plan and relapse prevention strategy that Walker and myself worked on together in order to achieve that goal. Yes, it took him another seven months to recover and enjoy his sex life, but at the end he had proven two things:

1) That PIED can be cured by abstaining from porn and connecting with a real-life partner.

2) That he can handle the wedding night without thousands of pornographic images in his brain.

What the Research Tells Us

From my observations and the research that follows, it's clear that regular viewing of pornography can interfere with arousal and healthy sexual function. A recent Reddit community survey of members of NoFap® (a community-based porn addiction recovery website) discussed the effects of porn on their lives. Although the results are anecdotal, the statistics are worth considering.

Many of the participants reported experiencing a decline in arousal with the same partner—however, after committing to no porn or masturbation, 60% noticed an improvement in their sexual function, and 67% experienced increased productivity and energy levels. Of the survey participants aged between 27–31 years old, over 30% experience erectile dysfunction and have problems reaching orgasm, 19% experience premature ejaculation and a quarter have no interest in having sex with their partner.

When asked about the amount of time spent watching porn, 59% of those surveyed said they watched it up to fifteen hours per week. One fifth of those surveyed admitted to feeling controlled by their sexual desires and 64% reported a heightened taste for deviant or extreme porn. Just over half started watching porn between the ages of twelve and fourteen, with 16% admitting they started before they turned twelve. Interestingly, half of those on NoFap® reported that their experience of sex was purely digital—they had never experienced sexual intimacy with a real-life partner.

How Porn Impacts Sex

Many people think that porn will enhance their sex life, but they soon discover this isn't true. There are many reasons for this, from the loss of libido to a disconnection between love and sex, and we explore some of these in detail below.

Sex is Less Enjoyable
Porn limits the frequency of enjoyable sex. For women with porn addict partners, they often feel that sex was simply a show because they needed to perform the sexual acts that their husbands or boyfriends had seen on pornographic videos. Eventually, the partners lose true intimacy and they feel disengaged. Women often find it difficult to be vulnerable with their man. Over time, any sexual act becomes a negative experience.

Development of Extreme Sexual Tastes
If you're a pornography user who frequently watches violent porn, including humiliating or degrading scenes, or extreme fetishes, you are conditioning the arousal of your brain even if you originally think that these scenes are unacceptable or disgusting. Eventually, you will consume extreme content because you need to experience the same dopamine rush you had from the start. Your brain will crave for it until you fall deep into the Internet's dark corners. You may not realize it, but your template for sexual arousal changes. You start to associate sexual pleasure with extreme sexual tastes.

Sexual Dysfunctions
Grown men can still struggle with porn's negative effects, particularly sexual dysfunction like delayed ejaculation and erectile dysfunction. Men in their prime often suffer from these issues because of their use of online porn. However, the issue isn't about the frequency of orgasm and masturbation, but about your penchant for masturbating to online pornography. Over time, you won't find your real-life partner stimulating anymore because endless visuals parade through your mind. You create an emotional disconnection that manifests as sexual dysfunction with your partner.

Sex Without Porn

Some of the signs of sexual dysfunction induced by porn include:

- Struggling to achieve orgasms or erections with a real-life partner, but achieve them with porn easily
- No libido when making love with your partner because you no longer feel turned on
- If orgasms are achieved with partners, it takes a long time to reach them
- Partner complains that you seemed disengaged during sex and she feels like "the other woman"
- Can maintain erections with a real-life partner, but orgasm is reached when porn scenes are replayed in his mind
- Prefers pornography and finds it more engaging and more intense than real-life sex
- Keeps secrets, such as frequency of watching porn, kinds of porn watched, etc., from his real-world partner

Sexual dysfunction not only affects men, but their romantic partners as well. A man's failure to reach orgasm or maintain erections makes his partner feel diminished sexual pleasure.

No Longer Aroused by the Partner

Porn excites the brain's arousal center. If orgasm occurs with it, it causes a chemical reaction and eventual release of hormones. The brain begins to associate eroticism with a video, idea, or image, instead of a person.

If you don't watch porn and save yourself until marriage, you release the hormones and chemicals with your spouse. Therefore, the union creates an intense bond between the couple. However, spending time on porn can teach the brain to associate release and arousal with porn, and not with a real person anymore. A man, having sex with a real-life partner, needs to watch or fantasize about porn first.

Becomes Lazy Sexually
With porn, you don't need to exert effort to arouse your partner because it's automatic. You don't have to indulge in foreplay. Therefore, your partner begins to think that it's her fault if she isn't aroused. You don't expect to show affection to help your partner jumpstart the arousal process. You have no intention to please your partner because porn teaches that sex is about getting what you want first. It's not about experiencing the wonders of sex as one.

Loss of Intimacy
The brain's arousal and pleasure centers associate sexual intercourse with intimacy and physical pleasure. However, porn doesn't have a real sense of intimacy, so it simply produces pleasure. It creates an idea that anonymous is sexy and being intimate isn't. If you're a frequent user of porn, you find it difficult to become intimate during sex because the pleasure and arousal centers focus only on the body. You tend to degrade or objectify your real-life partner to achieve pleasure.

Regular Sex Becomes Boring
Porn focuses on the body and not on intimacy. You watch porn and achieve a "high", but before long, you want to achieve a greater "high" so you watch weird porn. In contrast to the time when *Playboy* was king, today's porn consists of violent, degrading, and ugly images. It doesn't depict regular intercourse, so you get a warped view about sex. A problem arises when you think that weird porn is sexy.

Lack of Tenderness
Porn watching makes it difficult for you to be tender while having sex because it makes you view sex as rushed, impersonal, and forced.

You may not necessarily rape your partner, but porn shows violent sex without foreplay. You don't wait to arouse your partner, you want to get what you want immediately. In your brain, sex and tenderness don't go hand in hand.

How Quitting Porn Improves Your Sex Life

If your addiction to porn has negatively impacted your sex life, it is time to take steps to turn things around. There is no quick-fix solution, but with commitment and resolve the strategies below can help you regain your sexual health and intimacy with your real-life partner.

Recovery from Porn-Induced Sexual Dysfunction
The best and most effective method to reverse the damage caused by porn is to stop watching it. It is difficult to predict exactly when your erectile health will return to normal once you stop porn, masturbation, and porn fantasy completely. Often, cravings and withdrawal symptoms occur immediately, then, after the first week you should feel your confidence start to return.

After week one, you may feel increased flaccidity, and absence of erections and libido, and such symptoms may continue up to the eighth week. You may take time to exit and may even re-experience a flatline period. Libido and morning erections will return gradually. You may experience occasional spontaneous erections.

Some males may recover within a few weeks because their brain may have remained unchanged by porn addiction. Older men, who grew up without the Internet and online porn, may recover after around eight weeks. A few men may take up to six months or longer.

Factors that impact recovery from porn-induced sexual dysfunction include:

- Consistency in not viewing porn
- Age when the person voluntarily used porn—you may have a brain with stronger wiring for porn if you began watching porn early
- Frequency of sex with a real-life partner—if you started porn early with little or no sexual intimacy experience, you may take longer to rewire for sexual arousal
- If you have a real-life partner, you may recover quickly because you can rewire sexual response to your human partner immediately
- Length of porn use—if you used porn longer, it may take longer to recover
- Length of time for using porn for masturbation
- Previous experience of abstinence from porn—if you had recent experience of abstinence, you may recover quickly
- Kind of porn you use for masturbation—your brain may have been damaged and take longer to rewire if you use shocking or disturbing porn
- Porn-induced fetishes—recovery may take longer for "vanilla" sex arousal
- Initial sensitivity of your brain to addiction
- Kind of masturbation you used
- Edging without ejaculation

Loss of Objectification
Instead of sex being a communal and sacred gift, porn dehumanizes it and makes you lose the authentic connection. When you quit porn, your brain kills the dirty fantasy loops slowly and you will start to talk to women without the sexual layers in your head. It

takes time for healthy interaction, but you will begin to appreciate the real thing again and bring back authenticity.

Renewed Intimacy and Connection
Porn provides constancy in a world full of uncertain, clumsy, and messy intimacy that contains no promise or guarantee of reciprocity. Porn is a robotic yes-man that does not challenge, but only flatters. Ultimately, it says NO to real and authentic connection, where your partner returns the same love that you give. By quitting porn, you risk the erratic maze of human experience. Although you may feel safe with a computer every time, porn makes you less human. The goal of connection, intimacy, discipline, and faith is to make you more human.

CHAPTER 5

Health Without Porn

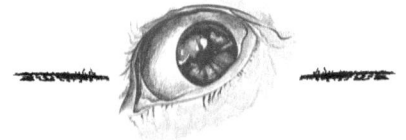

I'm sure you've seen those successful entrepreneurs online speaking about the importance of health, wealth, happiness, knowledge, business, and so on. They produce well-structured videos, sheets, e-books, and courses to show you how they've achieved their great empires, in the hope you will join their magical programs and become the next millionaire in a couple of months or so. Some of them, of course, are genuine, but many are just frauds. But one of the common traits they share is highlighting the importance of improving your health. In life, your health is the ultimate treasure.

So, how does pornography affect your health?

Jacqueline is a young married lady who has always been energetic, enthusiastic, and cheerful. She was introduced to Internet pornography at a very young age, but as she said: "*It was not that bad. I would sneak into an image or two and that would be enough for me to discharge and move on.*" For Jacqueline, pornography was an occasional experience with no signs of heavy addiction to the content she used to watch. "*I was more concerned about my discharge and orgasm. It was too quick with a touch or two and that was it. But I knew that porn was the main contributor to this pleasure, because the feeling associated with watching was very ecstatic and I would not be able to continue as a result of this discharge. Plus, I would only watch every couple of months or so. But then, the experience became more frequent after I got married, because I started to notice that my orgasm had almost completely disappeared when I was with my husband. I experienced none of the feelings of excitement, enjoyment or the rush that I used to get with pornography.*"

What Jacqueline was experiencing is known as *anorgasmia*, or more accurately, *situational anorgasmia*, where due to conditioning in the brain, orgasm can only be easily reached during a specific situation.

Jacqueline could experience orgasm very quickly when she watched porn—but with her husband, she hardly felt anything. It was an ongoing issue that left her frustrated, sad, and unable to respond to any sexual stimulation from her husband that would provide her with any satisfaction. Like PIED for men, anorgasmia inhibits the ability to experience real sexual intimacy and pleasure.

Jacqueline saw many doctors, but they were unable to assist her physically. She did not suffer from any serious illnesses that would lead to this condition, had no history of previous surgeries, no cancerous diseases that may affect orgasm, no pain during intercourse, no heavy medication that could contribute to this issue, she had never used drugs or alcohol in her life, she's too young to consider the possibility that she may be losing some of her hormones that contribute to orgasm. She's a sports woman who is in good shape. So physically, she is fit and well.

Several psychologists saw Jacqueline as well. And all reports were positive. She did not suffer from any mental health complications, she's very confident about her body, she's financially stable so there's no stress or anxiety involved, she's not feeling guilty of having sexual interaction and she was not traumatized from past sexual experiences. She was absolutely fine.

The only explanation that remained was through neuroscience and how she had situated her brain to activate the orgasm experience through pornography and touching herself a few times. That was the situation that her brain had registered for sexual pleasure and as a result she cannot experience the same with her husband.

Another young boy of twenty-two had contacted me via e-mail begging for help. He said that he's been addicted to pornography and masturbation for ten years straight which caused him a lot of physical problems. His symptoms were similar to those experienced by sufferers of Peyronie's disease which is a condition caused by the formation of a tissue on or inside the penis, which leads to a very painful erection. Not only that, he was also experiencing physical erectile dysfunction, or ED (which is different from Porn Induced Erectile Dysfunction). In the e-mail, he explained that he also suffered from a reduced fertility, which was observed by his physician when he examined his semen. I do not claim that Peyronie's disease is directly caused as a result of porn use. However, aggressive masturbation to pornography for that long could injure the penis which may lead to such a condition.

These stories are not meant to scare you or to bring shame into your life. They are only meant to remind you of one thing: that your health is worth every minute of the struggle to get rid of your addiction because, just like me and everyone else, we do not want to experience those conditions, ever.

What the Research Tells Us

Porn use is far more common and widespread than most people realize. In 2019, the website Pornhub had 42 billion visits, which equates to about 115 million visitors *per day*. It experienced an increase of 14 billion visits compared to 2017. According to Dr. Matthew Christman, urologist at the San Diego Naval Medical Center, there is a relationship between sexual dysfunction and porn addiction. With the widespread usage across the world, this equates to a large percentage of men and women who are experiencing dysfunction and poor sexual health.

Sexually transmitted diseases (STDs) are also found in much higher numbers in the pornography industry. In a study of 168 adult film actors, forty-seven of them reported having at least one sexually transmitted disease, particularly gonorrhea. Of the forty-seven actors, eleven found out they had an STD through the adult film industry's testing method. In April 2018, the adult entertainment industry shut down production in the US because a male actor tested positive for HIV. While there are no statistics currently available on the rate of STDs among porn users, there is a higher risk for those who are engaging multiple partners to satisfy their addiction.

How Porn Impacts Your Health

If you are watching porn on a regular basis, there is a high chance you are damaging your physical and mental health. Sexual dysfunction not only stops you performing physically, it causes serious mental anguish for you and your partner too. There are many other areas where your health can be affected by porn use, and I'll explain some of these in more detail below.

Erectile Dysfunction
Erectile dysfunction (ED) can be extremely distressing for a man. Research on porn-induced ED has found mixed results. Some studies say that a correlation between porn and erectile dysfunction exists—but there are other results that have shown that porn can help solve erectile dysfunction. Therefore, while porn may be a factor, it is unlikely that it is the only factor.

Research supporting the correlation between porn and ED shows that porn can desensitize your response to sex and that many young men seek help for erectile dysfunction because of hardcore porn.

Pornography can make men dissatisfied with their bodies, so they become anxious during sex. They need to increase sex stimulation progressively to maintain arousal.

We know that porn use changes the reaction of the brain to arousal, which means you can become less aroused with your real-life partner. In addition, sex toys may desensitize the nerves in your penis, making it harder to get an erection due to the nerves needing additional physical stimulation.

Decreased Sexual Satisfaction
A 2018 study conducted by Australian toxicology expert Professor Paul Wright looked at the effects of porn on sexual satisfaction, and found that frequent porn viewing could result in low sexual satisfaction. By analyzing statistics, the researchers discovered that religious males in a committed relationship suffered a decline in sexual satisfaction when they used porn a few times yearly. On the other hand, single and less religious females suffered a decrease in sexual satisfaction when they used porn at least once a month. The researchers found no correlation between porn and increased sexual satisfaction.

So why would sexual satisfaction decrease with increasing porn use? In a review of the fifty most famous videos on Pornhub, the study showed that only 18% of the female actors had orgasms, compared to 78% of males. Of the women who had an orgasm, 45% occurred when they had vaginal intercourse while 35% of them had an orgasm during anal intercourse.

As such, if porn is a how-to manual, it isn't overly successful in teaching individuals about sexual satisfaction. Porn portrays sexual pleasure inaccurately and may lead to infrequent orgasm and low-quality sex.

HIV and STD Infections

The adult film industry has a long list of STD and HIV outbreaks in its heterosexual segment. Accumulate data from 2004–2008 showed that 18–26% of actors had at least one infection of chlamydia or gonorrhea yearly. Moreover, 72% of actors who had a diagnosed infection were women. Almost 25% of STD cases in women were reinfections that occurred within a year and 15% of women actors visited STD and family planning clinics. A comparison between these women performers and other LA County residents of similar age range showed that the number of female actors diagnosed with chlamydia was seven times higher. Also, the prevalence of gonorrhea was fifteen times higher than the other LA County residents.

Adult film performers have a huge sexual network and are a bridge population for the transmission of STD. They don't just have sex with fellow performers, but also with individuals belonging to the general population. A UK study revealed that approximately 75% of adult performers had at least one sexual partner outside of work and 90% of them reported that they didn't use a condom regularly.

Viagra Addiction

Viagra and the Internet were released in the same decade, and they continue to play significant roles in today's culture. Many young men have become addicted to either one or the other, or both.

Viagra is an accessible drug and is used by men with prostate cancer and diabetes to treat their erectile dysfunctions. However, its most common users are young men, aged 15–30. These young adult men use it with alcohol or other drugs to gain a highly sensualized state. Viagra is like a silver bullet that boosts self-confidence and overcomes symptoms of physical or psychological impotence. However, as users build tolerance over time, they need higher doses to gain a similar effect. Thus, they become increasingly dependent on the drug.

Researchers point to modern sexual culture as a reason for the Viagra addiction. Young men who take the drug claim that it combats performance anxiety because of the porn they watch on the Internet. Internet addiction creates a dependency on the behavioral process. Its accessibility and popularity create correlations with other substances like Viagra and new disorders like porn-induced erectile dysfunction.

Hypersexual Disorder in Women
Hypersexual disorder in women is characterized by high rates of porn use and masturbation. Sexual medicine researchers and psychiatrists can't agree on what level of sexual activity is required for it to be classified as a disorder. However, research often ignores hypersexuality in women.

Researchers conducted a survey in Germany that consisted of about 1,000 women, mostly college students. They asked about the frequency of the respondents' porn use or masturbation, and the number of sexual partners they had. They assessed the participants' hypersexual behavior through the Hypersexual Behavior Inventory, suggesting that a person who scored high on the questionnaire may need to undergo therapy.

In the research, about 3% of the participants scored high on the hypersexual questionnaire. The results confirmed that women who frequently masturbate or watch porn were more likely to score higher on the questionnaire. Also, those respondents who had many sexual partners also had high hypersexuality scores.

Hypersexual behavior is a hotly debated topic because experts cannot agree if it is a disorder or not. The American Psychiatric Association's mental health bible the *Diagnostic and Statistical Manual of Mental Disorders 5th Edition*, stated there isn't enough evidence to prove that hypersexuality is a mental health issue. However, experts say that it can still be a problem for some individuals because it causes shame or stress and may even result in a negative consequence like loss of a job.

How Quitting Porn Improves Your Health

Watching porn frequently and regularly can cause significant damage to your health and well-being. However, in many cases the damage can be reversed by quitting porn and masturbation, as outlined below.

May Cure Erectile Dysfunction
If you're finding it difficult to maintain an erection during sex, but not when watching porn, you may have porn-induced erectile dysfunction, especially if you're under forty. Dopamine signaling to your penis is extremely significant to erection when you see a mating partner. If the dopamine pathway is healthy, it can maintain an erection. If you're a porn addict, dopamine floods your brain. The problem is that your brain has limited dopamine receptors. Thus, you will have trouble getting an erection because the receptors don't pick up many of the dopamine signaling that will trigger erection.

Moreover, porn projects perfection. You can choose the category that you like. Unfortunately, your expectation is far from reality, which disappoints you. Thus, you have trouble in having erections with a real-life partner. If you spend a lot of time masturbating without lubrication, your penis becomes desensitized, so you won't be able to ejaculate naturally. You may ejaculate extremely fast or masturbate to finish properly. You can eradicate your problem of porn-induced erectile dysfunction if you stop watching porn.

Better Sex
Masturbation can desensitize your penis. Thus, you won't find sex with a real-life partner pleasurable anymore. Your decision to stop or avoid watching porn will make you enjoy sex and ejaculation more. You'll also experience hard erections during intimacy. Of course, it may not happen instantly, but if you continue avoiding porn, you'll discover that sex and ejaculations become more pleasurable to you and your partner too.

CHAPTER 6

Productivity Without Porn

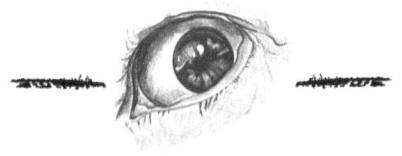

As I sit down to reflect over the next story of this chapter, I could not help but remember my own miserable time with pornography. I was newly married, and never thought the old days of porn would strike back after marriage. I had received an offer to leave my beautiful city, Alexandria in Egypt and move to Cairo for a better job and bigger income. The worst part of it was (which was for me the **best** deal ever at that time), the kind business owner had offered me free accommodation within the company. So the deal was great, and everyone was happy.

But—there was a huge ***BUT*** here that ruined everything. I was left alone at night with unlimited access to the company's Internet which I've never experienced before. So, I'd get ready for work by 9:00 a.m., meet clients, visit worksites, get trained, sell products and by 5:00 p.m. I'd be all alone in the company. After wasting some time chilling, watching a bit of TV and eating dinner, it would be 8:00 p.m. and my eyes would still be wide open looking for more activities and ways to spend my time. As I was new in town, with no close friends and still unfamiliar with Cairo, I decided to remain indoors. And it happened. The Internet was my world, specifically pornography.

For a whole year, I'd spend almost eight hours on porn or chatting programs trying to find a catch until 8:00 a.m. in the morning. Then I would rush for a quick shower, before my colleagues would arrive to start the day at work at nine. By 5:00 p.m. I'd be alone again, would nap for an hour, get up to eat and jump into porn until the next morning and so on and so forth for a whole year. A cycle of unproductivity and stupidity. A worthless life.

When my life was later changed for the better, I realized how much we can do if our time is utilized wisely. For example, my first book,

Productivity Without Porn

Beat It: 50 plus shades of hope, was written, compiled and published in a matter of six months. Aside from the assistance of the creative system of the publisher, I was focused and managed myself by doing what is necessary. Imagine if my life was still stuck within pornography sites for hours every day. Definitely three published books and hundreds of workshops and trainings around the world would never have been possible

Pornography is the greatest enemy to productivity. The two *Ps* cannot go hand in hand. In fact, if one is present, the other can never survive. Just as Samuel explains. He was addicted to gaming, pornography, and marijuana. Multiple addictions, which we call "cross addiction." Samuel described his days of addictions as: *"The most wasted years of my life. I was lazy, overweight, socially anxious, lying all the time and worst of all, postponing and/or neglecting important tasks for the sake of my fixes."* Now, after battling his addictions for years, Samuel is living a very healthy life as a personal fitness trainer with his own successful gym and martial arts school.

As I mentioned earlier, the moment you become productive, that's the moment of punching pornography hard to a nearly knockout moment.

One story that amazes me is that of Edric, co-author of the book *Why You Should Homeschool*. By his own admission, he got into pornography and masturbation at the age of twelve, which left him addicted for many long years until he got married. Even though he was able to quit and start afresh, he realized that his porn consumption had negatively affected his views on how women should be treated. He attributed his victory over porn addiction to a higher being/God, but another element that is very apparent in his book was the homeschooling system that he and his wife established. It was the amount of effort they exhorted to raise and homeschool their six bright, healthy, and intelligent children. Homeschooling isn't easy, it requires full-time dedication to the tasks at hand. Because of that dedication, hard work and productivity, Edric was able to live a life of freedom from the shackles of pornography and unhealthy sexual activities.

So here you have it. Either you engage yourself in productive work, activities, beneficial social gatherings, reading, sport and so on, or boredom will fill up your schedule with something else—and it could be porn and undesirable sexual behaviors. So, within this chapter lies a very simple but effective solution for porn addicts: just be busy.

What the Research Tells Us

In 2016, people around the world watched a total of 4.599 trillion hours on one famous porn site. Those people could have done so many other things and achieved so much more with all those hours, if they weren't dedicating them watching them to porn. The idea of productivity lost to porn is backed up by a Reddit community survey of NoFap® members, where 67% said they felt more productive and had higher energy levels when they stopped watching porn.

It also appears that viewing porn in the workplace is a real issue. Research conducted by the Nielsen Company in 2010, showed that 28% of employees who use a computer check sexually oriented sites. Their average visit to a porn site can last for about thirteen minutes. Thus, an average worker can spend about one hour and thirty-eight minutes each month on porn sites.

Using these statistics, based on the average hourly rate of $23.23 (Bureau of Labor Statistics 2012), the average loss of productivity because of porn use is $38 per month per employee. This monthly loss accounts to a $456 yearly loss for every employee who visits porn sites.

In the book *Porn @ Work: Exposing the office's no. 1 addiction* author Michael Leahy claims, 70% of porn viewing happens during business hours, and at least 60% of human resources employees discovered erotic content on computers in the office.

In 2015, the Judicial Conduct Investigations Office in Britain removed three judges while another judge resigned after discovering porn on their computers. While in 2018, the Inspector General of the US Department of the Interior discovered that malware infected the US Geological Survey network in South Dakota, particularly at its satellite imaging facility the EROS Center, after an employee visited tons of porn pages. The employee kept the porn images in his Android phone and an unauthorized USB device, which he used to connect to his work computer.

How Porn Impacts Your Productivity

It's not difficult to imagine the many things you could achieve if you gave up porn and chose to spend your time more productively. Whether at home or work, your productivity is severely affected once you take up porn as a pastime. Some specific examples follow to further illustrate this.

An Inactive Lifestyle
When you watch porn, your brain releases the happy chemicals serotonin and dopamine, which are the same chemicals released when

you exercise. As such, you tend to choose porn instead of exercise because you get the same feelings without the effort. If you exercise regularly, you are less likely to spend time watching porn for the same reason; your system is already full of happy chemicals. When you stay active and focus on physical exercise, you can ditch porn more easily.

Block Opportunities
Watching porn takes away your time for other activities like hanging out with friends, reading a book, cooking dinner for the family, volunteering in the community, or playing with your children. Since you spend your time and energy on porn, you are less motivated to do other things.

Watching porn causes a huge loss of productivity because you stop investing your time and energy on other significant endeavors. You no longer seek out opportunities that will enhance your life because so much of your focus is on porn.

Difficulty in Reaching Goals
You, like all human beings, have goals in life, but you know that to realize them, you need hard work, dedication, and time. By spending time and energy in porn, you also push aside working towards the realization of your dreams that will provide lasting and real happiness. Watching porn may bring you short-term happiness, but in the longer term you will not feel fulfilled and may experience anxiety and depression later on.

Poor Memory and Concentration
Different studies have linked watching porn to poor cognitive and mental-emotional health outcomes. However, some addiction neuroscientists have also proven that addiction to internet porn can produce long lasting, if not permanent, memory and concentration problems.

Neuroscientists started to isolate brain changes due to addiction to monitor cognitive impairment like disorganized white matter and decreased gray matter. They showed that people who are Internet addicts have increased impulsivity and impaired inhibitory control. Moreover, some brain studies discovered that Internet addicts have impaired concentration measured through the decline in dopamine signals. Dopamine is responsible for motivation, concentration, memory formation, and focus. Low dopamine signals relate to ADHD and poor working memory.

It is suggested that a lack of motivation causes the inattention as Internet addicts find tasks uninteresting or boring. Past neurological studies on sex and porn addicts showed similar brain changes as those in drug and Internet addicts. They also identified neurological desensitization and habituation that showed a reduction in reward system dopamine signaling. Some studies also reported impairment of executive control or dysfunctional prefrontal circuits among pornography users. Both impairment and desensitization of executive functioning bring about poor cognitive operations.

Loss of Revenues
As porn becomes more accessible than ever, young male employees are making regular online porn watching a habit. According to former sex addict and author George Collins, porn viewing results in a loss of productivity that equates to millions of dollars of lost revenue every year. Porn use can also prevent employees from achieving promotions or raises due to stunted or poor performance. In some rare cases, some employees sued employers for creating unsuitable work environments.

How Quitting Porn Improves Your Productivity Levels

When you give up porn, you instantly create more time in your life to do the things that matter. You can also begin to repair your brain which will enhance your memory and concentration as explained in more detail below.

Renewed Productivity
If you watch porn for more than fifteen hours each week, you're losing sleep, time, and mind-space. The time spent on porn is time for your hobbies, practice, and projects. If you've been watching porn for fifteen years, you've lost two years of your life that you could have used to practice your craft. When you decide to quit porn, you'll realize you have free hours monthly that you can use for your self-development and growth. Moreover, quitting porn can increase your work quality because you feel well rested in the morning and your dopamine levels become normal. You feel a renewed sense of excitement with what you're set to do for the day.

Increased Motivation
Sex drive, among men, serves as a motivation for them. In *Think and Grow Rich* by Napoleon Hill, in one chapter the author talks about transforming this sex drive into becoming productive. David Asprey of Bulletproof blog fame also talked about his deal with his wife about not ejaculating until he made $250,000. With the added motivation, he took home that big amount (at the time) in just a month.

Elevated Energy
In the NOBNOM (No Booze, No Masturbation) blog, author, investor, and entrepreneur Tim Ferris promoted the idea of abstaining for thirty days from ejaculating, porn, and masturbation to increase

energy and productivity. By the way, you're still allowed to have sex according to some anecdotes, so we do not promote celibacy here. We are saying that porn, masturbation and orgasm *that is associated with it* could ruin your level of energy and productivity.

Become an Early Riser
Productivity is a choice and not being productive is an option. Your mind and body may resist your decision to be a high performing and productive person, but if you can summon all your energies to resist the urge to be lax, you will generate the reward of having concise, clear, and levelheaded thinking that can help you reach your goals.

Being productive isn't just keeping busy; it's the sense of achievement that you finished a project, goal, or task, right and in a timely manner. When you are no longer staying up all night feeding your porn addiction, you can start your day fresh. By waking up early, you realign your priorities and decrease the probability of wallowing in the night-owl lifestyle. You'll have more hours each day to spend with your partner and family than before. In short, you can achieve the happiness that you've always been seeking.

Improved Quality of Work
As an example, let's say you spend around fifteen hours watching porn weekly. You lose sleep and mind-space. Moreover, you lose time for personal hobbies, practice, and projects. In fifteen years, you lose about two years of your life just watching porn. You could have used the time you spent on porn to learn a new language or skill on self-improvement.

When you quit porn, you'll suddenly have extra hours available each month to do something worthwhile. You'll notice an improvement

Aware

in the quality of your work because you go to work rested from the previous night, which in turn gives you a heightened level of excitement in what you do.

CHAPTER 7

Career Without Porn

Ashraf, is a very respected member of his community. With two kids and a very supportive wife, he was working as a sales manager before being promoted to head the department in one of the biggest companies in Morocco. As Ashraf explained: *"Pornography has always*

been a disturbing part of my life, however, due to my busy schedule and heavy loads of work, I would visit these sites only occasionally. Until one day. My boss called me to his office and revealed to me the plan to expand the company over the next year, taking it far and wide within the country. I was so happy and excited, but then he said that he was also called by potential customers in Egypt who would like to have the same establishment in their city and wanted someone to train the employees. And guess what? I was selected to be in Egypt for an entire year."

You might've guessed what happened next already. With the offer of a great promotion and pay rise, a big apartment and a whole shift in his career and financial stability, Ashraf had accepted without hesitation. He left his beloved family and promised to visit them as many times as he could.

As it was, Ashraf, being a very intelligent young man with a lot of experience in his field, shined in Egypt and reports kept pouring into the headquarters' e-mail address in Morocco about how great and professional Ashraf was.

A few months along this journey and Ashraf notices the following: *"As the company in Egypt started to become more stable and sustainable, I became less busy and more bored being alone. Then pornography kicked in once more, but this time very heavily, I mean like never before. A few times a day, masturbating a few times every night, and I started to lose focus and control over my sexual impulses. Every time I'd think of my wife, I'd feel terrible, yet I wasn't able to stop. Relying on the success that I had accomplished in Egypt already, I started neglecting going to work with lame excuses that were noticeable and unacceptable by everyone around me."*

You may think by now that Ashraf's story is over, right?
Not just yet.

Career Without Porn

The e-mails started to pour back into the headquarters' office, but this time with loads of complaints about how Ashraf has become unavailable, lazy and never punctual anymore. And of course, acting very defensively a couple of times for which his boss was convinced that perhaps the people are jealous at his amazing performances and outstanding results. Until one day, the boss himself had planned a visit to see his new empire in Egypt and meet all staff members for the first time. Nine months after Ashraf's promotion and relocation, a meeting was scheduled. Everyone was aware of the boss' arrival and a whole-day program was planned for this unique occasion, but someone very important was missing.

"Call me idiot, stupid, and moron as you please." Ashraf told me during our chat. *"I woke up at 3:00 p.m. that day, the meeting was supposed to take place at 8:30 a.m. When I got up, I found forty-one missed calls and around twenty plus text messages begging me to come immediately. It was right then that my boss had realized that I messed up and failed his expectations. It was only then that he'd believed the e-mail messages of complaints about me from the last few months. By the time I rushed to the company, which was about thirty minutes away from where I live, I was told by one of my colleagues not to go up there as the boss is going mad. I had literally a few minutes to come up with a very convincing lie to explain my absence. But I could not come up with any. The truth is, I was up all night watching porn and masturbating. I was knocked out around 6:00 a.m., I set my alarm but I could not hear it. This was it: pornography had ruined my career."*

Ashraf was told to pack his stuff, return to Morocco and report to work on an appointed date and time. With no choice of his own anymore, he returned back home with lies to convince his wife that he had to come earlier because he had finished the required job earlier. However, his wife came to know the entire story when he returned to her a week later with the sad news. *"I got fired."*

Ashraf had no way to lie anymore and could only explain with transparency the whole story of what happened to him while in Egypt. And this is how Ashraf came to know about my coaching services in this space, and this is how he got started with his journey towards recovery from pornography addiction.

What the Research Tells Us

It is surprisingly easy to fall deep into porn addiction if you have the time, space, and the means. In 2013, staff, peers, and Members of Parliament in the UK tried accessing porn sites 309,316 times *more* than the previous year using their work-issued computers. According to Huffington Post UK, around 850 attempts to access porn sites were blocked daily.

As mentioned earlier, research conducted by The Nielsen Company in 2010 discovered that 28% of employees who work with computers visit porn sites for an average of thirteen minutes per week. This not only results in financial and productivity losses for business, but also impacts career progression—and in severe cases like Ashraf, could result in job loss.

How Porn Impacts Your Career

As discussed, watching porn regularly takes away not only valuable time from your day, but it also adversely affects your memory, focus and motivation levels. If it gets out of hand it will stall or derail your career, and can also cause issues with productivity and interactions with colleagues as explored below.

Creates a Hostile Work Environment
These days, the vast majority of employers include conditions regarding use of the Internet and computers at work in their employment contracts or employee handbook. They have strict rules regarding accessing porn and other inappropriate materials at work and can terminate the employment of staff for gross misconduct if the rules are broken. A few employee contracts even prohibit the usage of the employee's device in accessing porn during work hours. In court, you can't say that you're doing your best in your workplace while watching porn.

According to the Equality and Human Rights Commission in the UK, displaying sexually graphic photos, posters, and pictures is a form of sexual harassment. So, if your coworker sees the porn images on your workstation, even briefly, it constitutes harassment. Your employer needs to act swiftly if your coworker notifies him because they need to avoid a hostile work environment.

Intimidation or Harassment of Female Employees
Porn also becomes a weapon to intimidate or harass female employees. According to the Trades Union Congress in the UK, 10% of female employees are exposed to displays of porn drawings or photos in their office. Sexism is alive in the workplace around the world. Some women reported receiving porn images from their superiors. Others witnessed their fellow employees accessing porn through their gadgets during office hours. In one example, a woman discovered her head on a Photoshopped porn image being circulated in her office. Her colleagues branded her as a "prude" when she pointed it out and complained.

Emotional Damage to Performers
An often forgotten but significant factor in the porn industry is the sex workers themselves. At work they attempt to separate sex and intimacy and receive money for sex to reduce their intrinsic enjoyment of it. However, the ripple effect impacts their lives because they repeat the phony enjoyment of sex. Thus, they condition themselves to believe the hype. If you're a porn actor, you become incapable of experiencing intimate and authentic relationships because you base your self-worth on sex.

Porn performers don't have career longevity and haven't the foresight to form a labor union. Eventually the psychological toll on performers weighs heavily and they become tired of feeling like a prostitute. Unfortunately, their history will also stand as a stumbling block in the future when they seek an alternative career later in life. Although rehabilitations and professional treatments are available, the reality we live in is that your past often determines your future.

Less Support for Gender Equality at Work
Porn activates abstract scripts that form opinions regarding social issues, primarily on gender equality. It depicts women as sexual objects that deserve aggression and degradation. Men who watch porn hold various antisocial attitudes to women, which means they are less likely to support policies that facilitate women's success in the workplace. Although only a minority of men watch porn at work, their actions affect women in the workplace, especially in team settings. Watching porn results in an increase in sexual harassment and leads to loss of focus and disunity.

Financial Loss
As a porn addict, you've likely spent countless hours watching porn at night. As such, you are not in your best form when you wake

up the following morning. You lack restful sleep so you can't give your best work performance for the day. If you establish a routine of porn watching, your sleep deprivation will reflect on the kind of work you produce. You don't have the zeal to acquire new clients. You feel like a zombie because you lack sleep. Eventually, your superiors will notice your under-performance and may decide to fire you, especially if they catch you watching porn during office hours.

The financial loss can impact employers in other ways too. When porn is an issue with team members, managers need to redirect their time and attention to behavioral meetings, disciplinary actions, lawsuits, and termination cases due to increased sexual harassment cases in the workplace. These activities divert their attention away from where it is needed which is another reason why porn is extremely costly for companies.

How Quitting Porn Improves Your Career

If you're looking to progress in your career, it's clear that you need to quit wasting your time and energy on watching porn. Once you do, the door is open to all kinds of possibilities, some of which are discussed below.

Delayed Gratification
If you constantly watch porn, you don't develop the skill of delayed gratification, which is a trait many successful people share. Instead, your brain's focus is on what you find pleasurable, rather than actively controlling and directing your life. Often, if you're a porn addict, you're also an underachiever in other areas.

Without porn, you can develop delayed gratification. When you do, you'll feel more confident and will have more control over your earthly desires. Once you master delayed gratification, you also increase your chances of success in other areas of your life.

Set Goals and Rewards
Many porn addicts fail to set and reach personal goals and often struggle with their careers, finances, and relationships. Self-gratification can't exist together with achievement of worthy goals. You may not realize it, but if you watch porn often and masturbate, your brain gets excess dopamine—then, you become desensitized slowly to its effects and look for additional stimulation by watching more porn. The excess dopamine in your brain breaks the reward circuitry. If you stop watching porn, you can repair the damage by setting meaningful goals and rewards for yourself.

Establish Clear Thinking
When your motivation levels are high, your brain works more effectively to solve difficult cognitive problems. However, sexual exhaustion due to excessive porn watching makes you slower physically and mentally. After you've finished your sexual mission for the day, your hormones and body send signals to you that you've already accomplished your significant tasks. Thus, your brain goes into relaxation mode early. Observe how you feel sleepy after sex. You may wonder why you felt fitter years ago than today—it's because your daily porn watching is having a negative impact on how you function.

Increased Creativity
Porn addiction clouds your imagination and kills your creativity. It can overshadow your greatest thoughts and become deadly to yourself and success. Why is this so? It's because your thoughts

become clouded with adult content, which is based on fantasy and generally does not happen in real-life situations. And as a result, you lose your ability to think clearly.

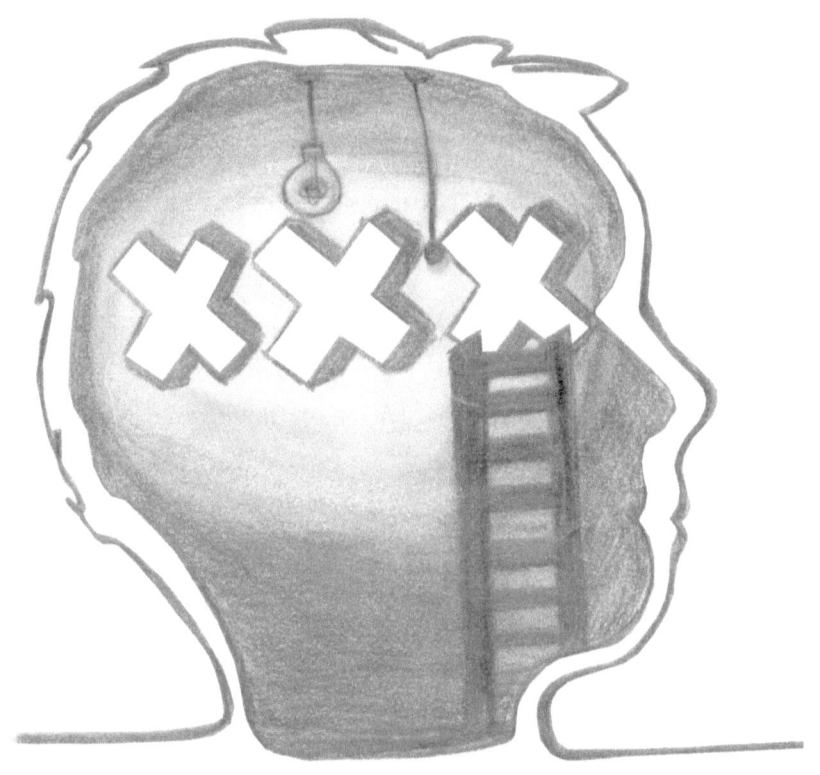

CHAPTER 8

Mental Health Without Porn

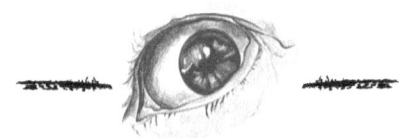

Aware

"*I am desperately in need of your guidance.*" This is one opening line I see on many of the e-mails that I receive on a daily basis, and it always grabs my attention. This time it was from Gulani, who started her message by describing how her husband is such a nice human being, kindhearted and caring. However, he's been trapped in the cycle of pornography for over twenty years.

She went on to say: "*It (pornography) destroyed my psychological well-being. This problem has affected our relationship from the very beginning of our marriage to a great extent. He doesn't want to hurt me, but it seems he's so helpless to get rid of it on his own.*"

The key phrase that I wanted to highlight in her message here is that *pornography had destroyed her psychological well-being.* She's been tortured mentally and cannot make sense of anything around her anymore. Gulani has been struggling for four years since the day she knew about her husband's addiction to porn. In her own words she continued to say: "*This thing (pornography) is stealing my peace of mind. I want to break free from this suffocation.*" **Look at what your addiction can do to others.** She is not addicted and does not have anything to do with porn herself, yet her husband's behavior has led her close to a mental breakdown. That's why I always say, pornography is no longer an individual choice or action that may affect the consumer only. I've seen in my practice so far children being traumatized by the actions of their parents in regard to their porn use. And now Gulani is going through similar drama as a result of her husband's addiction to porn.

Gulani had joined one of our recovery programs at the Aware Academy but she wasn't sure how would she convince her husband to join and benefit from the treatment. Although she signed up for the program, completed her payment and committed to the contract, yet she kept on delaying the time to start until her husband is ready and willing to cooperate. And the reason is, in her own words: *"My husband has lost confidence in himself. He's always alone, sad, sobbing at night, and very emotional almost all day. It has become so painful to bear this type of life. On one hand I am very upset and angry at him for his unacceptable behavior, but on the other hand I feel so sorry for him being in this condition."*

I could relate more than one story here on the harmful impacts that pornography could cause to your mental health, whether it is depression, anxiety, or stress. The main problem that I wanted you to take away from this chapter is, that pornography does not only affect the individual consumer anymore, it can extend to their loved ones, just like Gulani in the story above.

What the Research Tells Us

While pornography provides users with a short-term high, this is replaced with ongoing mental health issues such as depression, anxiety and low self-esteem. In a self-selected sample of 400 porn-using males, Dr. Kevin B. Skinner discovered that men who use porn daily often suffer from depression. Within the group, eighty-nine reported using porn between 3–5 times a week and all had experienced depression, ranging from mild to severe.

Marcus Squirrell, a Swinburne University of Technology PhD student in Melbourne, Australia discovered a relationship between the time spent in online sex activity and the severity of depression. In his survey of 1,325 Australian and American men, 27% of the respondents reported moderate to severe depression, 30% experienced anxiety, and over a third suffered from stress.

How Porn Impacts Your Mental Health

In today's fast-paced world, looking after your mental health has never been more important. Often those who watch porn report that they started doing so for stress relief or to escape their worries. While this may have worked in some way initially, prolonged and regular viewing of porn negatively impacts your mental health in multiple ways as explained below.

Low Self-Esteem
Low self-esteem can make you vulnerable to addictive behaviors. It can drive you to find ways to feel important, in control, and accepted—so, you start watching porn because it connects you with people you see on the screen. You do it to escape any negative feelings, like worthlessness, you may have. Unknowingly, you are only making matters worse. You fall into a vicious pattern because once you get up and go back to real life, you will find it boring compared to the porn images and videos. You start feeling less enthusiastic about almost everything, including yourself.

Guilt
No person who watches porn thinks that he's doing a noble act. Some teenagers believe that watching porn is a very grown-up thing to do and may even brag about it. On the other hand, older people may perceive watching porn as a common or necessary activity and downplay the kind of unrest their soul is having. However, no one feels that what he's doing is honorable or virtuous.

Guilt is prevalent among porn users and causes changes in physiology and a decline in mental health. For porn users, they only have two options. First, they can dull or turn off the conscience so that they won't feel guilty. Second, they can stop using porn. The former will further deteriorate their state of mental health.

Depression

Porn users become compulsive, at-risk cybersex users who experience anxiety, depression, and guilt. Moreover, these experiences can lead to other negative behaviors. Although it is difficult to ascertain which comes first, porn or depression, porn temporarily makes users forget about their fears, boredom, sadness, and anger. Porn use can lead to depression and depression can lead to porn use. Of course, you don't want to find yourself in either of the two scenarios because it is detrimental to your mental health.

Porn and other addictions trigger the release of dopamine that will make you feel good. However, you will feel its effects less and less over time and you suddenly find yourself searching for hardcore porn. Some porn users substitute watching pornography for happiness. They become numb with graphic sex videos and images. They miss building amazing and real relationships with their partners, family, friends, and community.

Low Mood

Because of personal factors like anxiety, interpersonal stress, loneliness, or depression, people may find pleasure in watching pornography because it changes their negative mood. However, porn addiction affects your overall emotional, physical, and mental health. You may cover up how you feel about yourself and your relationships. Ultimately, you miss experiencing real love and you feel worse about yourself and your situation.

You feel shame and guilt due to your sex addiction which can make you question your self-worth, your interactions with other people, and your accomplishments. Your struggle with porn will pull you down and will make you despise yourself as you continue with your destructive behaviors.

Impulsiveness
Some research points to the existence of a relationship between impulsive behaviors and Internet porn use. This is true of the occasional porn user, not just porn addicts.

Disconnection
Obsession or compulsion to porn generally has a negative effect on relationships. People need a sense of community and social interaction, not the fake intimacy that porn offers. If you become hooked on porn, you miss out on building real relationships and connections. As you turn to porn and sex addiction, you lose your desire to have real sex and you withdraw from people you love. Your obsession pulls you away from your family and friends. You miss and disconnect from the people you love.

When you watch porn, you carry a secret that creates distance. You often think how people will react if they know that you're watching porn. This kind of thinking affects your mental health because you'll feel that even your closest friendships are fake or superficial.

Objectification of People
In the porn world, individuals aren't loved, assisted, and heard because they are used, evaluated, and ranked. If you spend many hours watching porn, you begin to assimilate such values. You fail to see other people as unique individuals who deserves your respect. When you treat people this way, your mental health will eventually suffer.

Inability to Manage Unpleasant Emotions
Watching porn is a stress reliever for many people. However, this passive approach to stress management makes you incapable of managing unpleasant emotions. Thus, you will likely suffer more from depression, anxiety, and other distresses. If you watch porn regularly, you condition yourself to believe that normal conflicts in your life and relationships that occur every day are unbearable.

Your mental health is stable if you remain resilient even in the middle of unpleasant circumstances or emotions. Porn provides an escape from processing your unpleasant emotions in a healthy manner, which reinforces the belief that stress mustn't exist.

Loss of Focus
Mindfulness allows you to maintain your focus, even under adverse circumstances, which contributes to your mental health and well-being. On the other hand, porn has the opposite effect, because it pulls you from the real world into a world of fantasy through sound, tactile, and sight sensation. It presents an enticing narrative that makes it difficult for you to focus your attention on less stimulating activities.

You may disengage from essential activities that lack the same excitement. For instance, you can lose focus on basic life management tasks, because you avoid anything mundane. However, this eventually catches up with you, as when you consistently perform poorly on basic life management activities it has a negative impact on your mental health.

No Time for Constructive Activities
The time you spend viewing porn, takes away from the time you have available to do something constructive. Excessive porn watching means you don't invest time on meaningful and substantive things

that can improve your mental and physical health. Porn robs you of time that you could have spent doing something worthwhile that enables you to develop and grow.

The CUBIS Model
You may wonder about the connection between mental issues like anxiety and depression, and porn addiction. This is explained through the CUBIS Model which focuses on the following five areas: Chemical imbalance, Unresolved issues, Beliefs, Inability to cope, and Stimulus-response relationship.

Chemical Imbalance: Depression and anxiety can occur because some neurochemicals in the brain don't produce at the expected levels, resulting in mental health issues like paranoia, fear, depression, and anxiety. Porn and sex addiction can regulate the imbalance temporarily so you may feel better by distracting yourself with these destructive and undesirable behaviors.

Unresolved Issues: Trauma, abandonment, grief, abuse, and loss can make you find ways to escape or numb yourself from these challenges. You may avoid these issues whenever they pop up, so you turn to porn and cybersex to suppress these feelings or thoughts and help you to escape, forget, or distract yourself from your mental health issues.

Beliefs: You grew up with a set of beliefs that you received from your family, neighbors, and community. This belief system is your benchmark in how you see things, people, and yourself. However, some beliefs are distorted, irrational, and untrue. For instance, a healthy relationship starts with friendship then moves on to trust, commitment, love, and sex—but, some people believe that sex is a way to develop friendship and that it can meet their unmet needs.

This irrational and distorted belief can lead to an unhealthy cycle of addiction.

Inability to Cope: If you're a porn addict, you treat it as your best friend that you can rely on 24/7. When reality becomes unpredictable, you turn to porn and cybersex because they always deliver what they promise. Moreover, your addiction becomes equal with your partner, family, and friends. Unfortunately, it may even be your number one. If you want to get well, you need to give up your best friend that is porn.

Stimulus-Response Relationship: The prefrontal cortex and the midbrain play an important role in addiction. The former is where decision-making, personality, and morality exist while the latter is responsible for reinforcing behaviors. The midbrain releases dopamine that reinforces behaviors required for survival. However, addictive behaviors like porn and sex can also trigger the release of the chemical.

The release of dopamine will flood the prefrontal cortex and shut down the brain's logical, rational, and decision-making part. It also triggers the release of glutamate, the memory neurochemical, which makes the midbrain remember that you need these addictive behaviors to survive. Society views addiction as a morality issue and responds by treating it with guilt, coercion, shame, blame, and incarceration.

How Quitting Porn Improves Your Mental Health

There are so many ways your mental health will improve once you quit porn. Not only will you lose the guilt and shame associated with your secret habit, you'll also start making healthy lifestyle choices which will boost both your physical and mental health, including some that are listed below.

Better and Restful Sleep
When you spend hours watching porn at night, you wreak havoc on your physical and mental health. Porn, masturbation, and orgasm allows you to escape from your problems, but they also suck the life out of you. When you shun porn, you get proper sleep which helps you to strengthen your creativity, become emotionally stable and reduce stress levels.

Time for Exercise
Once you decide to stop using porn, you can use the time to exercise instead, which can prevent diseases and improve your health. If you become physically active, you boost your confidence and are better equipped to deal with stress and depression.

Mindfulness
Avoiding porn will allow you to practice mindfulness so you can pay attention on purpose and become physically present without judgment. When you become mindful, conscious, and aware of what is happening around you, you will start to live in the present and stop reacting on an external stimulus automatically. Mindfulness is your tool to fight against compulsive behaviors. It allows you to disengage from automatic harmful habits, thoughts, and unhealthy behavior patterns.

Positive Self-Image
A positive self-image is about self-acceptance. The more you think positively about yourself, the easier it is for you to accept other people. If you have a positive image about yourself, you can also practice

self-acceptance and self-confidence. Eventually, other people will notice it and will want to spend more time with you, and you'll gain a desire to spend more time socializing.

CHAPTER 9

Your Brain Without Porn

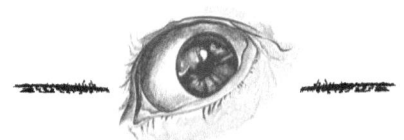

While I was in Indonesia some time ago conducting a two-day workshop on the harmful impact of pornography, I had the pleasure of meeting the "Iron Lady" of Indonesia, Elly Risman, an activist, researcher and a very committed, passionate and dedicated lady when it comes to the health and well-being of her people. When I met her, a couple of years ago she was sixty-eight years old with the energy of a teenager.

Elly had carried out research which aimed to determine the effect of pornography addiction on the brain's function, structure, and activity, and also the sexual behavior mainly on young minds. A sample of teenagers with addiction and non-addiction to porn aged 12–16 years were selected. The selection of age groups, I was told, was based on the findings of Kita and Buah Hati Foundation in 2016, which found that of 2045 children in grade 4–6 SD, 97% had been exposed to pornography. In addition, the age is chosen in order to represent the level of education from elementary to high school as other research conducted across the world tends to focus on older student and adult respondents.

As I sat with her for hours, she explained that the research used *purposive sampling technique,* where respondents were chosen in accordance with the criteria and objectives of the study. The research process was conducted from February to May 2017. The data collection process was started by screening to select the respondent according to the exclusion and inclusion criteria. Exclusion criteria started with interviews to find out the age of the respondent, the history of pregnancy and birth, physical and psychological deveuleopment, indication of psychological and neurological disorders, and history of injuries and diseases affecting the head of the respondent. The inclusion criteria was set to diagnose whether the respondent was experiencing pornographic or non-addiction based on the result validated Pornography Addiction Test (PAT) which can be used on the respondent's age group. Respondents who scored low on the PAT were categorized as non-addictive. Conversely, respondents who scored high were categorized as addictive. Respondents from both categories are entitled to follow the taking of psychological data related to sexual behavior and cognitive ability, MRI examination at Abdi Waluyo Hospital, and EEG examination at UHAMKA Neuroscience Center.

I just wanted you to imagine the difficult and detailed work that such an old lady (although truly very young at heart, and full of passion and energy) had to go through before sharing with us her finding. The research results came in, showing just what she and the other experts would expect:

1) From the perspective of neuroscience, pornographic exposure proved to cause addiction can damage a teenager's brain and affect the brain very negatively.

2) Porn addiction can damage brain connectivity, especially in the prefrontal cortex. The disruption can impact some brain functions, such as compulsivity, self-control, managing priorities and making decisions, flexibility, attention, motivation, learning, and memory.

3) Brain volumetric analysis shows change, both functional and structural, in respondents with porn addiction, as seen in those with drug or other substance addiction.

4) Porn addiction becomes a predisposition of prefrontal lobe shrink up to 4.4%. This shrinkage could lead to a limited base for emotional and spiritual intelligence.

5) The addicted respondents' brains showed dominance of delta wave, which indicates that hypofrontal syndrome is happening. Hypofrontal syndrome is degradation of brain activity caused by reduction of blood flow and brain volume. This syndrome may give impact to the braking system, a system that allow humans to control themselves from doing wrong actions. People with a damaged braking system will not be able to control themselves since they cannot tell whether one act is wrong or not and cannot think further about the impact.

6) In the brain of addicted respondents, they also found domination of gamma wave, which accounted for tendency to behave impulsively compared to non-addiction respondents. Individuals with impulsive behavior tend to fulfill their needs without properley thinking it thorough.

7) Respondents with pornography addiction had a higher tendency to participate in pre-marital sexual behavior compared to non-addiction respondents. (We are talking about teenagers who are 12–16 years old here.)

8) Addicted respondents were more likely to masturbate compared to non-addicted respondents. Of course this is a result of the brain being over stimulated with countless pornographic imagery, and the need to relieve yourself is always high with porn addicts.

9) Based on cognitive assessment, there is no difference in intelligence ability between addicted and non-addicted respondents.

10) Parenting tests showed that parents' involvement, through awareness and proper education, can protect their children from the harms of pornography addiction.

11) Warm relationships between parents and their children will not be enough to prevent their children from risky sexual behavior. They need parental controls as well.

The above study is not the first of its kind. The University of Cambridge conducted a study that covered much of the same content and it produced very similar findings.

What the Research Tells Us

The Internet's accessibility and anonymity permits porn to reach a huge audience. And so, it is important that we start a discussion about the consequences to ensure the information passes through to people to help them make educated decisions.

In an Australia study, over half of the respondents claimed that porn had a positive effect on them. Educational insights, stress relief, and open-mindedness were some of the cited benefits. In the same study, only 7% claimed that porn had a negative impact on them, naming porn addiction and unrealistic expectations in particular. It is clear that many porn users believe there are benefits in watching it, however, most are unaware of the negative and damaging effects on the brain that emerging research is uncovering.

How Porn Impacts Your Brain

Watching porn regularly conditions your brain in a range of negative ways. It sets unrealistic expectations and a warped perspective on relationships. The brain responds in the same way as it does to any addiction, producing feel-good hormones that compel you to keep watching , which in turns depletes your supply so that over time it is harder to experience the same feeling. Below, I look at some of the ways the brain is affected by frequent porn.

Effect of Violent Themes on the Brain
Violent content in porn is common although the amount of violation can vary. Also, how science determines what is violent (and what isn't) is vague and troublesome to measure. But, for our purpose, it is beneficial to determine how porn violence affects the brain and why we should be concerned about it.

In the early 1990s, researchers discovered mirror neurons in masque monkeys. They found that the F5 region of the brain is activated when the monkeys grasped peanuts and were surprised to discover that the same neurons were activated when the monkeys watched someone else grasp the nuts. Additional research showed that the same mirror system existed in humans. The mirror neurons suggest that they are active when you watch porn and when you have actual sex. Such research is still speculative, but it is interesting to know if such mirror neurons can affect your sexual perception. According to UCLA psychiatry professor Marco Jacoboni, these neurons can spread violent behavior because of the way they contribute to mimicking behaviors in people.

Different theories exist about the operation of mirror neurons. Some researchers believe that they mediate action understanding while some of them say that these neurons facilitate the imitation of action. The latter group of scientists also suggests a probable relationship between watching violence and imitating it through the mirror neurons. However, this belief requires more research.

Porn Addiction
In the past, addiction has been scientifically defined and recognized as dependence on a substance. However, the American Society of Addiction Medicine included substances and behaviors in their addiction definition in 2011. It explained that addiction also encompasses the reward circuitry dysfunction of the brain when a person pursues a specific reward habitually through a particular substance or behavior. However, at the time of writing, porn addiction hasn't yet been officially recognized as an addiction although modern day neuroscientist studies agree with the addiction model.

Dopamine may be responsible for porn addiction. It is responsible for the "feel-good" feeling that comes from the brain's reward systems. Often, the reward circuit reacts to natural rewards like having sex, eating food, and other functions that are significant for survival. The use of substances like opioids, methamphetamines, and cocaine highjack it by exaggerating the release of large amounts of dopamine.

Because there is too much dopamine in the brain while you view porn, you can potentially become addicted to it. Porn and addictive substances have the same effects on your brain. However, they differ significantly from the reaction your brain has for natural and healthy pleasures like sex or food. For example, when you eat a snack or enjoy a romantic activity, you will notice a drop in your cravings because you feel satisfied.

According to the director of The National Institute of Drug Abuse, Nora Volkow, dopamine stops firing after recurring use of the natural reward. However, for addictive drugs, dopamine levels continue to increase without let up. Using drugs continuously can increase the level of dopamine. Then, you will feel a stronger urge to use more drugs and will find it hard to stop.

Brain Shrinkage
In 2014, a study in the *JAMA Psychiatry* journal found that frequent porn consumption could shrink the brain and cause fewer connections to the brain's reward circuitry. However, it is also possible that the brain shrinks because porn viewers become used to watching porn images, so they find them less rewarding. Moreover, the same parts of the brain become smaller if you are an alcoholic, depressed, busy, or not in a relationship. Thus, when you watch porn, you may also be suffering from depression.

Quieting the Visual Imagery Process
According to a study published in the *Journal of Sexual Medicine* in 2012, porn consumption tended to quiet a brain part responsible for processing visual imagery. Although it isn't clear why it happens, researchers speculated that the brain diverts blood to more important things instead of allowing it to flow to the visual cortex.

If you view porn, you focus more on the sexually explicit image instead of the finer details of the image background. Thus, you won't be aroused if you take time scanning the horizon. However, according to the researchers, you needed to feel safe and be free from the requisite of searching for potential dangers to experience arousal.

Immediate Gratification

If you watch porn, you value immediate gratification over delayed payoffs. This finding was the overall theme of a study published in the *Journal of Sex Research* in September 2015. Abstaining from porn for three weeks resulted in a willingness to wait longer for a reward. This indicates that if you avoid porn, you can retrain your brain to focus on bigger plans over the longer term, rather than short-term gains.

Rewiring of the Brain

Modern science has found that the brain changes throughout one's lifetime. The brain rewires and lays down fresh connections constantly. Because of fierce competition among the brain pathways, parts not frequently used become replaced. Porn does an incredible job of creating new and long-lasting brain pathways. Most activities can't compete with it, even real-life sex. It can overpower the natural ability of your brain to engage in real sex. According to author and psychiatrist Dr. Norman Doidge, porn can release the right chemicals and create the perfect conditions to change your brain over the long term.

Desensitization and Sensitization

If you bombard the normal reward system of your brain with heightened dopamine levels, it begins to shut down, as the neurons that receive the dopamine shut down to protect their receptors from overstimulation. However, the sending neurons don't stop sending dopamine. Dopamine depletion and nonresponse to the brain chemical occur. You will find it troublesome to experience pleasure. You'll feel lousy. The only thing that can release the much-needed dopamine is for you to watch more porn.

Sensitization can also occur as your brain familiarizes itself with what it hopes to see. If your brain expects to see porn, you start seeing through a sexualized filter where other people's bodies become sexualized objects for you. Adapting your brain in this way makes it difficult for you to reverse the effects.

Bypass and Weaken the Prefrontal Cortex
Porn viewing can bypass and weaken the prefrontal cortex responsible for decision-making and impulse control because it sends a powerful dopamine dose directly to your brain's limbic system where impulse and pleasure reside. You will feel better, but not for long. Then, you'll have a strong desire to watch porn again.

Over time, porn use can damage the pleasure center of your brain to make you less able to feel normal pleasure. You will need stronger and higher dopamine doses, which can increase your desire to search for extreme kinds of porn. You may even indulge in riskier behavior. You develop an abnormal brain that is overactive in some areas and underactive in others. Your brain will have craters and bumps that are visible in scans.

How Quitting Porn Improves Your Brain Function

As highlighted in this chapter, the brain has the ability to replace unused neural pathways with new ones over time. When you quit porn, you give your brain the chance to heal.

Creation of New Brain Pathways
When you stop watching porn, your brain will create new pathways to replace the old ones created by your habit. The "feed the right wolf" analogy is true for this case. If you continue watching porn, you become powerless and porn gets a hold of you. However, if

you decide to stay away from it, you regain your power and porn becomes powerless on you. The process won't be instantaneous, but over time, the brain pathways created by your porn habit will begin to shrink and new pathways can be formed based on healthy and positive actions.

Regaining Brain Sensitivity

As mentioned earlier, porn use affects the brain's reward center. The overused center produces less happy chemicals and becomes less responsive to them. It means that you need more porn to make you feel good. If you stop using it, you effectively remove the primary source of the release of chemicals. Your brain begins searching for new sources.

If you connect to constructive things in your life, you will gain back your physical, mental, emotional, and social health. You may need to start small, but eventually the new pathways will replace the old ones.

Recovery of Damaged Frontal Lobes

Addiction causes adverse changes in your brain. A common outcome is the shrinkage of the frontal lobe, which is responsible for reasoning, logic, and choice. Compulsions and addiction, according to scientists, can cause the harmful changes. You may feel that you're not making any healthy choices due to continuous porn use, but quitting can help you bring back what you've lost and avoid the unwanted behaviors.

Your frontal lobes can recover, although it may take time. Practicing mindfulness can help you achieve daily victories. The process is like that of muscle building. Your muscles become stronger and bigger when you use them often. The more you avoid porn, the healthier your brain becomes and the easier your recovery will be.

Further Reading
Before closing this chapter, I wanted to leave you with an extensive list of neuroscience-based reviews and neurological studies assessing the brain structure and functioning of porn users and sex addicts.

https://www.yourbrainonporn.com/relevant-research-and-articles-about-the-studies/brain-studies-on-porn-users-sex-addicts/#brain

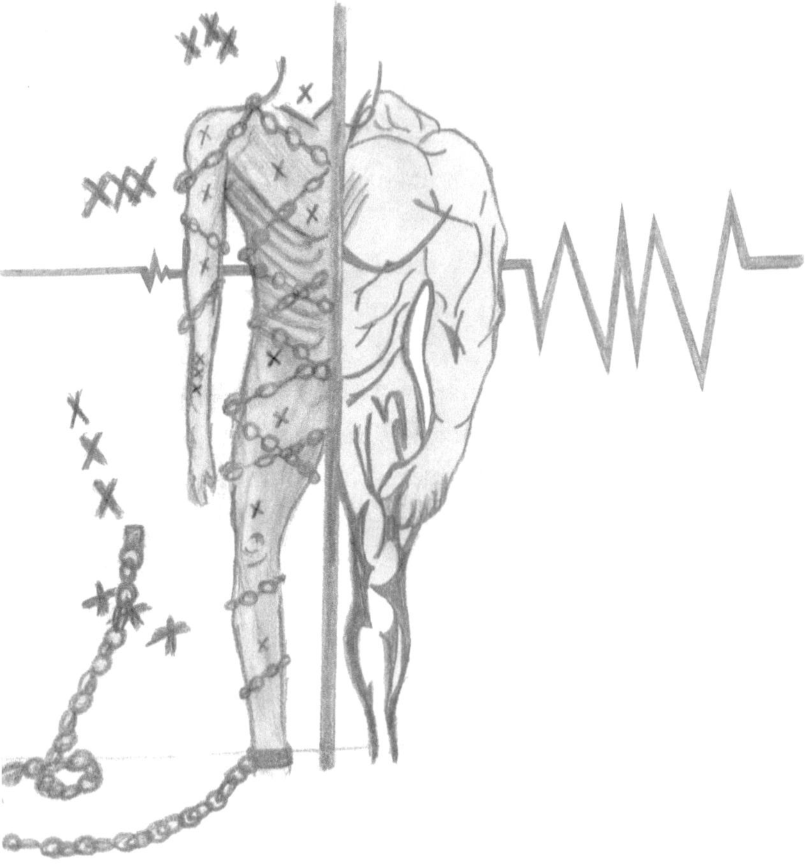

CHAPTER 10

Real Men Without Porn

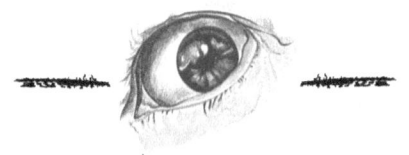

Aware

A teacher once taught me a great lesson, a life lesson we usually don't receive in a classroom. But then, this teacher was different. I never saw him as young, he always looked in his late 60s, with gray hair, a milky white beard and wrinkled skin. Yet, he was strong, muscular, very active, always playing soccer with students during recess, lunchtime and during occasional competitions, was always the first to initiate physical exercises and training. We always used to argue whether he had a six or eight pack!

One day I saw him in the market when I was with my father. He knew my father back in the days when they were neighbors, long before I was born. My father greeted him, talked for a few minutes then we all departed. On the day he was pushing an old lady in a wheelchair. I did not remember my father's conversation with him, all I was thinking was, "Who was that lady?" Since my father was a man who does not concern himself with the business of others, I dared not ask him about it.

A few days later, I was playing soccer in the school and my teacher came in as usual with full enthusiasm and energy asking if he could join. And who dared to say no? Of course, he joined in and we enjoyed the game, his movements and his excellent skills. I remember that day very well. After we finished, he purchased drinks for all students who participated in the match, another reason we loved this teacher. For me though, I was only curious about one thing: Who was that lady he was pushing in a wheelchair? So, I collected myself, grabbed all the courage in the world, and went up to him and said, "Sir, may I ask you a personal question but please do not get mad at me?" He immediately smiled and said something amazing that I won't forget. *"Wael, I do not have anything personal that I am ashamed of, so go ahead and ask, I'd be happy to answer if it would benefit you in your future."* Wow. Didn't expect that. So, I went ahead and asked him. "Do you remember when I met you with my dad in the market a few days ago?" "Yes, I do," he said. "I saw you pushing an old lady in a wheelchair," I continued, "Who is she if you don't mind me asking?" My teacher then started to laugh kindly before answering, "She is my beloved wife."

Please note: He could've said *"She is my wife"* without adding the word *"beloved"* – but he deliberately chose his words very carefully.

Then he said something that I didn't expect, yet I was dying to ask him about it. "You may wonder how someone like me, very healthy, is married to such an old, paralyzed and mute lady huh?" I was dumbfounded and could not even swallow my saliva out of fear and embarrassment. I did not even think that she was paralyzed, let alone being mute! I only thought that she was an old lady who cannot walk like the rest of us. But he kept going. "My wife has been the best thing ever to happen to my life. I was once a very poor man. Ask your dad, he knows me well and the rest of my family. I grew up hearing about the three meals per day but never experienced more than one meal. My parents have struggled a lot to get my siblings and I into university so that we may experience a better life in the future. That was my condition before meeting my beloved wife. Then she came into my life. We met in uni, she was full of life, a bright student, always at the top, charitable and always organizing events to help the poor and needy, not only in our surroundings, but far and wide in different places around the world. She noticed that I never had a meal with them during lunchtime, and she learned about me without my knowledge. She approached me once and said – *"So are you going to live and die in this condition? Aren't you going to do something else to change your life and your family's future? Why are you sitting and waiting for the world to change for your sake? It is not going to happen. You need to do something."* He said he is giving me the short version of the story, I wish I could've asked him to dig into the details of what happened, but anyways, after they became so close, my teacher started to organize fitness classes after university work to earn extra income, and it was through him that his family started to experience what it means to have dinner.

He gave the credit of this shift in his life to his beloved wife. She was the one who encouraged him to be energetic, an initiator of goodness, to always think of an alternative, and never to give up when life becomes tough. He added: *"My wife suffered from a shock that she experienced a couple of years ago when our daughter passed away. She could not bear the news and as a result her health has deteriorated to the condition that you have witnessed. Many people have advised me to find another wife, and my response has always been, I will never hurt her."*

Real men are not driven by their desires, they are driven by situations that would make them act sensibly and responsibly. My teacher, despite his great shape and energy, still remembers his wife's favor upon him and even though she may have lost her physical beauty and function, he said: *"Her soul's beauty would remain forever."*

If you wish to be a real man, do not ever surrender to your physical desire. Instead, get in control of your own life and find a solace in the people around you to soothe any pain that you may experience.

What the Research Tells Us

As mentioned earlier, Pornhub, is the number one publisher of professional and amateur pornographic videos and photos. In 2019, they received 42 billion visitors with an average of 115 million visitors each day—this is equivalent to 962 searches *every second*. Only 29% of visits to the site were made by women, which shows that over two thirds of the visitors are men.

Around the world, significant events caused site traffic to fluctuate. This illustrates the impact that positive events and celebrations can have on reducing the need to view porn, while also showing that some events have the opposite effect and traffic significantly jumps. The statistics are shown below:

- Academy Awards (down 6%) and Emmy Awards (down 5%)
- First Annual Pornhub Awards (up 5%)
- Royal Wedding of Prince Harry and Meghan Markle (down 10%)
- When the servers of YouTube went down on October 16 (up 21%)
- In the US during the Super Bowl (down 26%)
- 2018 World Cup Final (down 55% in France and 66% in Croatia)
- In the US on Christmas Eve (down 34%) and Christmas Day (down 17%)
- In the US, on Valentine's Day (up 7%)
- **Pornhub's annual Free Valentine's Day Premium event (up 308%)**
- Worldwide on New Year's Eve (down 44%)

How Porn Impacts Real Men

A real man respects a woman and her individuality. He considers her as his equal. Although the relationship with her takes effort, he values this and respects her for who she is. On the other hand, porn objectifies women and turns them into "things" which gratify the sexual urge of men. It eliminates the need to connect with women intellectually or emotionally which makes it difficult to develop and maintain meaningful relationships.

Objectification of Women
Insiders in the porn industry believe that women satisfy men's desire. As such, they don't care about these women. In fact, most porn themes revolve about stories of men putting women in their rightful place and getting even with them. They portray women as powerless against men of authority. You have manliness issues if you watch porn just so you can feel like a man. Real men don't objectify women.

Support for a Filthy Industry
Real men don't pay for sex because it violates propriety. However, porn is prostitution with only a few deleted steps. You may rationalize or slice it, but you are indeed paying for sex when you watch porn. If you take a step back, you're spending money to watch other people have sex.

If you have a sister, would you want her to star in a porn video? Definitely not. So, why is it okay for you to watch someone else's sister star in a porn movie? The more you watch porn, the more you encourage the making of more porn. Even if you're watching in the privacy of your room, you still contribute to the problem and allow the porn industry to flourish.

Unrealistic Expectations of Sex
You may not realize it, but you create unrealistic expectations about sex and love when you watch too much porn. Women in porn movies

always appear hot and on the go. They look perfect because they don't nag their partners. When you watch porn, you don't interact with the women, so you just satisfy yourself until you're done.

In general, real-life women won't have sex with you every single time. Not all women are sexy and most of them love to talk a lot. If you are obsessed with porn, you find it difficult to have a meaningful relationship with a woman because you keep comparing every female you meet with those woman actors you watch on porn videos. Any sociologist will tell you that you see your girlfriend or wife through a "porn filter." You prefer impersonal fantasy than having real sex because your partner's love can't satisfy you.

You may also push your partner to do things she doesn't want to, like acting out erotic scenes you've watched on porn films. In your mind, you believe that all women are like those female actors in porn, but that's not the case.

Cyclical Diminishment of Pleasure from Sex
Moderation is the key to happiness. Your brain has sensitive pleasure receptors. For instance, if you try something new, you can activate your receptors easily. However, if you continuously expose yourself to the stimuli, you experience pleasure plateaus and will find yourself wanting more. If you watch porn, you'll find yourself wanting to watch more porn to experience pleasure. Unfortunately, you get into a vicious cycle where you seek more stimulation to experience the same pleasure you had when you first watched porn. Eventually, you'll numb and overwhelm your pleasure receptors.

Society encourages you to view more sexual images than before to make you happy. However, this is ineffective because constant exposure to these images diminishes your capacity to be joyful.

You tend to associate orgasm with something or someone that will turn you on, but focusing on an endless stream of sexual images will dilute Eros and not turn you on.

Extinguishing Manly Confidence
Porn will sap much of your confidence. If you watch porn because of depression and loneliness, you become lonelier and more depressed because you experience intimacy impersonally. You feel empty and this may lead you to watch more porn.

Erection Problems
If you're a moderate porn user, you may notice that you have difficulty sustaining erections with your real-life partner. You'll be horny as ever, yet you need constant visual erotic stimulation to hold your focus. Real sex may become under-stimulating for you. You may also have premature ejaculation due to consistent watching of porn. You might notice you can climax after watching a short video. Your body gets used to climaxing quickly, but your partner's aroused body may not be in tune with yours. If you really value your partner's enthusiasm, you'll feel concerned.

Failure to Have Powerful Interactions with Real Women
Men in Western culture often fail to interact powerfully with real women they find attractive. They fail to approach women in honorable, effective, and respectful ways. Thus, you allow your silent crushes to slip away and suffer a life of regret. Often, you masturbate to take the edge out of your frustrations that you failed to muster the courage to interact with a real woman.

Unrealistic Expectations of Women
Porn makes you think that you can get women to bed easily. You may think that if you're more aggressive, clever, or bold, you may get laid

more. This thinking at times can be true because Western men are bolder with women. However, it comes at the cost of genuine care.

In porn videos, women let a man to do whatever he wants with them. However, real women don't just open their legs due to male aggression. They want to create an intimate and authentic relationship.

Support for Human Trafficking, Rape, Slavery, and Blackmail of Women
If you watch porn, you are a party to the manipulation and outright blackmail of women. In most videos, the camera only shows the face of the woman, not the man's face. Also, countless examples of criminal cases involve men who created porn with women they trafficked and enslaved. These men kept the women captive in buildings where they suffer from physical violence, threats of being exposed to their families and are forced to do sex acts.

How Quitting Porn Makes You A Real Man

When you give up porn, you take a huge step closer to a more fulfilling life. If you don't engage in porn, you don't take part in its fantasy world. You can begin to build real sexual experiences and relationships. Everything about porn is fake and while you are addicted to this world you can never be a real man.

Improvement in Behavior
Porn allows you to be aroused by things that disgust you. You begin to like them even though you know it's wrong to do so. Watching porn regularly makes you believe that such behaviors are common and normal. The destructive behaviors presented by porn compromise your beliefs, relationships, and ideas. You expect your partner to live

up to or do the pornographic scenes—but when you stop watching porn, you can reverse these destructive behaviors.

Build Deeper Connections
Porn objectifies and commoditizes women and sex. You won't find any romance or reality in porn sex—it disconnects you from reality. If you are regularly consuming porn, you will find it difficult to connect intimately with a real woman. But when you quit, you'll begin to feel complete again, and will be able to form real connections.

Become Appreciative of Your Body
Subconsciously, you compare yourself with the men you watch in porn videos. You begin to overthink and develop low self-esteem. If you kick your porn habit, you can reinstate confidence and restore your healthy body image.

Appreciate the Opposite Sex
If you don't watch porn, you tend to appreciate the opposite sex more. Porn turns women into sexual objects and you subconsciously learn to see them as a complete fictional version of what women are. Turning away from porn can get you excited about your partner again and appreciate her for who she is without objectifying her.

Withdraw Support to Sex Trafficking
When you stop watching porn, you also stop supporting human sex trafficking. Less demand for porn will see the need for actors to perform sex on camera reduced. If you don't click on a porn video, you refuse to contribute to the exploitation of porn actors.

Be a Better Parent, Partner, and Friend
If porn has no effect on you, you have more time for your partner, children, and friends. Spending time watching porn makes you

neglect and betray the people you love because you choose to bond with your screen rather than with them. When you cut ties with porn, you can focus on building healthy relationships with the people who matter in your life.

Gain Back Control of Your Life
Some porn users feel that their sexual desires control them, and feel something is wrong because real people no longer turn them on. They then turn to more porn, because they feel that doing so works. If you quit porn, you start connecting with real people and controlling your sexual desires. As you turn away from porn, you also nurture back your sexuality. Instead of reenacting what you've watched on porn, you attune yourself to what you and your partner want. You also increase your sexual energy when you stop watching porn because you begin to show interest in your partner and your sexual intimacy with her.

CHAPTER 11

Women Without Porn

Hager, is a young teenager who got into porn by chance. She used to strip naked online for her boyfriend, but without her knowledge, he was recording every bit of it and uploading it online. Hager didn't know anything about what was happening until one day her cousin (who was addicted to pornography herself) told her, "*Last night I saw you on a pornographic website.*" Hager couldn't believe what she'd heard and what she later saw for herself. She confronted her boyfriend but in a matter of a few hours he blocked her and vanished.

Hager was naturally upset and frustrated, and even thought about killing herself. At the same time, she was desperate to get the footage off the Internet, but unfortunately, as they said, "*What's online remains online.*"

Hager then started to receive messages from strangers asking her to perform to them on certain applications. She was disgusted at first, until she heard the amount of money she will receive if she goes naked for a few minutes. And this is exactly what happened. Hager had entered the world of pornography as a star from the comfort of her bedroom.

Five years went by and Hager was happy making money by pleasing men, who were/are probably addicted to porn and other fetishes. Until one day Hager was proposed to for marriage by a decent guy who had no clue that his beloved girl is porn star. She really wanted to settle down and live a clean life, but unfortunately, her past was always a stumbling block in her way to achieve goodness and live a life that she's always wanted.

After weeks of chatting with her potential spouse, she decided to tell him everything. They went out together for a meal where she was to reveal to him her big secret. She told me that she had texted him earlier saying: *"Hi Majeed, thought I'd let you know that today is a big day for me. Please take whatever I say to you in a spirit of gentleness and ease because it has been so hard for me already and I am not prepared to experience yet another negative reaction to add to my misery."* So, in a way, the guy was prepared to hear something ugly. So, he came on time, worried and breathing heavily, waiting for the shock. Then bam she said it.

Both then departed and a time was granted for Majeed to respond whether he wished to proceed with the proposal or not. And a few days later, she receives his response via text message telling her: *"Hi Hager, I thought over what you mentioned, I think I won't be able to continue. Wish you all the best."* And that was it.

She recalled the days when he would be sending tons of messages just for her to respond and pay attention to him. She said: *"Just because my dark side was exposed to him, he ended it without even trying to help me."* The question now is, did Hager quit her porn business? Unfortunately, no, and this is how bad it was for her.

What the Research Tells Us

According to a 2016 survey by The Independent, 28% of porn users are women. Of the women who watch porn, 30% reported watching it a few times a month, while 31% said they watch it weekly. Almost all (90%) watched the porn online, with two thirds doing so on their smartphone.

Interestingly, in 2017 Pornhub reported that, "Porn for women" was the most used search words, and between 2016 and 2017, the website experienced a 359% increase in women visitors.

How Porn Impacts Women

As we have learned throughout this book, porn objectifies and demeans women. It negatively impacts women who are involved in the industry as well as those who have partners who are addicted in many ways, including those outlined below.

Violence Against Women
There have been many reported incidents from young women of violent and vile things that their husbands or boyfriends do to them as a result of their pornography habits. According to Maree Crabbe, author of *In the Picture*, men often demand that their partners mirror what they watched in porn. Even junior high school girls can be victims of their male classmates, who may ask for naked pictures. Due to the prevalence of porn online, it is no longer surprising that boys and men make real-life requests that are degrading and violent. Expectations can affect healthy relationships and can carry into marriage. It takes time to unlearn what porn teaches about intimacy.

A Painful Legacy
Porn users don't think about the future of the women in the films. According to a former porn star Brittni Ruiz, even though she left the industry and married a pastor, her images and videos are still online. Porn companies make a profit from her past contracts up to now. Another former porn star fears that her children will accidentally find out about her past life online. Porn transforms these women into people who others consume for pleasure. It affects the humanity and dignity of these women.

Addiction
Porn addiction and use isn't just for men only. Women need safe spaces to talk about their addictions too. Sexual templates are for

both sexes. Sexual violence can attract teenage girls and adult women. At first, they may watch soft-core and romantic porn. Then, they will develop the desire to watch degrading and violent sexual acts. They will hide from their family to watch porn. Eventually, they will think that they also deserve to experience pain, abuse, domination, and disrespect just like the women they see in porn.

Gets All the Blame
The media has become the sex educator and online porn prepares boys for dating. Research conducted by Sociology Professor Gail Dines, found that our culture removed the onus on the media and made women take responsibility. Rape occurs because of the over-conformity to the currently structured gender system. Media created hypersexualized boys, and teen girls may become victims, because boys tend to act out what they watch in violent porn movies.

Harassment and Domination
Porn users tend to desire deviant or more explicit images because they experience increased dopamine levels which creates a yearning for the same high feeling they had when they first watched porn. Their brain gets a high sense of excitement and pleasure because it connects such feelings to the images. Thus, they gradually watch more explicit or shocking porn materials that at first disgusted them. Porn users have been known to harass and dominate women. They also become less compassionate to rape victims and victims of violence and may even commit violence themselves.

Sexual Objects
Porn turns women into sexual objects by portraying them as orifices that are ready anytime a man wants them. It shows women without any sexual or human needs. A woman is just a useful object for a

man's gratification. Often, she is a slut, and whore. Porn desensitizes and kills empathy towards a woman's humanity.

Low Self-Esteem and Self-Image

Porn can hijack a user's self-esteem and self-image and can cause undue stress because of the incongruity between actions, values, and beliefs. A woman who watches porn can feel guilt because she knows she's doing something wrong, but she feels trapped because of her addiction. She'll feel powerless and may tend to minimize or justify porn's significance. Whenever she sees the images and scenes, she can feel demoralized and hypocritical.

Lack of Support

Women who watch porn find themselves irritable, angry, annoyed, or depressed. The conflicting feelings are due to their beliefs about porn use. For instance, they realize that society frowns upon porn users as perverts or deviants. Thus, they keep their porn habit a secret. However, they find themselves fantasizing about what they watched even when they're doing other things. They feel ashamed of what they do.

The feelings of shame and isolation women experience and the dopamine rush with watching porn are the same feelings that men experience. Women can also lose interest in sex because they prefer the extreme material that porn offers, and this can lead to the breakdown of romantic relationships. If they want to talk about how their habit is affecting them negatively, they often can't find anyone to listen.

Women can find themselves in deeper problems because they also feel shameful about seeking help. Psychosexual therapist Lisa Etherson noted that women have greater feelings of shame about porn addiction because of the sexual double standard of society. They prefer to keep things secret instead of seeking help.

Undermining Relationships
Aside from the effects of porn use on relationships and individuals, porn also has a pervasive societal effect and contributes to the undermining of women's rights. The exposure of women to porn at an early age makes them more accepting of the fantasy myths of rape.

Also, porn use may have a correlation with relationship instability because the user can have intimacy, attachment, and bonding issues. Men watch porn more often than women and often watch alone for solo masturbation. On the other hand, women generally watch porn as part of lovemaking. Researchers discovered that the relationship quality of women porn users doesn't relate to their porn use, but men's relationship quality may suffer negatively in correlation with their porn use. Porn may also change relationship perceptions that can cause users to have multiple partners or to downgrade monogamy. Porn often leads users to have unrealistic sexual expectations that can lead to the deterioration of real romantic relationships.

Shutdown of the Brain
According to research at the University of Groningen Medical Center, women who watched porn experience a decrease in blood that flows to the visual cortex. While watching a TV show or reading a blog can make a woman absorb all the visual details, porn watching has the opposite effect.

The research showed that the more explicit the video the women watch, the less blood flows into the visual cortex. They opined that the blood goes to the other brain regions involved in sexual arousal.

According to uro-neurologist Gert Holstege, the brain doesn't want to expend energy, so when some of its parts aren't necessary for high level functioning, it shuts them down. Holstege claimed that individuals can't be turned on and be afraid at the same time. According to him, a man needs to generate a safe situation for his partner if he wants to have sex. Some studies showed that, for women, their orgasms could relieve their anxiety.

The desire of researchers to study the woman's brain is as interesting as their conclusions. According to the scientist Beverly Whipple, who discovered the G-Spot, women were not the subjects of studies until after 1993. Men were often the central figure in most research studies and the results were just extrapolated to women. However, researchers discovered that the sexes differ from each other. For Whipple and her team, they believe that although both sexes feel orgasms, they differ with the sexual responses. For example, women can climax through imagination of sensory stimulation.

The studies of the University of Groningen and the team of Whipple suggest that they are opening a new era where the female brain is as interesting and profound as the male brain. Social constraints that once prevented them from studying the sexuality of women are now fading away.

Feelings of Betrayal
Instead of the usual "other woman," the wife of a porn user is betrayed by various fantasy images that get her into thinking that she isn't on par with them. The feeling is devastating because it evokes various ranges of emotions. Research says that the feeling is as painful as a traditional affair. Therefore, it isn't surprising that divorce is on the upswing due to porn.

Porn causes relational, spiritual, and psychological harm. In North America, women expect intimate and marital relationships based on equality founded on honesty, mutual respect, and shared power. Porn, on the other hand, eroticizes and promotes balances of power, disrespect, voyeurism, detachment, discrimination, abuse, and objectification that are the antitheses of the ideals of a married Western woman.

Whenever a married woman discovers her partner is a secret porn user, she feels devastated, because it threatens the foundation of her relational world. Moreover, she faces various assumptions and misconceptions about the reasons why her husband watches porn. Sometimes, society blames her, because her man wouldn't seek porn if she was more sexually available. Also, some people may surmise that she has a bad marriage or that her man is more sexually creative and open-minded than her.

Most women then feel intense isolation because of the blame, judgment, shame, and implications of disclosure. They experience spiritual and psychological crises as they search for help on what to do. Society often dismisses these women as overreacting, frigid, and pathological. The wives are regarded as psychologically unfit while the porn stars are just performers. No one wins.

Empathetic Porn Viewer
Women experience empathy for the porn performers, instead of focusing on the physical sexual acts. They will comment on the possible feelings and facial expressions of actors on different sexual activities. For instance, they may notice if the actor is having real sexual pleasure or not.

Unfortunately, the perception of the women on the enjoyment of the performers can have implications on their arousal. When they sense that the performers' sexual activity is unrealistic, they also find the sexual act less enjoyable and pleasurable.

Insecurity About Their Bodies
Women who watch porn will evaluate the bodies of performers, then reflect on how they feel about their own bodies. Some women become insecure about their bodies after watching porn because they feel that they don't measure up to the physiques of the porn stars. However, others may feel more normal because they see similarities with the performers, while some may even feel better about their own bodies.

Feeling Threatened
Women have different preferences and comfort levels when they watch porn and they differ in how they incorporate porn into their relationship. For instance, some women report that porn arouses them whenever they watch it with their partners. They get ideas and inspirations for the various kinds of sexual activities they can do.

On the other hand, some women feel threatened whenever their partners watch porn because they don't like that their husband or boyfriend experiences arousal for other women. Also, some women report that watching porn is a right of their partner. They don't have problems with the viewing behaviors of their partner as long as he does it privately. Little do they know the huge impacts that it can later have on their relationships.

Cognitive Dissonance
Women may report having a particular porn perspective that doesn't align with their behaviors. For example, they say that porn watching is sexually arousing, but they think that it is socially inappropriate to enjoy watching. They feel conflicted with what they think is

enjoyable and what they feel is socially acceptable. Furthermore, some women may have negative porn perceptions, but still watch it for sexual stimulation. They find it difficult to reconcile their feelings with their moral and cognitive beliefs about porn.

How Quitting Porn Helps Women

While some women enjoy watching porn, alone or with their partners, most report negative feelings of various degrees. Porn rarely results in any improvement to their sexual relationships—in fact, it's generally the opposite, as they find connection, intimacy and arousal increase once they and their partners quit porn. Some of the reasons for this is explained in more detail below.

Enhanced Sexual Confidence
Some people spread a toxic lie that porn can offer new ideas to a couple's sex life. However, the porn user's partner often feels insignificant and insufficient. If the porn user stops watching obscene images and videos, he is saying that his partner is more desirable and significant than the airbrushed beauties of fantasy. Woman can reconnect intimately with their partners and feel more confident in their relationship and sexuality. Their sex life can become satisfying and more frequent.

Reconnect with Love and Intimacy
Curbing porn addiction means that a woman no longer feeds their mind with artificial sexual script to feel momentary connection and satisfaction. Deciding to quit porn can be challenging, but the resulting feelings of real love, connection and intimacy are far more satisfying.

Healthier View of Themselves and Others
Porn conveys women as individuals who can take abuse from their partners. Ditching the porn habit can allow users to see things differently. It can also change the perception about sex and sexuality. Staying away from all forms of porn can improve the understanding about men, women, and relationships. Porn can greatly influence a person on an emotional level, but staying porn-free allows you to develop better views about yourself and other people that can make everyone happier.

Ending Sexual Exploitation
When people stop consuming porn, it helps to improve the lives of others. Because of the high demand for porn, sexual exploitation exists. There are thought to be over 24 million human trafficking victims around the world and 19% of them are victims of sexual exploitation that rake in about $99 billion profits annually.

Millions of women, men, and even children are subject to violence and abuse for someone's sexual entertainment. Staying away from porn can help the victims used in the production of porn films. If you decide not to consume porn anymore, you also contribute to putting a stop to sexual exploitation.

CHAPTER 12

Faith Without Porn

Whether you are a Jew, Christian or a Muslim, pornography does not know faith.

Being a Muslim myself, I've been contacted by thousands of Muslims from around the world complaining about their porn use and begging for some help. As a faith-based community, who are driven by their religious obligations, they are some of the most negatively affected. They are faced with the multiple problems caused by pornography explained in earlier chapters, and on the top of that, they are also faced with the hypocrisy threat. They feel that they are double faced and are not living in harmony with what they believe in. Sometimes they are praying to God with devotions and love, and other times they are disobeying Him by visiting what they believe to be prohibited and abhorred. As a result, some end up leaving their faith altogether.

One thing we need to clarify here is that any addict, whether religious or not, what he may experience as a result of his addiction is in no way recognized as hypocrisy. This is a limited belief that addicts may adapt, which is completely wrong. Hypocrisy is to pretend to be someone who you are not, or to act out being a believer when you are not, which is not what you usually experience as porn addict. You are compelled beyond your control to repeat an unwanted activity against your will. And this is NOT hypocrisy. In fact, I praise anyone who keeps on fighting within himself or herself to free themselves from the shackles of any addiction. If you relapse for any reason during this battle of purity, it does not mean that you are lying to yourself or to your Creator, it means that you have lost the battle once but there are chances for you to stand back up and knockout your enemy. So, keep on fighting and rectify the situation in your favor as soon as you can.

What the Research Tells Us

Various research points to widespread porn usage in religious men and women, with similar numbers reporting unhealthy porn habits as those in the wider community. According to a study by the Barna Group in 2014, almost 40% of self-identified Christian males who were surveyed said that they watch too much porn. Of these, 64% of men accessed porn at least once each month, which is almost identical to the 65% of non-Christian men who also watch porn at least once monthly. While 87% of Christian women admitted to watching porn on occasion, the numbers for regular viewing are lower in comparison, with 15% of Christian females and 30% of non-Christian women admit to using porn at least once every month.

Over half of the pastors who took part revealed that married men had come to them to seek help for their porn habit, while 70% of youth pastors said at least one teenager sought help. Many pastors also said porn has adversely affected the church, and some reported that porn addiction is the most damaging problem in the congregation. Despite this, only 7% of the surveyed pastors said their congregation has a program to help people struggling with porn.

In a survey I conducted for the Aware Academy, we noticed that over 85% of the Muslim community in places like Indonesia, Sri Lanka, the Philippines and Australia have recognized pornography as harmful. And a similar percentage have confessed that they know someone, whether themselves or their partners who is struggling with pornography.

How Porn Impacts Your Faith

If you are a man or woman of faith, porn addiction can be particularly disturbing on an emotional and moral level. You are likely acutely aware of the conflict between your porn use and your beliefs but feel powerless to quit porn and live according to your spiritual values. This then leads to a range of negative feelings and behaviors that significantly impact your mental health as discussed below.

Sexual Shame and Difficulties
In research conducted by the team at Volk, a model was created that showed the progression from childhood religiosity to sexual shame regarding porn use. The model is significant and useful for clinical intervention because it understands how religious porn users experience difficulties and shame. Clinicians can assist the individuals to examine their moral and religious values about porn instead of addressing porn use alone. They can help patients deal with their shameful feelings and sense of addiction.

That's why, I always encourage religious communities to discuss these "less talked about" topics in their sermons and lectures to educate—this is the first step. Secondly, they should aim to normalize the conversation around taboo issues so that a suitable solution can be found.

Feelings of Anger towards God
Research by the group at Wilt, showed that the moral disapproval of using porn causes feelings of anger towards God. You feel distressed when you watch porn, and although you've been praying for a cure, you feel that God had abandoned you for some reason. When watching porn, a religious person generates an increased general irritability and anger towards God for not "helping him"

to cope with his addiction. What the addict fails to realize here is, that your addiction should be treated through multi-model solutions and not only spiritually. Just like a patient of any disease, he or she does not rely on praying ONLY, rather they visit doctors to seek medical solutions as well.

Therapists must help the individuals manage their anger and anxiety, as well as explore the dissonance between moral disapproval and porn use. They can offer nonjudgmental therapeutic relationships through mindfulness techniques instead of providing clinical interventions only.

Violations of Sexual Values
The level of negative perception about your sexual values violations depends on your religion and religious values. If you have strong religious beliefs, you will feel more negatively whenever you violate your sexual values by doing what is abhorred. Moreover, you will identify your violations as having a more negative effect on your partner.

Spiritual Struggle and Sexual Anxiety
The conflict between your actual sexual behaviors and your religiously driven sexual values is the main contributor to your spiritual struggle and sexual anxiety. The higher the conflict, the more likely you will experience depression and low sexual self-esteem. A person with a high level of porn use experiences no psychological or moral conflict if he feels that his sexual behaviors and values are congruent.

Higher Level of Depression
According to the research of Reid, Hook, and Carpenter, religious sex addicts experience higher levels of depression. However, both religious and nonreligious patients experience almost the same levels

of stress and shame. Moreover, they both have comparable levels of porn and masturbation use. However, religious patients have fewer sexual partners, and lower levels of drug and alcohol use. Another noteworthy finding is that 57% of the patients in the study are in committed and religious relationships. It shows that sex addiction can be a concept developed around the foundations of monogamy and religion.

Relationship Anxiety
In a study by Leonhardt, Young-Petersen, and Willoughby it was revealed that porn use affects relationship anxiety of the individual, especially when he thinks of himself as "damaged goods." The damaged goods hypothesis is a concept where people see themselves as tainted, immoral, or deficient because of their sexual behaviors, or after being a victim of sexual abuse or rape. A "damaged" individual begins to isolate himself from personal engagement and social supports that can help counteract his feelings of negativity.

Relationship anxiety causes relationships to fail because you believe that you are doomed and rejected by other people when they learn about you being "damaged goods." Thus, you will become secretive of your porn use.

Hinders spiritual growth
Religion calls on the individual to be pure and holy. Secret sin distracts your spiritual life from reaching that goal. You have trouble experiencing true closeness to God, performing your prayers and rituals, and studying religion. Not only that, but porn use is looked at by religion as a sinful act, which makes its user struggle to repent due to the compulsive nature of the habit.

Subversion to God's Will

A porn addict cannot fully surrender himself to God. Failure, pain, frustration, and loneliness are the results of pursuing selfish desires. Porn use distorts how you hear God's words and commands. God's purpose is for you to honor, glorify and worship Him. He created you for this reason and pornography snatches you away from that path. It isn't His purpose to live a life following your lusts and unwanted desires. Thus, sexual exploitation is a rebellion against the divine plan of God in your life.

Culture paints the human body as a product of random chance, and not as something special created by God. Taking Him out of the picture makes you believe that you have complete freedom to live a life that you desire without any consideration. However, claiming that fulfilling lustful passions is your only purpose makes you destroy and undermine the moral standards of human dignity and decency that serve as the foundation of free and just societies.

Consequences-bound

In Jesus's Sermon on the Mount, He reminded the faithful not to commit adultery. He said that anyone who looks at a woman with lust has committed adultery. Aside from the prohibition of stealing another person's wife, He prohibits lusting. Therefore, if you watch porn, there is a chance your addiction will escalate into an actual act of adultery.

In the Qur'an too, the believers are reminded to lower their gaze in order to protect their chastity and private parts, and that any sexual desire attained through means other than the constitution of marriage is considered to be a transgression against God Almighty.

Habitual porn users will have to face some negative consequences as a result of watching porn and engaging in any sexual immorality.

Dishonor God
As faithful to God, no matter what your religion is, you have a duty to honor Him through obedience. And obeying God requires both, heartily acts of worship, like sincere devotions, good intentions, etc., and also physical acts through ritualistic prayers and supplications. If you indulge in porn, you dishonor Him. Firstly, because your body isn't created for sexual immorality, and secondly, your body doesn't belong to you to damage it. He is your Creator, so you should keep the trust (*your body*) as healthy as it was given to you the first time.

Foolish Waste of Life
Spending time watching porn is foolishness. Life on this earth is short; thus, you must use your time wisely. Indulging in porn is not only a time waster, but money and energy waster too. You waste the life that God gave you and cripple your faith by refusing to invest your time, energy, and money into spreading the good teachings of your religion. You become a slave to your desires instead of being a slave of the One who created you in the first place.

Betrayal of the Family
Even if you're not yet married, loyal love is a commitment that you have with your wife that brings kind deeds. A covenant loyalty makes you prefer to die instead of being unfaithful to her. If you use porn, you don't love your wife and break the promise you have with her. Also, you betray and commit adultery against her if you persist in your actions due to the escalation of your addiction. You

make her compete with the pornographic images and videos that can ruin your relationship.

Your porn use doesn't only ruin your relationship with your wife, but with your children as well. You no longer have moral authority with them. Your faltering relationship with your family can lead to divorce, as I have witnessed many times in the course of my practice. You and your wife aren't the only ones that will suffer. Your children will hurt the most.

Ruins the Conscience and the Mind
Porn use ruins your thinking about sex, which is God's gift for you and your partner joined in marriage. Sex, within the realms of marriage, is beautiful. Yet, porn perverts and corrupts sex. Continuous use of porn makes you desire your wife less and increase your desire for illegal sexual activities. Eventually, you'll no longer delight in sex with her at all.

If you indulge in porn, you think of women as just objects to satisfy your lusts. However, God created women to be a companion to men, not a sex provider. Indulging in porn allows you to think of your wife as a sex object. Moreover, porn ruins your thinking process because it rewires your brain destructively, thus warping your affections and love toward her.

Consequently, porn ruins your conscience, which differentiates right from wrong. If you use porn, you allow the desensitization of your conscience by silencing and suppressing it and rationalizing away your sin. In the end, you damage your conscience by not condemning your sinful act, in other words you begin to tolerate what you know is wrong.

Participation in Sex Slavery
Watching porn allows you to feed a system harmful to women. You take part in harming women by ruining how they think about themselves. Your porn use could lead women to become insecure about their bodies. They become depressed and even have eating disorders because they feel a need to compete with the unreasonable porn standards. Porn also harms women because they become sex slaves. It sustains the demand for what is known now as "acceptable prostitution."

An anti-trafficking center notes that more than one third of the victims were also used in producing porn. In another study of 900 prostitutes living in nine countries, about 50% reported that they were used in porn while in prostitution. Anyone who indulges in porn creates a demand for more prostitutes.

How Quitting Porn Enhances Your Faith

When you quit porn, you let go of a life of shame and contradiction, and a huge weight is lifted from your shoulders. You can begin to live according to your religious beliefs and values which leads to feelings of freedom, joy and contentment that will enhance your life on every level. Below are some of the many ways a life free of porn can enhance your religion.

A Change of Heart
The goal of teaching sexual ethics to any faithful isn't to encourage them to abstain from sex. It's not to highlight that the stove is hot so do not approach. Rather, to discipline humankind by becoming *kind* to each other emotionally before the physical and sexual part takes place.

Porn may stir up your lustful cravings, but your manners and your love of God becomes your new source of higher cravings, the craving of respect and honoring what God has revealed, and what He had entrusted you with, i.e. your spouse.

Regulations, rules, and laws may tell you when something is bad and what isn't bad. However, they can't change your lusts for sinful things. You need new cravings, new affections to counter your lustful cravings. Your love of God and your love to obey Him could be the starting point of a new craving that would fill your heart with contentment and patience.

Get Closer to The Creator
If you're a porn addict, you'll realize that guilt plays a huge part in the cycle of addiction. It's a feeling that you're culpable for something you did and you're not sure how to rectify the situation. If you're guilty, you want reconciliation and absolution. When you long for these two things, you create penance modes to soothe your conscience. You perform rituals to make you feel good.

You try to become clean by doing things to recover from your moral lapse. You renew your commitment to God by means of prayers and obedience to His commands, join community activities, or donate your time and talents to worthy causes. You need the right understanding of who God is to realize that sinning against Him is huge. And when you come to that understanding, you will enjoy the closeness to Him who had created you for higher purpose than pleasuring yourself to damnation.

Avoid Undesirable Activities
When you avoid porn, you will also avoid some of the deadliest acts than anyone could commit.

- **Adultery**
  The desire or deed to be involved with somebody sexually other than your spouse is a sin. Pornography addiction does not remain on one level. What was pleasurable in the past is no longer getting you excited, so what do you do? Just like any other addiction, you start looking for stronger doses and harder content. And as a result, your addiction escalates until you desire to act out your fantasy with someone else, and adultery with prostitutes or other partners could be your fate.

- **Deceit**
  You are also guilty of committing the sin of deceit when you watch porn and conceal or misrepresent your actions. Porn makes you shameful; thus, you try to hide or deny confession about it to the one that you are hurting the most. Deleting your browsing history so that your family won't find out about your porn use, you are being deceitful. When you don't confess your porn habit proactively to an accountability partner, you are being deceitful too. I know it is hard to confess this secretive act to anyone, but it is harder to live your entire life lying to yourself and to your loved ones.

- **Greed**
  You are greedy if you commit sexual sin because you take advantage of an individual by defrauding that person of something. If you take something from somebody greedily, you allow your greed to motivate fraud. You use that individual illegitimately and unfairly for your purpose. And this is exactly what you do when you watch porn.

- **Sexual Assault**
  If you watch sexual assault for your titillation, you are also guilty of the same thing. Most porn scenes are violent in nature because they show men taking advantage of the opposite sex. Some women volunteer for degradation, but some of them are raped or forced to do the scenes against their will. If you watch the scenes and enjoyed them, you are also a participant in it.

I'd like to remind you once more before I close this chapter, that religion or spirituality is not the only solution to get rid of your undesirable sexual activities and addiction. It could be a very powerful tool in your journey of recovery but should not be the only strategy you rely on. Addiction is a brain disease, it can change the brain's structure physically to a point where a person loses control over his own actions, and thus a multi-model approach is needed.

Pray as much as you can, supplicate to God with a sincere heart, bow down to Him in humility and repent every day and every night—however, I recommend you also seek out professional help to speed up your recovery.

Final Word

On every level, as we have observed through the chapters of this book, pornography has the potential to destroy your life. Whether you are a young child or taking care of a child, a teenager growing up in an over-sexualized society, a married couple, a business person with a successful career, an intelligent individual with a super powerful brain, a muscular man with high sexual urges, a healthy individual whether physically or mentally, a great looking man or woman with great reputation, or a faithful individual who honors his Creator and is proud being part of his religion—it does not really matter, because pornography could easily rob you of all the goodness associated with the areas mentioned above.

This book is not an invitation for you to hate sex or anything pleasurable associated with it. It is a call to look at the facts, which tell us that pornography has nothing to do with sex or pleasure. It sneaks into your life with three-second pleasurable moments at a time and ends with nothing but pain, regret, and a miserable lifestyle. So, if you have been suffering and nearly suffocating from the negative impact of pornography, then you owe it to yourself to seek the necessary help as soon as you can. The Aware Academy provides that help for those who are serious about their recovery, however, if you think that porn has done nothing negative to you, then there's no harm done. I just hope and pray that your children won't come to you one day telling you, *"Dad, Mum, why didn't you warn me about the negative effects of pornography?"* And if they do, I hope that on that day, you will be able to assist them and help them cope with their struggles.

Wael Ibrahim

You may contact the below e-mail if you wish to join our recovery programs:
wael@wael-ibrahim.com

References

CHAPTER 1: CHILDREN WITHOUT PORN

Baxter, A. (2018, January 9). *How Pornography Harms Children: The Advocate's Role.* Retrieved from American Bar Association: https://www.americanbar.org/groups/child_law/resources/child_law_practiceonline/child_law_practice/vol-33/may-2014/how-pornography-harms-children--the-advocate-s-role/

De Robien, M. (2018, April 4). *A family therapist reveals the worst effects of adult content on children.* Retrieved from Aleteia: https://aleteia.org/2018/04/04/a-family-therapist-reveals-the-worst-affects-of-porn-on-children/

Digital Kids Initiative. (2014, August). *Children and Pornography.* Retrieved from Digital Kids Initative: https://digitalkidsinitiative.com/wp-content/uploads/2014/08/Children_and_Pornography_Factsheet-Revised-August-2014.pdf

Fight the New Drug. (2018, March 16). *4 Studies That Show How Porn-Obsessed Brains Can Heal Over Time.* Retrieved from Fight the New Drug: https://fightthenewdrug.org/4-studies-that-prove-porn-addicted-brains-can-return-to-normal/

Fight the New Drug. (2017, July 27). *Kids Who Find Hardcore Porn Want To Repeat What They've Seen, Study Shows.* Retrieved from Fight the New Drug: https://fightthenewdrug.org/massive-study-reveals-what-kids-are-watching-learning-from-online-porn/

Garner, D. (2016, September 15). *Counselor Shares 5 Strategies to Keep Kids from Porn Addiction.* Retrieved from Protect Young Minds: https://protectyoungminds.org/2016/09/15/counselor-strategies-porn-addiction/

MacLaughlin, K. (2017, December 19). *The Detrimental Effects of Pornography on Small Children.* Retrieved from Net Nanny: https://www.netnanny.com/blog/the-detrimental-effects-of-pornography-on-small-children/

Moore, A. (2018, June 26). *Does My Child Need Counseling? Reassuring Advice from a Porn Addiction Therapist.* Retrieved from Protect Young Minds: https://protectyoungminds.org/2018/06/26/does-child-need-counseling-advice-porn-addiction-therapist/

Muresan, R. (2016, September 20). *One in 10 visitors of porn sites is under 10 years old.* Retrieved from Hot for Security: https://hotforsecurity.bitdefender.com/blog/one-in-10-visitors-of-porn-sites-is-under-10-years-old-16675.html

National Society for the Prevention of Cruelty to Children. (2016, April 6). *50% of children admit to seeing sexual and violent material online.* Retrieved from National Society for the Prevention of Cruelty to Children: https://www.nspcc.org.uk/what-we-do/news-opinion/net-aware-reveals-risky-social-media-sites/

National Society for the Prevention of Cruelty to Children. (2018, August 30). *New survey reveals risks children and young people face online.* Retrieved from National Society for the Prevention of Cruelty to Children: https://www.nspcc.org.uk/what-we-do/news-opinion/new-survey-online-risks-wild-west-web/

Perry, L. (2016, June). *The Impact of Pornography on Children.* Retrieved from American College of Pediatricians: https://www.acpeds.org/the-college-speaks/position-statements/the-impact-of-pornography-on-children

Primack, B.A., Gold, M.A., Schwarz, E.B. & Dalton. M.A. (2009, April). *Degrading and Non-Degrading Sex in Popular Music: A Content Analysis.* Retrieved from Science Daily: https://www.sciencedaily.com/releases/2009/02/090224132903.htm

Ross, C. C. (2012, August 13). *Overexposed and Under-Prepared: The Effects of Early Exposure to Sexual Content.* Retrieved from Psychology Today: https://www.psychologytoday.com/us/blog/real-healing/201208/overexposed-and-under-prepared-the-effects-early-exposure-sexual-content

CHAPTER 2: TEENAGERS WITHOUT PORN

Baxter, A. (2018, January 9). *How Pornography Harms Children: The Advocate's Role.* Retrieved from American Bar Association: https://www.americanbar.org/groups/child_law/resources/child_law_practiceonline/child_law_practice/vol-33/may-2014/how-pornography-harms-children--the-advocate-s-role/

Beck, J. (n.d.). *How Pornography Affects Teenagers [and Children].* Retrieved March 22, 2019, from Ever Accountable: https://everaccountable.com/blog/how-pornography-affects-teenagers-and-children/

Blair, L. (2016). *How Difficult is it to Treat Delayed Ejaculation Within a Short-Term Psychosexual Model? A Case Study Comparison.* Retrieved from Taylor & Francis Online: https://www.tandfonline.com/doi/abs/10.1080/14681994.2017.1365121?journalCode=csmt20&Covenant Eyes. (2015). *Pornography Statistics.* Owosso: Covenant Eyes.

Culture Reframed. (2017, June 27). *Extensive Research into the Harms of Pornography on Children and Young People.* Retrieved from Culture Reframed: https://www.culturereframed.org/researched-harms/

References

De Robien, M. (2018, April 4). *A family therapist reveals the worst effects of adult content on children.* Retrieved from Aleteia: https://aleteia.org/2018/04/04/a-family-therapist-reveals-the-worst-affects-of-porn-on-children/

Digital Kids Initiative. (2014, August). *Children and Pornography.* Retrieved from Digital Kids Initative: https://digitalkidsinitiative.com/wp-content/uploads/2014/08/Children_and_Pornography_Factsheet-Revised-August-2014.pdf

Fight the New Drug. (2015). *3 Reasons Why Watching Porn is Harmful (And Research is Proving It).* Retrieved from Medium: https://medium.com/@FightTheNewDrug/3-reasons-why-watching-porn-is-harmful-and-research-is-proving-it-bc572b1b0abf

Fight the New Drug. (2018, March 16). *4 Studies That Show How Porn-Obsessed Brains Can Heal Over Time.* Retrieved from Fight the New Drug: https://fightthenewdrug.org/4-studies-that-prove-porn-addicted-brains-can-return-to-normal/

Fight the New Drug. (2017, July 27). *Kids Who Find Hardcore Porn Want To Repeat What They've Seen, Study Shows.* Retrieved from Fight the New Drug: https://fightthenewdrug.org/massive-study-reveals-what-kids-are-watching-learning-from-online-porn/

Fight the New Drug. (2018, June 20). *Let's Talk About Porn. Is It As Harmless As Society Says It Is?* Retrieved from Fight the New Drug: https://fightthenewdrug.org/3-reasons-why-watching-porn-is-harmful/

Garner, D. (2016, September 15). *Counselor Shares 5 Strategies to Keep Kids from Porn Addiction.* Retrieved from Protect Young Minds: https://protectyoungminds.org/2016/09/15/counselor-strategies-porn-addiction/

Green, L., Brady, D., Olafsson, K., Hartley, J. & Lumby, C. (2011). *Risks and Safety for Australian Children on the Internet.* Retrieved form Edith Cowan University: https://ro.ecu.edu.au/ecuworks2011/2/

Huerta, D. (n.d.). *Seven Strategies to Combat Teen Porn Use.* Retrieved March 23, 2019, from Focus on the Family: https://www.focusonthefamily.com/parenting/sexuality/kids-and-pornography/seven-strategies-to-combat-teen-porn-use

MacLaughlin, K. (2017, December 19). *The Detrimental Effects of Pornography on Small Children.* Retrieved from Net Nanny: https://www.netnanny.com/blog/the-detrimental-effects-of-pornography-on-small-children/

Marripedia. (n.d.). *Effects of Pornography on Adolescents.* Retrieved March 22, 2019, from Marripedia: http://marripedia.org/effects_of_pornography_on_adolescents

Moore, A. (2018, June 26). *Does My Child Need Counseling? Reassuring Advice from a Porn Addiction Therapist.* Retrieved from Protect Young Minds: https://protectyoungminds.org/2018/06/26/does-child-need-counseling-advice-porn-addiction-therapist/

Muresan, R. (2016, September 20). *One in 10 visitors of porn sites is under 10 years old.* Retrieved from Hot for Security: https://hotforsecurity.bitdefender.com/blog/one-in-10-visitors-of-porn-sites-is-under-10-years-old-16675.html

National Society for the Prevention of Cruelty to Children. (2016, April 6). *50% of children admit to seeing sexual and violent material online*. Retrieved from National Society for the Prevention of Cruelty to Children: https://www.nspcc.org.uk/what-we-do/news-opinion/net-aware-reveals-risky-social-media-sites/

National Society for the Prevention of Cruelty to Children. (2018, August 30). *New survey reveals risks children and young people face online*. Retrieved from National Society for the Prevention of Cruelty to Children: https://www.nspcc.org.uk/what-we-do/news-opinion/new-survey-online-risks-wild-west-web/

Perry, L. (2016, June). *The Impact of Pornography on Children*. Retrieved from American College of Pediatricians: https://www.acpeds.org/the-college-speaks/position-statements/the-impact-of-pornography-on-children

Peter, J. & Valkenburg, P. (2008). *Adolescents' Exposure to Sexually Explicit Internet Material, Sexual Uncertainty, and Attitudes Towards Uncommitted Sexual Explorations: Is There a Link?* Retrieved from ResearchGate: HYPERLINK "https://www.researchgate.net/publication/249683186_Adolescents'_Exposure_to_Sexually_Explicit_Internet_Material_Sexual_Uncertainty_and_Attitudes_Toward_Uncommitted_Sexual_ExplorationIs_There_a_Link" https://www.researchgate.net/publication/249683186_Adolescents'_Exposure_to_Sexually_Explicit_Internet_Material_Sexual_Uncertainty_and_Attitudes_Toward_Uncommitted_Sexual_ExplorationIs_There_a_Link

Pizzol, D., Bertoldo, A. & Foresta, C. (2016). *Adolescents and Web Porn: A New Era of Sexuality*. Retrieved from NCBI: https://www.ncbi.nlm.nih.gov/pubmed/26251980

Quadarra, A., El-Murr, A., & Latham, J. (2017, December). *The effects of pornography on children and young people*. Retrieved from Australian Institute of Family Studies: https://aifs.gov.au/publications/effects-pornography-children-and-young-people-snapshot

Ross, C. C. (2012, August 13). *Overexposed and Under-Prepared: The Effects of Early Exposure to Sexual Content*. Retrieved from Psychology Today: https://www.psychologytoday.com/us/blog/real-healing/201208/overexposed-and-under-prepared-the-effects-early-exposure-sexual-content

Ybarra, M. L., & Thompson, R. (2017, July 7). *Predicting the Emergence of Sexual Violence in Adolescence*. Retrieved from John Hopkins University: https://jhu.pure.elsevier.com/en/publications/predicting-the-emergence-of-sexual-violence-in-adolescence

Your Brain on Porn. *Research Confirms Sharp Rise in Youthful Sexual Dysfunctions*. Retrieved from Your Brain on Porn: https://www.yourbrainonporn.com/rebooting-porn-use-faqs/research-confirms-sharp-rise-in-youthful-sexual-dysfunctions/

CHAPTER 3: RELATIONSHIPS WITHOUT PORN

Baxter, A. (2018, January 9). *How Pornography Harms Children: The Advocate's Role*. Retrieved from American Bar Association: https://www.americanbar.org/groups/child_law/resources/child_law_practiceonline/child_law_practice/vol-33/may-2014/how-pornography-harms-children--the-advocate-s-role/

Becca. (2019, March 20). *How Pornography Affects Marriage*. Retrieved from The Dating Divas: https://www.thedatingdivas.com/pornography-affects-marriage/

References

Beck, J. (n.d.). *How Pornography Affects Teenagers [and Children]*. Retrieved March 22, 2019, from Ever Accountable: https://everaccountable.com/blog/how-pornography-affects-teenagers-and-children/

Brenner, G. (2017, July 17). *Pornography and Broken Relationships*. Retrieved from Psychology Today: https://www.psychologytoday.com/us/blog/experimentations/201707/pornography-and-broken-relationships

Covenant Eyes. (2015). *Pornography Statistics*. Owosso: Covenant Eyes.

Culture Reframed. (2017, June 27). *Extensive Research into the Harms of Pornography on Children and Young People*. Retrieved from Culture Reframed: https://www.culturereframed.org/researched-harms/

Daubney, M. (2017, March 29). *Men's lives are being ruined by pornography. So why aren't we angry about it?* Retrieved from The Telegraph: https://www.telegraph.co.uk/men/thinking-man/mens-lives-ruined-pornography-arent-angry/

De Robien, M. (2018, April 4). *A family therapist reveals the worst effects of adult content on children*. Retrieved from Aleteia: https://aleteia.org/2018/04/04/a-family-therapist-reveals-the-worst-affects-of-porn-on-children/

Digital Kids Initiative. (2014, August). *Children and Pornography*. Retrieved from Digital Kids Initative: https://digitalkidsinitiative.com/wp-content/uploads/2014/08/Children_and_Pornography_Factsheet-Revised-August-2014.pdf

Douglas, Z. (2015, May 18). *5 Ways Porn Ruins Relationships*. Retrieved from Relevant Magazine: https://relevantmagazine.com/life5/relationships/5-ways-porn-ruins-relationships/

Doyel, J. (2012, June 4). *How Do I Keep My Husband from Looking at Pornography*. Retrieved from Covenant Eyes: https://www.covenanteyes.com/2012/06/04/how-do-i-keep-my-husband-from-looking-at-pornography/

Fight the New Drug. (2017, February 3). *3 Reasons Why Relationships And Porn Don't Mix*. Retrieved from Fight the New Drug: https://fightthenewdrug.org/3-reasons-why-relationships-and-porn-dont-mix/

Fight the New Drug. (2018, March 16). *4 Studies That Show How Porn-Obsessed Brains Can Heal Over Time*. Retrieved from Fight the New Drug: https://fightthenewdrug.org/4-studies-that-prove-porn-addicted-brains-can-return-to-normal/

Fight the New Drug. (2017, July 27). *Kids Who Find Hardcore Porn Want To Repeat What They've Seen, Study Shows*. Retrieved from Fight the New Drug: https://fightthenewdrug.org/massive-study-reveals-what-kids-are-watching-learning-from-online-porn/

Fight the New Drug. (2018, June 20). *Let's Talk About Porn. Is It As Harmless As Society Says It Is?* Retrieved from Fight the New Drug: https://fightthenewdrug.org/3-reasons-why-watching-porn-is-harmful/

Garner, D. (2016, September 15). *Counselor Shares 5 Strategies to Keep Kids from Porn Addiction*. Retrieved from Protect Young Minds: https://protectyoungminds.org/2016/09/15/counselor-strategies-porn-addiction/

Goulston, M. (2010, January 7). *Why Men Use Porn (and How to Get Yours to Stop)*. Retrieved from Psychology Today: https://www.psychologytoday.com/us/blog/just-listen/201001/why-men-use-porn-and-how-get-yours-stop

Huerta, D. (n.d.). *Seven Strategies to Combat Teen Porn Use*. Retrieved March 23, 2019, from Focus on the Family: https://www.focusonthefamily.com/parenting/sexuality/kids-and-pornography/seven-strategies-to-combat-teen-porn-use

MacLaughlin, K. (2017, December 19). *The Detrimental Effects of Pornography on Small Children*. Retrieved from Net Nanny: https://www.netnanny.com/blog/the-detrimental-effects-of-pornography-on-small-children/

Marripedia. (n.d.). *Effects of Pornography on Adolescents*. Retrieved March 22, 2019, from Marripedia: http://marripedia.org/effects_of_pornography_on_adolescents

McKay, B., & McKay, K. (2009, May 11). *The Problem With Porn*. Retrieved from Art of Manliness: https://www.artofmanliness.com/articles/the-problem-with-porn/

Moore, A. (2018, June 26). *Does My Child Need Counseling? Reassuring Advice from a Porn Addiction Therapist*. Retrieved from Protect Young Minds: https://protectyoungminds.org/2018/06/26/does-child-need-counseling-advice-porn-addiction-therapist/

Muresan, R. (2016, September 20). *One in 10 visitors of porn sites is under 10 years old*. Retrieved from Hot for Security: https://hotforsecurity.bitdefender.com/blog/one-in-10-visitors-of-porn-sites-is-under-10-years-old-16675.html

National Society for the Prevention of Cruelty to Children. (2016, April 6). *50% of children admit to seeing sexual and violent material online*. Retrieved from National Society for the Prevention of Cruelty to Children: https://www.nspcc.org.uk/what-we-do/news-opinion/net-aware-reveals-risky-social-media-sites/

National Society for the Prevention of Cruelty to Children. (2018, August 30). *New survey reveals risks children and young people face online*. Retrieved from National Society for the Prevention of Cruelty to Children: https://www.nspcc.org.uk/what-we-do/news-opinion/new-survey-online-risks-wild-west-web/

Perry, L. (2016, June). *The Impact of Pornography on Children*. Retrieved from American College of Pediatricians: https://www.acpeds.org/the-college-speaks/position-statements/the-impact-of-pornography-on-children

Quadarra, A., El-Murr, A., & Latham, J. (2017, December). *The effects of pornography on children and young people*. Retrieved from Australian Institute of Family Studies: https://aifs.gov.au/publications/effects-pornography-children-and-young-people-snapshot

Regnerus, M., Gordon, D. & Price, J. (2016). Documenting Pornography Use in America: A Comparative Analysis of Methodological Approaches. Retrieved from NCBI: https://www.ncbi.nlm.nih.gov/pubmed/26683998

Rissel, C., Ricters, J., Oliver de Visser, R. & McKee, A. (2016). *A Profile of Pornography Users in Australia: findings from the Second Australian Study of Health and Relationships*. Retrieved from ResearchGate: www.researchgate.net/publication/305362715_A_Profile_of_Pornography_Users_in_Australia_Findings_From_the_Second_Australian_Study_of_Health_and_Relationships

References

Ross, C. C. (2012, August 13). *Overexposed and Under-Prepared: The Effects of Early Exposure to Sexual Content.* Retrieved from Psychology Today: https://www.psychologytoday.com/us/blog/real-healing/201208/overexposed-and-under-prepared-the-effects-early-exposure-sexual-content

Stritof, S. (2018, September 27). *What to Do When Your Husband Won't Stop Watching Pornography.* Retrieved from Very Well Mind: https://www.verywellmind.com/husband-wont-stop-watching-pornography-2303586

Weiss, R. (2019, January 30). *3 Ways Porn Is Affecting Your Relationship (And What You Can Do About It).* Retrieved from Mind Body Green: https://www.mindbodygreen.com/0-27470/3-ways-porn-is-affecting-your-relationship-and-what-you-can-do-about-it.html

Wiley, W. (n.d.). *9 Reasons Why Porn Will Ruin Your Marriage.* Retrieved April 1, 2019, from Debt to Life: http://www.debttolife.com/9-reasons-why-porn-will-ruin-your-marriage

Ybarra, M. L., & Thompson, R. (2017, July 7). *Predicting the Emergence of Sexual Violence in Adolescence.* Retrieved from John Hopkins University: https://jhu.pure.elsevier.com/en/publications/predicting-the-emergence-of-sexual-violence-in-adolescence

CHAPTER 4: SEX WITHOUT PORN

Baxter, A. (2018, January 9). *How Pornography Harms Children: The Advocate's Role.* From American Bar Association: https://www.americanbar.org/groups/child_law/resources/child_law_practiceonline/child_law_practice/vol-33/may-2014/how-pornography-harms-children--the-advocate-s-role/

Becca. (2019, March 20). *How Pornography Affects Marriage.* From The Dating Divas: https://www.thedatingdivas.com/pornography-affects-marriage/

Beck, J. (n.d.). *How Pornography Affects Teenagers [and Children].* Retrieved March 22, 2019 from Ever Accountable: https://everaccountable.com/blog/how-pornography-affects-teenagers-and-children/

Brenner, G. (2017, July 17). *Pornography and Broken Relationships.* From Psychology Today: https://www.psychologytoday.com/us/blog/experimentations/201707/pornography-and-broken-relationships

Covenant Eyes. (2015). *Pornography Statistics.* Owosso: Covenant Eyes.

Culture Reframed. (2017, June 27). *Extensive Research into the Harms of Pornography on Children and Young People.* From Culture Reframed: https://www.culturereframed.org/researched-harms/

Daubney, M. (2017, March 29). *Men's lives are being ruined by pornography. So why aren't we angry about it?* From The Telegraph: https://www.telegraph.co.uk/men/thinking-man/mens-lives-ruined-pornography-arent-angry/

De Robien, M. (2018, April 4). *A family therapist reveals the worst effects of adult content on children.* From Aleteia: https://aleteia.org/2018/04/04/a-family-therapist-reveals-the-worst-affects-of-porn-on-children/

Digital Kids Initiative. (2014, August). *Children and Pornography*. From Digital Kids Initative: https://digitalkidsinitiative.com/wp-content/uploads/2014/08/Children_and_Pornography_Factsheet-Revised-August-2014.pdf

Douglas, Z. (2015, May 18). *5 Ways Porn Ruins Relationships*. From Relevant Magazine: https://relevantmagazine.com/life5/relationships/5-ways-porn-ruins-relationships/

Doyel, J. (2012, June 4). *How Do I Keep My Husband from Looking at Pornography*. From Covenant Eyes: https://www.covenanteyes.com/2012/06/04/how-do-i-keep-my-husband-from-looking-at-pornography/

Fight the New Drug. (2017, February 3). *3 Reasons Why Relationships And Porn Don't Mix*. From Fight the New Drug: https://fightthenewdrug.org/3-reasons-why-relationships-and-porn-dont-mix/

Fight the New Drug. (2017, April 11). *3 Ways Porn Damaged Our Relationship & Killed Our Sex Life*. From Fight the New Drug: https://fightthenewdrug.org/3-ways-porn-damaged-our-relationship-killed-our-sex-life/

Fight the New Drug. (2018, March 16). *4 Studies That Show How Porn-Obsessed Brains Can Heal Over Time*. From Fight the New Drug: https://fightthenewdrug.org/4-studies-that-prove-porn-addicted-brains-can-return-to-normal/

Fight the New Drug. (2018, August 19). *How My Obsession With Extreme Porn Impacts My Ability To Be Naturally Aroused*. From Fight the New Drug: https://fightthenewdrug.org/true-story-how-porn-twisted-my-sexuality/

Fight the New Drug. (2017, July 27). *Kids Who Find Hardcore Porn Want To Repeat What They've Seen, Study Shows*. From Fight the New Drug: https://fightthenewdrug.org/massive-study-reveals-what-kids-are-watching-learning-from-online-porn/

Fight the New Drug. (2018, June 20). *Let's Talk About Porn. Is It As Harmless As Society Says It Is?* From Fight the New Drug: https://fightthenewdrug.org/3-reasons-why-watching-porn-is-harmful/

Garner, D. (2016, September 15). *Counselor Shares 5 Strategies to Keep Kids from Porn Addiction*. From Protect Young Minds: https://protectyoungminds.org/2016/09/15/counselor-strategies-porn-addiction/

Goulston, M. (2010, January 7). *Why Men Use Porn (and How to Get Yours to Stop)*. From Psychology Today: https://www.psychologytoday.com/us/blog/just-listen/201001/why-men-use-porn-and-how-get-yours-stop

Gregoire, S. W. (2014, March 18). *Top 10 Effects of Porn on Your Brain, Your Marriage, and Your Sex Life*. From To Love, Honor, & Vacuum: https://tolovehonorandvacuum.com/2014/03/effects-of-porn-on-your-marriage/

Huerta, D. (n.d.). *Seven Strategies to Combat Teen Porn Use*. Retrieved March 23, 2019 from Focus on the Family: https://www.focusonthefamily.com/parenting/sexuality/kids-and-pornography/seven-strategies-to-combat-teen-porn-use

MacLaughlin, K. (2017, December 19). *The Detrimental Effects of Pornography on Small Children*. From Net Nanny: https://www.netnanny.com/blog/the-detrimental-effects-of-pornography-on-small-children/

References

Marripedia. (n.d.). *Effects of Pornography on Adolescents.* Retrieved March 22, 2019 from Marripedia: http://marripedia.org/effects_of_pornography_on_adolescents

McKay, B., & McKay, K. (2009, May 11). *The Problem With Porn.* From Art of Manliness: https://www.artofmanliness.com/articles/the-problem-with-porn/

Moore, A. (2018, June 26). *Does My Child Need Counseling? Reassuring Advice from a Porn Addiction Therapist.* From Protect Young Minds: https://protectyoungminds.org/2018/06/26/does-child-need-counseling-advice-porn-addiction-therapist/

Muresan, R. (2016, September 20). *One in 10 visitors of porn sites is under 10 years old.* From Hot for Security: https://hotforsecurity.bitdefender.com/blog/one-in-10-visitors-of-porn-sites-is-under-10-years-old-16675.html

National Society for the Prevention of Cruelty to Children. (2016, April 6). *50% of children admit to seeing sexual and violent material online.* From National Society for the Prevention of Cruelty to Children: https://www.nspcc.org.uk/what-we-do/news-opinion/net-aware-reveals-risky-social-media-sites/

National Society for the Prevention of Cruelty to Children. (2018, August 30). *New survey reveals risks children and young people face online.* From National Society for the Prevention of Cruelty to Children: https://www.nspcc.org.uk/what-we-do/news-opinion/new-survey-online-risks-wild-west-web/

Park, J. S. (2016, December 1). *4 Unexpected Things That Happen When You Quit Porn.* From XXX Church: https://www.xxxchurch.com/men/4-unexpected-things-that-happen-when-you-quit-porn.html

Perry, L. (2016, June). *The Impact of Pornography on Children.* From American College of Pediatricians: https://www.acpeds.org/the-college-speaks/position-statements/the-impact-of-pornography-on-children

Quadarra, A., El-Murr, A., & Latham, J. (2017, December). *The effects of pornography on children and young people.* From Australian Institute of Family Studies: https://aifs.gov.au/publications/effects-pornography-children-and-young-people-snapshot

Ross, C. C. (2012, August 13). *Overexposed and Under-Prepared: The Effects of Early Exposure to Sexual Content.* From Psychology Today: https://www.psychologytoday.com/us/blog/real-healing/201208/overexposed-and-under-prepared-the-effects-early-exposure-sexual-content

Scott, C. (2013, November 20). *10 Reasons Why You Should Quit Watching Porn.* From GQ: https://www.gq.com/story/10-reasons-why-you-should-quit-watching-porn

Stritof, S. (2018, September 27). *What to Do When Your Husband Won't Stop Watching Pornography.* From Very Well Mind: https://www.verywellmind.com/husband-wont-stop-watching-pornography-2303586

Weiss, R. (2019, January 30). *3 Ways Porn Is Affecting Your Relationship (And What You Can Do About It).* From Mind Body Green: https://www.mindbodygreen.com/0-27470/3-ways-porn-is-affecting-your-relationship-and-what-you-can-do-about-it.html

Weiss, R. (2014, January 20). *Is Male Porn Use Ruining Sex?* From Psychology Today: https://www.psychologytoday.com/us/blog/love-and-sex-in-the-digital-age/201401/is-male-porn-use-ruining-sex

Wiley, W. (n.d.). *9 Reasons Why Porn Will Ruin Your Marriage*. Retrieved April 1, 2019 from Debt to Life: http://www.debttolife.com/9-reasons-why-porn-will-ruin-your-marriage

Ybarra, M. L., & Thompson, R. (2017, July 7). *Predicting the Emergence of Sexual Violence in Adolescence*. From John Hopkins University: https://jhu.pure.elsevier.com/en/publications/predicting-the-emergence-of-sexual-violence-in-adolescence

Your Brain on Porn. (n.d.). *How long will it take to recover from Porn-Induced Sexual Dysfunction?* Retrieved April 6, 2019 from Your Brain on Porn: https://www.yourbrainonporn.com/porn-induced-sexual-dysfunctions/how-long-will-it-take-to-recover-from-porn-induced-sexual-dysfunction/

CHAPTER 5: HEALTH WITHOUT PORN

American Public Health Association. (2010, November 9). *Prevention and Control of Sexually Transmitted Infections and HIV in the Adult Film Industry*. Retrieved from American Public Health Association: https://www.apha.org/policies-and-advocacy/public-health-policy-statements/policy-database/2014/07/28/15/23/prevention-and-control-of-sexually-transmitted-infections-and-hiv-in-the-adult-film-industry

Baxter, A. (2018, January 9). *How Pornography Harms Children: The Advocate's Role*. Retrieved from American Bar Association: https://www.americanbar.org/groups/child_law/resources/child_law_practiceonline/child_law_practice/vol-33/may-2014/how-pornography-harms-children--the-advocate-s-role/

Becca. (2019, March 20). *How Pornography Affects Marriage*. Retrieved from The Dating Divas: https://www.thedatingdivas.com/pornography-affects-marriage/

Beck, J. (n.d.). *How Pornography Affects Teenagers [and Children]*. Retrieved March 22, 2019, from Ever Accountable: https://everaccountable.com/blog/how-pornography-affects-teenagers-and-children/

Brenner, G. (2018, March 5). *4 Ways Porn Use Causes Problems*. Retrieved from Psychology Today: https://www.psychologytoday.com/intl/blog/experimentations/201803/4-ways-porn-use-causes-problems

Brenner, G. (2017, July 17). *Pornography and Broken Relationships*. Retrieved from Psychology Today: https://www.psychologytoday.com/us/blog/experimentations/201707/pornography-and-broken-relationships

Covenant Eyes. (2015). *Pornography Statistics*. Owosso: Covenant Eyes.

Culture Reframed. (2017, June 27). *Extensive Research into the Harms of Pornography on Children and Young People*. Retrieved from Culture Reframed: https://www.culturereframed.org/researched-harms/

Daubney, M. (2017, March 29). *Men's lives are being ruined by pornography. So why aren't we angry about it?* Retrieved from The Telegraph: https://www.telegraph.co.uk/men/thinking-man/mens-lives-ruined-pornography-arent-angry/

References

De Robien, M. (2018, April 4). *A family therapist reveals the worst effects of adult content on children*. Retrieved from Aleteia: https://aleteia.org/2018/04/04/a-family-therapist-reveals-the-worst-affects-of-porn-on-children/

Digital Kids Initiative. (2014, August). *Children and Pornography*. Retrieved from Digital Kids Initative: https://digitalkidsinitiative.com/wp-content/uploads/2014/08/Children_and_Pornography_Factsheet-Revised-August-2014.pdf

Douglas, Z. (2015, May 18). *5 Ways Porn Ruins Relationships*. Retrieved from Relevant Magazine: https://relevantmagazine.com/life5/relationships/5-ways-porn-ruins-relationships/

Doyel, J. (2012, June 4). *How Do I Keep My Husband from Looking at Pornography*. Retrieved from Covenant Eyes: https://www.covenanteyes.com/2012/06/04/how-do-i-keep-my-husband-from-looking-at-pornography/

Fight the New Drug. (2017, February 3). *3 Reasons Why Relationships And Porn Don't Mix*. Retrieved from Fight the New Drug: https://fightthenewdrug.org/3-reasons-why-relationships-and-porn-dont-mix/

Fight the New Drug. (2017, April 11). *3 Ways Porn Damaged Our Relationship & Killed Our Sex Life*. Retrieved from Fight the New Drug: https://fightthenewdrug.org/3-ways-porn-damaged-our-relationship-killed-our-sex-life/

Fight the New Drug. (2018, March 16). *4 Studies That Show How Porn-Obsessed Brains Can Heal Over Time*. Retrieved from Fight the New Drug: https://fightthenewdrug.org/4-studies-that-prove-porn-addicted-brains-can-return-to-normal/

Fight the New Drug. (2018, August 19). *How My Obsession With Extreme Porn Impacts My Ability To Be Naturally Aroused*. Retrieved from Fight the New Drug: https://fightthenewdrug.org/true-story-how-porn-twisted-my-sexuality/

Fight the New Drug. (2017, July 27). *Kids Who Find Hardcore Porn Want To Repeat What They've Seen, Study Shows*. Retrieved from Fight the New Drug: https://fightthenewdrug.org/massive-study-reveals-what-kids-are-watching-learning-from-online-porn/

Fight the New Drug. (2018, June 20). *Let's Talk About Porn. Is It As Harmless As Society Says It Is?* Retrieved from Fight the New Drug: https://fightthenewdrug.org/3-reasons-why-watching-porn-is-harmful/

Frank. (2018, April 9). *5 Life-Changing Health Benefits of Nofap*. Retrieved from My Wealth Shop: https://www.mywealthshop.com/health-benefits-of-nofap/

Garner, D. (2016, September 15). *Counselor Shares 5 Strategies to Keep Kids from Porn Addiction*. Retrieved from Protect Young Minds: https://protectyoungminds.org/2016/09/15/counselor-strategies-porn-addiction/

Gholiphour, B. (2014, July 7). *Hypersexuality in Women Linked to High Porn Use*. Retrieved from Live Science: https://www.livescience.com/46687-hypersexuality-women.html

Goulston, M. (2010, January 7). *Why Men Use Porn (and How to Get Yours to Stop)*. Retrieved from Psychology Today: https://www.psychologytoday.com/us/blog/just-listen/201001/why-men-use-porn-and-how-get-yours-stop

Gregoire, S. W. (2014, March 18). *Top 10 Effects of Porn on Your Brain, Your Marriage, and Your Sex Life*. Retrieved from To Love, Honor, & Vacuum: https://tolovehonorandvacuum.com/2014/03/effects-of-porn-on-your-marriage/

Huerta, D. (n.d.). *Seven Strategies to Combat Teen Porn Use*. Retrieved March 23, 2019, from Focus on the Family: https://www.focusonthefamily.com/parenting/sexuality/kids-and-pornography/seven-strategies-to-combat-teen-porn-use

Los Angeles Daily News. (2012, November 2). *STDs In Porn Industry Higher Than Reported*. Retrieved from HuffPost: https://www.huffpost.com/entry/stds-porn-industry_n_2064639

MacLaughlin, K. (2017, December 19). *The Detrimental Effects of Pornography on Small Children*. Retrieved from Net Nanny: https://www.netnanny.com/blog/the-detrimental-effects-of-pornography-on-small-children/

Marripedia. (n.d.). *Effects of Pornography on Adolescents*. Retrieved March 22, 2019, from Marripedia: http://marripedia.org/effects_of_pornography_on_adolescents

McKay, B., & McKay, K. (2009, May 11). *The Problem With Porn*. Retrieved from Art of Manliness: https://www.artofmanliness.com/articles/the-problem-with-porn/

Moore, A. (2018, June 26). *Does My Child Need Counseling? Reassuring Advice from a Porn Addiction Therapist*. Retrieved from Protect Young Minds: https://protectyoungminds.org/2018/06/26/does-child-need-counseling-advice-porn-addiction-therapist/

Morris, C. (2018, April 18). *Adult Entertainment Industry Remains Shut Down After Positive HIV Test*. Retrieved from Fortune: http://fortune.com/2018/04/18/adult-entertainment-industry-shut-down-positive-hiv-test-porn/

Muresan, R. (2016, September 20). *One in 10 visitors of porn sites is under 10 years old*. Retrieved from Hot for Security: https://hotforsecurity.bitdefender.com/blog/one-in-10-visitors-of-porn-sites-is-under-10-years-old-16675.html

National Society for the Prevention of Cruelty to Children. (2016, April 6). *50% of children admit to seeing sexual and violent material online*. Retrieved from National Society for the Prevention of Cruelty to Children: https://www.nspcc.org.uk/what-we-do/news-opinion/net-aware-reveals-risky-social-media-sites/

National Society for the Prevention of Cruelty to Children. (2018, August 30). *New survey reveals risks children and young people face online*. Retrieved from National Society for the Prevention of Cruelty to Children: https://www.nspcc.org.uk/what-we-do/news-opinion/new-survey-online-risks-wild-west-web/

Park, J. S. (2016, December 1). *4 Unexpected Things That Happen When You Quit Porn*. Retrieved from XXX Church: https://www.xxxchurch.com/men/4-unexpected-things-that-happen-when-you-quit-porn.html

Perry, L. (2016, June). *The Impact of Pornography on Children*. Retrieved from American College of Pediatricians: https://www.acpeds.org/the-college-speaks/position-statements/the-impact-of-pornography-on-children

References

Pornhub. (2018, December 11). *2018 Year in Review*. Retrieved from Pornhub: https://www.pornhub.com/insights/2018-year-in-review

Quadarra, A., El-Murr, A., & Latham, J. (2017, December). *The effects of pornography on children and young people*. Retrieved from Australian Institute of Family Studies: https://aifs.gov.au/publications/effects-pornography-children-and-young-people-snapshot

Ross, C. C. (2012, August 13). *Overexposed and Under-Prepared: The Effects of Early Exposure to Sexual Content*. Retrieved from Psychology Today: https://www.psychologytoday.com/us/blog/real-healing/201208/overexposed-and-under-prepared-the-effects-early-exposure-sexual-content

Scott, C. (2013, November 20). *10 Reasons Why You Should Quit Watching Porn*. Retrieved from GQ: https://www.gq.com/story/10-reasons-why-you-should-quit-watching-porn

Stritof, S. (2018, September 27). *What to Do When Your Husband Won't Stop Watching Pornography*. Retrieved from Very Well Mind: https://www.verywellmind.com/husband-wont-stop-watching-pornography-2303586

The Edge. (2018, August 29). *Can Porn Addiction Lead to Viagra Addiction?* Retrieved from The Edge Rehab: https://www.theedgerehab.com/blog/can-porn-addiction-lead-to-viagra-addiction/

Thompson, D. (2017, May 12). *Study Sees Link Between Porn and Sexual Dysfunction*. Retrieved from WebMD: https://www.webmd.com/sex/news/20170512/study-sees-link-between-porn-and-sexual-dysfunction#1

Villines, Z. (2018, July 30). *How can porn induce erectile dysfunction?* Retrieved from Medical News Today: https://www.medicalnewstoday.com/articles/317117.php

Weiss, R. (2019, January 30). *3 Ways Porn Is Affecting Your Relationship (And What You Can Do About It)*. Retrieved from Mind Body Green: https://www.mindbodygreen.com/0-27470/3-ways-porn-is-affecting-your-relationship-and-what-you-can-do-about-it.html

Weiss, R. (2014, January 20). *Is Male Porn Use Ruining Sex?* Retrieved from Psychology Today: https://www.psychologytoday.com/us/blog/love-and-sex-in-the-digital-age/201401/is-male-porn-use-ruining-sex

Wiley, W. (n.d.). *9 Reasons Why Porn Will Ruin Your Marriage*. Retrieved April 1, 2019, from Debt to Life: http://www.debttolife.com/9-reasons-why-porn-will-ruin-your-marriage

Wright, P. J., Tokunaga, R., Kraus, A. & Klann, Elyssa. (2017) *Pornography Consumption and Satisfaction: A Meta-Analysis*. Retrieved from ResearchGate: https://www.researchgate.net/publication/314197900_Pornography_Consumption_and_Satisfaction_A_Meta-Analysis_Pornography_and_Satisfaction

Ybarra, M. L., & Thompson, R. (2017, July 7). *Predicting the Emergence of Sexual Violence in Adolescence*. Retrieved from John Hopkins University: https://jhu.pure.elsevier.com/en/publications/predicting-the-emergence-of-sexual-violence-in-adolescence

Your Brain on Porn. (n.d.). *How long will it take to recover from Porn-Induced Sexual Dysfunction?* Retrieved April 6, 2019, from Your Brain on Porn: https://www.yourbrainonporn.com/porn-induced-sexual-dysfunctions/how-long-will-it-take-to-recover-from-porn-induced-sexual-dysfunction/

Your Greatest Version. (2017, April 1). *10 Amazing Benefits of NoFap*. Retrieved from Your Greatest Version: https://www.yourgreatestversion.com/benefits-of-nofap/

CHAPTER 6: PRODUCTIVITY WITHOUT PORN

Addiction.com Staff. (2011, November 20). *Pornography At Work*. Retrieved from Addiction.com: https://www.addiction.com/7819/pornography-at-work/

American Public Health Association. (2010, November 9). *Prevention and Control of Sexually Transmitted Infections and HIV in the Adult Film Industry*. Retrieved from American Public Health Association: https://www.apha.org/policies-and-advocacy/public-health-policy-statements/policy-database/2014/07/28/15/23/prevention-and-control-of-sexually-transmitted-infections-and-hiv-in-the-adult-film-industry

Barrett, D. (2015, March 17). *Judges dismissed after watching pornography on court computers*. Retrieved from The Telegraph: https://www.telegraph.co.uk/news/uknews/law-and-order/11476880/Judges-dismissed-after-watching-pornography-on-court-computers.html

Baxter, A. (2018, January 9). *How Pornography Harms Children: The Advocate's Role*. Retrieved from American Bar Association: https://www.americanbar.org/groups/child_law/resources/child_law_practiceonline/child_law_practice/vol-33/may-2014/how-pornography-harms-children--the-advocate-s-role/

Becca. (2019, March 20). *How Pornography Affects Marriage*. Retrieved from The Dating Divas: https://www.thedatingdivas.com/pornography-affects-marriage/

Beck, J. (n.d.). *How Pornography Affects Teenagers [and Children]*. Retrieved March 22, 2019, from Ever Accountable: https://everaccountable.com/blog/how-pornography-affects-teenagers-and-children/

Brenner, G. (2018, March 5). *4 Ways Porn Use Causes Problems*. Retrieved from Psychology Today: https://www.psychologytoday.com/intl/blog/experimentations/201803/4-ways-porn-use-causes-problems

Brenner, G. (2017, July 17). *Pornography and Broken Relationships*. Retrieved from Psychology Today: https://www.psychologytoday.com/us/blog/experimentations/201707/pornography-and-broken-relationships

Chang, M. (2014, August 3). *Why Having Only ONE Orgasm a Month Leads to Success*. Retrieved from Next Shark: https://nextshark.com/this-is-why-the-key-to-productivity-and-success-is-having-only-one-orgasm-a-month/

Covenant Eyes. (2015). *Pornography Statistics*. Owosso: Covenant Eyes.

Culture Reframed. (2017, June 27). *Extensive Research into the Harms of Pornography on Children and Young People*. Retrieved from Culture Reframed: https://www.culturereframed.org/researched-harms/

Cushing, J. (2018, November 1). *Employee Watching Porn At Work Infected US Government Agency's Network*. Retrieved from TechDirt: https://www.techdirt.com/articles/20181031/11124040951/employee-watching-porn-work-infected-us-government-agencys-network.shtml

References

Daubney, M. (2017, March 29). *Men's lives are being ruined by pornography. So why aren't we angry about it?* Retrieved from The Telegraph: https://www.telegraph.co.uk/men/thinking-man/mens-lives-ruined-pornography-arent-angry/

De Robien, M. (2018, April 4). *A family therapist reveals the worst effects of adult content on children.* Retrieved from Aleteia: https://aleteia.org/2018/04/04/a-family-therapist-reveals-the-worst-affects-of-porn-on-children/

Digital Kids Initiative. (2014, August). *Children and Pornography.* Retrieved from Digital Kids Initative: https://digitalkidsinitiative.com/wp-content/uploads/2014/08/Children_and_Pornography_Factsheet-Revised-August-2014.pdf

Douglas, Z. (2015, May 18). *5 Ways Porn Ruins Relationships.* Retrieved from Relevant Magazine: https://relevantmagazine.com/life5/relationships/5-ways-porn-ruins-relationships/

Doyel, J. (2012, June 4). *How Do I Keep My Husband from Looking at Pornography.* Retrieved from Covenant Eyes: https://www.covenanteyes.com/2012/06/04/how-do-i-keep-my-husband-from-looking-at-pornography/

Fight the New Drug. (2017, February 3). *3 Reasons Why Relationships And Porn Don't Mix.* Retrieved from Fight the New Drug: https://fightthenewdrug.org/3-reasons-why-relationships-and-porn-dont-mix/

Fight the New Drug. (2017, April 11). *3 Ways Porn Damaged Our Relationship & Killed Our Sex Life.* Retrieved from Fight the New Drug: https://fightthenewdrug.org/3-ways-porn-damaged-our-relationship-killed-our-sex-life/

Fight the New Drug. (2017, April 2). *4 Hidden Problems With Watching Porn That You Might Not Know.* Retrieved from Fight the New Drug: https://fightthenewdrug.org/hidden-problems-with-watching-porn/

Fight the New Drug. (2018, March 16). *4 Studies That Show How Porn-Obsessed Brains Can Heal Over Time.* Retrieved from Fight the New Drug: https://fightthenewdrug.org/4-studies-that-prove-porn-addicted-brains-can-return-to-normal/

Fight the New Drug. (2018, August 19). *How My Obsession With Extreme Porn Impacts My Ability To Be Naturally Aroused.* Retrieved from Fight the New Drug: https://fightthenewdrug.org/true-story-how-porn-twisted-my-sexuality/

Fight the New Drug. (2017, July 27). *Kids Who Find Hardcore Porn Want To Repeat What They've Seen, Study Shows.* Retrieved from Fight the New Drug: https://fightthenewdrug.org/massive-study-reveals-what-kids-are-watching-learning-from-online-porn/

Fight the New Drug. (2018, June 20). *Let's Talk About Porn. Is It As Harmless As Society Says It Is?* Retrieved from Fight the New Drug: https://fightthenewdrug.org/3-reasons-why-watching-porn-is-harmful/

Frank. (2018, April 9). *5 Life-Changing Health Benefits of Nofap.* Retrieved from My Wealth Shop: https://www.mywealthshop.com/health-benefits-of-nofap/

Garner, D. (2016, September 15). *Counselor Shares 5 Strategies to Keep Kids from Porn Addiction.* Retrieved from Protect Young Minds: https://protectyoungminds.org/2016/09/15/counselor-strategies-porn-addiction/

Gholiphour, B. (2014, July 7). *Hypersexuality in Women Linked to High Porn Use*. Retrieved from Live Science: https://www.livescience.com/46687-hypersexuality-women.html

Goulston, M. (2010, January 7). *Why Men Use Porn (and How to Get Yours to Stop)*. Retrieved from Psychology Today: https://www.psychologytoday.com/us/blog/just-listen/201001/why-men-use-porn-and-how-get-yours-stop

Gregoire, S. W. (2014, March 18). *Top 10 Effects of Porn on Your Brain, Your Marriage, and Your Sex Life*. Retrieved from To Love, Honor, & Vacuum: https://tolovehonorandvacuum.com/2014/03/effects-of-porn-on-your-marriage/

Huerta, D. (n.d.). *Seven Strategies to Combat Teen Porn Use*. Retrieved March 23, 2019, from Focus on the Family: https://www.focusonthefamily.com/parenting/sexuality/kids-and-pornography/seven-strategies-to-combat-teen-porn-use

Los Angeles Daily News. (2012, November 2). *STDs In Porn Industry Higher Than Reported*. Retrieved from HuffPost: https://www.huffpost.com/entry/stds-porn-industry_n_2064639

MacLaughlin, K. (2017, December 19). *The Detrimental Effects of Pornography on Small Children*. Retrieved from Net Nanny: https://www.netnanny.com/blog/the-detrimental-effects-of-pornography-on-small-children/

Marripedia. (n.d.). *Effects of Pornography on Adolescents*. Retrieved March 22, 2019, from Marripedia: http://marripedia.org/effects_of_pornography_on_adolescents

McKay, B., & McKay, K. (2009, May 11). *The Problem With Porn*. Retrieved from Art of Manliness: https://www.artofmanliness.com/articles/the-problem-with-porn/

Mendoza, Edric and Joy (2018). Page 27. Why you should Homeschool. ABS-CBN Publishing Inc. Q.C., Philippines

Moore, A. (2018, June 26). *Does My Child Need Counseling? Reassuring Advice from a Porn Addiction Therapist*. Retrieved from Protect Young Minds: https://protectyoungminds.org/2018/06/26/does-child-need-counseling-advice-porn-addiction-therapist/

Morris, C. (2018, April 18). *Adult Entertainment Industry Remains Shut Down After Positive HIV Test*. Retrieved from Fortune: http://fortune.com/2018/04/18/adult-entertainment-industry-shut-down-positive-hiv-test-porn/

Muresan, R. (2016, September 20). *One in 10 visitors of porn sites is under 10 years old*. Retrieved from Hot for Security: https://hotforsecurity.bitdefender.com/blog/one-in-10-visitors-of-porn-sites-is-under-10-years-old-16675.html

National Society for the Prevention of Cruelty to Children. (2016, April 6). *50% of children admit to seeing sexual and violent material online*. Retrieved from National Society for the Prevention of Cruelty to Children: https://www.nspcc.org.uk/what-we-do/news-opinion/net-aware-reveals-risky-social-media-sites/

National Society for the Prevention of Cruelty to Children. (2018, August 30). *New survey reveals risks children and young people face online*. Retrieved from National Society for the Prevention of Cruelty to Children: https://www.nspcc.org.uk/what-we-do/news-opinion/new-survey-online-risks-wild-west-web/

References

Park, J. S. (2016, December 1). *4 Unexpected Things That Happen When You Quit Porn*. Retrieved from XXX Church: https://www.xxxchurch.com/men/4-unexpected-things-that-happen-when-you-quit-porn.html

Park, J. S. (2016, December 10). *4 Unexpected Things That Happen When You Quit Porn*. Retrieved from Christian Post: https://www.christianpost.com/news/4-unexpected-things-that-happen-when-you-quit-porn.html

Perry, L. (2016, June). *The Impact of Pornography on Children*. Retrieved from American College of Pediatricians: https://www.acpeds.org/the-college-speaks/position-statements/the-impact-of-pornography-on-children

Pornhub. (2018, December 11). *2018 Year in Review*. Retrieved from Pornhub: https://www.pornhub.com/insights/2018-year-in-review

Quadarra, A., El-Murr, A., & Latham, J. (2017, December). *The effects of pornography on children and young people*. Retrieved from Australian Institute of Family Studies: https://aifs.gov.au/publications/effects-pornography-children-and-young-people-snapshot

Ross, C. C. (2012, August 13). *Overexposed and Under-Prepared: The Effects of Early Exposure to Sexual Content*. Retrieved from Psychology Today: https://www.psychologytoday.com/us/blog/real-healing/201208/overexposed-and-under-prepared-the-effects-early-exposure-sexual-content

Scott, C. (2013, November 20). *10 Reasons Why You Should Quit Watching Porn*. Retrieved from GQ: https://www.gq.com/story/10-reasons-why-you-should-quit-watching-porn

Stritof, S. (2018, September 27). *What to Do When Your Husband Won't Stop Watching Pornography*. Retrieved from Very Well Mind: https://www.verywellmind.com/husband-wont-stop-watching-pornography-2303586

The Edge. (2018, August 29). *Can Porn Addiction Lead to Viagra Addiction?* Retrieved from The Edge Rehab: https://www.theedgerehab.com/blog/can-porn-addiction-lead-to-viagra-addiction/

Thompson, D. (2017, May 12). *Study Sees Link Between Porn and Sexual Dysfunction*. Retrieved from WebMD: https://www.webmd.com/sex/news/20170512/study-sees-link-between-porn-and-sexual-dysfunction#1

Villines, Z. (2018, July 30). *How can porn induce erectile dysfunction?* Retrieved from Medical News Today: https://www.medicalnewstoday.com/articles/317117.php

WebRoot. (n.d.). *Internet Pornography by the Numbers; A Significant Threat to Society*. Retrieved April 10, 2019, from WebRoot: https://www.webroot.com/us/en/resources/tips-articles/internet-pornography-by-the-numbers

Weiss, R. (2019, January 30). *3 Ways Porn Is Affecting Your Relationship (And What You Can Do About It)*. Retrieved from Mind Body Green: https://www.mindbodygreen.com/0-27470/3-ways-porn-is-affecting-your-relationship-and-what-you-can-do-about-it.html

Weiss, R. (2014, January 20). *Is Male Porn Use Ruining Sex?* Retrieved from Psychology Today: https://www.psychologytoday.com/us/blog/love-and-sex-in-the-digital-age/201401/is-male-porn-use-ruining-sex

Wiley, W. (n.d.). *9 Reasons Why Porn Will Ruin Your Marriage*. Retrieved April 1, 2019, from Debt to Life: http://www.debttolife.com/9-reasons-why-porn-will-ruin-your-marriage

Ybarra, M. L., & Thompson, R. (2017, July 7). *Predicting the Emergence of Sexual Violence in Adolescence*. Retrieved from John Hopkins University: https://jhu.pure.elsevier.com/en/publications/predicting-the-emergence-of-sexual-violence-in-adolescence

Your Brain on Porn. (n.d.). *6 Habits That Will (Indirectly) Help You Quit Porn*. Retrieved April 11, 2019, from Your Brain on Porn: https://www.yourbrainonporn.com/blogs-vlogs-by-friends-of-ybop/reboot-blueprints-blog/6-habits-that-will-indirectly-help-you-quit-porn/

Your Brain on Porn. (n.d.). *How long will it take to recover from Porn-Induced Sexual Dysfunction?* Retrieved April 6, 2019, from Your Brain on Porn: https://www.yourbrainonporn.com/porn-induced-sexual-dysfunctions/how-long-will-it-take-to-recover-from-porn-induced-sexual-dysfunction/

Your Greatest Version. (2017, April 1). *10 Amazing Benefits of NoFap*. Retrieved from Your Greatest Version: https://www.yourgreatestversion.com/benefits-of-nofap/

Your Internet on Porn. (n.d.). *Can porn use affect memory and concentration?* Retrieved April 10, 2019, from Your Internet on Porn: https://www.yourbrainonporn.com/rebooting-porn-use-faqs/can-porn-use-affect-memory-and-concentration/

CHAPTER 7: CAREER WITHOUT PORN

Addiction.com Staff. (2011, November 20). *Pornography At Work*. Retrieved from Addiction.com: https://www.addiction.com/7819/pornography-at-work/

American Public Health Association. (2010, November 9). *Prevention and Control of Sexually Transmitted Infections and HIV in the Adult Film Industry*. Retrieved from American Public Health Association: https://www.apha.org/policies-and-advocacy/public-health-policy-statements/policy-database/2014/07/28/15/23/prevention-and-control-of-sexually-transmitted-infections-and-hiv-in-the-adult-film-industry

AntiDopamine. (n.d.). *27 NoFap Benefits to Supercharge Your Manliness*. Retrieved May 12, 2019, from AntiDopamine: https://www.antidopamine.com/nofap/list-of-benefits/

Archebelle, C. (n.d.). *5 Ways Pornography Will Ruin Your Life... and How to Break Free*. Retrieved May 9, 2019, from Conquer Series: https://conquerseries.com/5-ways-pornography-will-ruin-life/

Bacter, P. (n.d.). *10 ADVANTAGES OF QUITTING PORN*. Retrieved May 12, 2019, from Steemit: https://steemit.com/steemit/@paulobacter/10-reasons-why-you-should-quit-porn

Baesler, A. J. (2017, June 19). *Effects of Pornography in the Workplace*. Retrieved from Slideshare: https://www.slideshare.net/AdamBaesler1/effects-of-pornography-in-the-workplace

Barrett, D. (2015, March 17). *Judges dismissed after watching pornography on court computers*. Retrieved from The Telegraph: https://www.telegraph.co.uk/news/uknews/law-and-order/11476880/Judges-dismissed-after-watching-pornography-on-court-computers.html

References

Baxter, A. (2018, January 9). *How Pornography Harms Children: The Advocate's Role.* Retrieved from American Bar Association: https://www.americanbar.org/groups/child_law/resources/child_law_practiceonline/child_law_practice/vol-33/may-2014/how-pornography-harms-children--the-advocate-s-role/

Becca. (2019, March 20). *How Pornography Affects Marriage.* Retrieved from The Dating Divas: https://www.thedatingdivas.com/pornography-affects-marriage/

Beck, J. (n.d.). *How Pornography Affects Teenagers [and Children].* Retrieved March 22, 2019, from Ever Accountable: https://everaccountable.com/blog/how-pornography-affects-teenagers-and-children/

Brenner, G. (2018, March 5). *4 Ways Porn Use Causes Problems.* Retrieved from Psychology Today: https://www.psychologytoday.com/intl/blog/experimentations/201803/4-ways-porn-use-causes-problems

Brenner, G. (2017, July 17). *Pornography and Broken Relationships.* Retrieved from Psychology Today: https://www.psychologytoday.com/us/blog/experimentations/201707/pornography-and-broken-relationships

Calonzo, A., & Heijmans, P. (2019, May 12). *The Philippines' Midterm Election Will Test Duterte's Presidency.* Retrieved from Bloomberg: https://www.bloomberg.com/news/articles/2019-05-11/duterte-set-to-gain-allies-shut-out-critics-in-midterm-vote

Chang, M. (2014, August 3). *Why Having Only ONE Orgasm a Month Leads to Success.* Retrieved from Next Shark: https://nextshark.com/this-is-why-the-key-to-productivity-and-success-is-having-only-one-orgasm-a-month/

Covenant Eyes. (2015). *Pornography Statistics.* Owosso: Covenant Eyes.

Culture Reframed. (2017, June 27). *Extensive Research into the Harms of Pornography on Children and Young People.* Retrieved from Culture Reframed: https://www.culturereframed.org/researched-harms/

Cushing, J. (2018, November 1). *Employee Watching Porn At Work Infected US Government Agency's Network.* Retrieved from TechDirt: https://www.techdirt.com/articles/20181031/11124040951/employee-watching-porn-work-infected-us-government-agencys-network.shtml

Darbyshire, M. (2017, December 14). *The consequences of looking at pornography at work.* Retrieved from Financial Times: https://www.ft.com/content/ead0956e-de96-11e7-a0d4-0944c5f49e46

Daubney, M. (2017, March 29). *Men's lives are being ruined by pornography. So why aren't we angry about it?* Retrieved from The Telegraph: https://www.telegraph.co.uk/men/thinking-man/mens-lives-ruined-pornography-arent-angry/

De Robien, M. (2018, April 4). *A family therapist reveals the worst effects of adult content on children.* Retrieved from Aleteia: https://aleteia.org/2018/04/04/a-family-therapist-reveals-the-worst-affects-of-porn-on-children/

Digital Kids Initiative. (2014, August). *Children and Pornography.* Retrieved from Digital Kids Initative: https://digitalkidsinitiative.com/wp-content/uploads/2014/08/Children_and_Pornography_Factsheet-Revised-August-2014.pdf

Douglas, Z. (2015, May 18). *5 Ways Porn Ruins Relationships*. Retrieved from Relevant Magazine: https://relevantmagazine.com/life5/relationships/5-ways-porn-ruins-relationships/

Doyel, J. (2012, June 4). *How Do I Keep My Husband from Looking at Pornography*. Retrieved from Covenant Eyes: https://www.covenanteyes.com/2012/06/04/how-do-i-keep-my-husband-from-looking-at-pornography/

Emezi, J. (n.d.). *How Pornography Erodes Your Masculinity*. Retrieved May 10, 2019, from Steven Aitchison: https://www.stevenaitchison.co.uk/pornography-erodes-masculinity/

Fight the New Drug. (2017, February 3). *3 Reasons Why Relationships And Porn Don't Mix*. Retrieved from Fight the New Drug: https://fightthenewdrug.org/3-reasons-why-relationships-and-porn-dont-mix/

Fight the New Drug. (2017, April 11). *3 Ways Porn Damaged Our Relationship & Killed Our Sex Life*. Retrieved from Fight the New Drug: https://fightthenewdrug.org/3-ways-porn-damaged-our-relationship-killed-our-sex-life/

Fight the New Drug. (2017, April 2). *4 Hidden Problems With Watching Porn That You Might Not Know*. Retrieved from Fight the New Drug: https://fightthenewdrug.org/hidden-problems-with-watching-porn/

Fight the New Drug. (2018, March 16). *4 Studies That Show How Porn-Obsessed Brains Can Heal Over Time*. Retrieved from Fight the New Drug: https://fightthenewdrug.org/4-studies-that-prove-porn-addicted-brains-can-return-to-normal/

Fight the New Drug. (2018, August 19). *How My Obsession With Extreme Porn Impacts My Ability To Be Naturally Aroused*. Retrieved from Fight the New Drug: https://fightthenewdrug.org/true-story-how-porn-twisted-my-sexuality/

Fight the New Drug. (2017, July 27). *Kids Who Find Hardcore Porn Want To Repeat What They've Seen, Study Shows*. Retrieved from Fight the New Drug: https://fightthenewdrug.org/massive-study-reveals-what-kids-are-watching-learning-from-online-porn/

Fight the New Drug. (2018, June 20). *Let's Talk About Porn. Is It As Harmless As Society Says It Is?* Retrieved from Fight the New Drug: https://fightthenewdrug.org/3-reasons-why-watching-porn-is-harmful/

Frank. (2018, April 9). *5 Life-Changing Health Benefits of Nofap*. Retrieved from My Wealth Shop: https://www.mywealthshop.com/health-benefits-of-nofap/

Garner, D. (2016, September 15). *Counselor Shares 5 Strategies to Keep Kids from Porn Addiction*. Retrieved from Protect Young Minds: https://protectyoungminds.org/2016/09/15/counselor-strategies-porn-addiction/

Gholiphour, B. (2014, July 7). *Hypersexuality in Women Linked to High Porn Use*. Retrieved from Live Science: https://www.livescience.com/46687-hypersexuality-women.html

Goulston, M. (2010, January 7). *Why Men Use Porn (and How to Get Yours to Stop)*. Retrieved from Psychology Today: https://www.psychologytoday.com/us/blog/just-listen/201001/why-men-use-porn-and-how-get-yours-stop

References

Gregoire, S. W. (2014, March 18). *Top 10 Effects of Porn on Your Brain, Your Marriage, and Your Sex Life*. Retrieved from To Love, Honor, & Vacuum: https://tolovehonorandvacuum.com/2014/03/effects-of-porn-on-your-marriage/

Huerta, D. (n.d.). *Seven Strategies to Combat Teen Porn Use*. Retrieved March 23, 2019, from Focus on the Family: https://www.focusonthefamily.com/parenting/sexuality/kids-and-pornography/seven-strategies-to-combat-teen-porn-use

Jacobs, T. (2017, June 14). *PORN VIEWING IMPACTS ATTITUDES ON WOMEN IN WORKPLACE*. Retrieved from Pacific Standard: https://psmag.com/social-justice/porn-viewing-impacts-attitudes-women-workplace-66280

Ketcham, J. (2012, November 11). *Pornography Does Lasting Harm to Performers*. Retrieved from The New York Times: https://www.nytimes.com/roomfordebate/2012/11/11/does-pornography-deserve-its-bad-rap/pornography-does-lasting-harm-to-performers

Los Angeles Daily News. (2012, November 2). *STDs In Porn Industry Higher Than Reported*. Retrieved from HuffPost: https://www.huffpost.com/entry/stds-porn-industry_n_2064639

MacLaughlin, K. (2017, December 19). *The Detrimental Effects of Pornography on Small Children*. Retrieved from Net Nanny: https://www.netnanny.com/blog/the-detrimental-effects-of-pornography-on-small-children/

Marripedia. (n.d.). *Effects of Pornography on Adolescents*. Retrieved March 22, 2019, from Marripedia: http://marripedia.org/effects_of_pornography_on_adolescents

McKay, B., & McKay, K. (2009, May 11). *The Problem With Porn*. Retrieved from Art of Manliness: https://www.artofmanliness.com/articles/the-problem-with-porn/

Moore, A. (2018, June 26). *Does My Child Need Counseling? Reassuring Advice from a Porn Addiction Therapist*. Retrieved from Protect Young Minds: https://protectyoungminds.org/2018/06/26/does-child-need-counseling-advice-porn-addiction-therapist/

Morris, C. (2018, April 18). *Adult Entertainment Industry Remains Shut Down After Positive HIV Test*. Retrieved from Fortune: http://fortune.com/2018/04/18/adult-entertainment-industry-shut-down-positive-hiv-test-porn/

Muresan, R. (2016, September 20). *One in 10 visitors of porn sites is under 10 years old*. Retrieved from Hot for Security: https://hotforsecurity.bitdefender.com/blog/one-in-10-visitors-of-porn-sites-is-under-10-years-old-16675.html

National Society for the Prevention of Cruelty to Children. (2016, April 6). *50% of children admit to seeing sexual and violent material online*. Retrieved from National Society for the Prevention of Cruelty to Children: https://www.nspcc.org.uk/what-we-do/news-opinion/net-aware-reveals-risky-social-media-sites/

National Society for the Prevention of Cruelty to Children. (2018, August 30). *New survey reveals risks children and young people face online*. Retrieved from National Society for the Prevention of Cruelty to Children: https://www.nspcc.org.uk/what-we-do/news-opinion/new-survey-online-risks-wild-west-web/

News.com.au. (2016, March 26). *Former porn star Bree Olson goes public: 'I'm shunned by society'*. Retrieved from News.com.au: https://www.news.com.au/entertainment/celebrity-life/former-porn-star-bree-olsen-goes-public-im-shunned-by-society/news-story/106695d7e5eec3e050538697cfac7d28

Park, J. S. (2016, December 1). *4 Unexpected Things That Happen When You Quit Porn*. Retrieved from XXX Church: https://www.xxxchurch.com/men/4-unexpected-things-that-happen-when-you-quit-porn.html

Park, J. S. (2016, December 10). *4 Unexpected Things That Happen When You Quit Porn*. Retrieved from Christian Post: https://www.christianpost.com/news/4-unexpected-things-that-happen-when-you-quit-porn.html

Perry, L. (2016, June). *The Impact of Pornography on Children*. Retrieved from American College of Pediatricians: https://www.acpeds.org/the-college-speaks/position-statements/the-impact-of-pornography-on-children

Pornhub. (2018, December 11). *2018 Year in Review*. Retrieved from Pornhub: https://www.pornhub.com/insights/2018-year-in-review

Quadarra, A., El-Murr, A., & Latham, J. (2017, December). *The effects of pornography on children and young people*. Retrieved from Australian Institute of Family Studies: https://aifs.gov.au/publications/effects-pornography-children-and-young-people-snapshot

Renaud-Komiya, N. (2013, SEptember 4). *Parliament's porn habit revealed as 300,000 attempts made to access 'adult' websites from work computers in last year*. Retrieved from Independent: https://www.independent.co.uk/news/parliaments-porn-habit-revealed-as-300000-attempts-made-to-access-adult-websites-from-work-computers-8797386.html

Ross, C. C. (2012, August 13). *Overexposed and Under-Prepared: The Effects of Early Exposure to Sexual Content*. Retrieved from Psychology Today: https://www.psychologytoday.com/us/blog/real-healing/201208/overexposed-and-under-prepared-the-effects-early-exposure-sexual-content

Scott, C. (2013, November 20). *10 Reasons Why You Should Quit Watching Porn*. Retrieved from GQ: https://www.gq.com/story/10-reasons-why-you-should-quit-watching-porn

Stritof, S. (2018, September 27). *What to Do When Your Husband Won't Stop Watching Pornography*. Retrieved from Very Well Mind: https://www.verywellmind.com/husband-wont-stop-watching-pornography-2303586

The Edge. (2018, August 29). *Can Porn Addiction Lead to Viagra Addiction?* Retrieved from The Edge Rehab: https://www.theedgerehab.com/blog/can-porn-addiction-lead-to-viagra-addiction/

Thompson, D. (2017, May 12). *Study Sees Link Between Porn and Sexual Dysfunction*. Retrieved from WebMD: https://www.webmd.com/sex/news/20170512/study-sees-link-between-porn-and-sexual-dysfunction#1

Villines, Z. (2018, July 30). *How can porn induce erectile dysfunction?* Retrieved from Medical News Today: https://www.medicalnewstoday.com/articles/317117.php

References

WebRoot. (n.d.). *Internet Pornography by the Numbers; A Significant Threat to Society.* Retrieved April 10, 2019, from WebRoot: https://www.webroot.com/us/en/resources/tips-articles/internet-pornography-by-the-numbers

WebRoot. (n.d.). *Internet Pornography by the Numbers; A Significant Threat to Society.* Retrieved 12 2019, May, from WebRoot: https://www.webroot.com/us/en/resources/tips-articles/internet-pornography-by-the-numbers

Weiss, R. (2019, January 30). *3 Ways Porn Is Affecting Your Relationship (And What You Can Do About It).* Retrieved from Mind Body Green: https://www.mindbodygreen.com/0-27470/3-ways-porn-is-affecting-your-relationship-and-what-you-can-do-about-it.html

Weiss, R. (2014, January 20). *Is Male Porn Use Ruining Sex?* Retrieved from Psychology Today: https://www.psychologytoday.com/us/blog/love-and-sex-in-the-digital-age/201401/is-male-porn-use-ruining-sex

Wiley, W. (n.d.). *9 Reasons Why Porn Will Ruin Your Marriage.* Retrieved April 1, 2019, from Debt to Life: http://www.debttolife.com/9-reasons-why-porn-will-ruin-your-marriage

Ybarra, M. L., & Thompson, R. (2017, July 7). *Predicting the Emergence of Sexual Violence in Adolescence.* Retrieved from John Hopkins University: https://jhu.pure.elsevier.com/en/publications/predicting-the-emergence-of-sexual-violence-in-adolescence

Your Brain on Porn. (n.d.). *6 Habits That Will (Indirectly) Help You Quit Porn.* Retrieved April 11, 2019, from Your Brain on Porn: https://www.yourbrainonporn.com/blogs-vlogs-by-friends-of-ybop/reboot-blueprints-blog/6-habits-that-will-indirectly-help-you-quit-porn/

Your Brain on Porn. (n.d.). *How long will it take to recover from Porn-Induced Sexual Dysfunction?* Retrieved April 6, 2019, from Your Brain on Porn: https://www.yourbrainonporn.com/porn-induced-sexual-dysfunctions/how-long-will-it-take-to-recover-from-porn-induced-sexual-dysfunction/

Your Greatest Version. (2017, April 1). *10 Amazing Benefits of NoFap.* Retrieved from Your Greatest Version: https://www.yourgreatestversion.com/benefits-of-nofap/

Your Internet on Porn. (n.d.). *Can porn use affect memory and concentration?* Retrieved April 10, 2019, from Your Internet on Porn: https://www.yourbrainonporn.com/rebooting-porn-use-faqs/can-porn-use-affect-memory-and-concentration/

CHAPTER 8: YOUR MENTAL HEALTH WITHOUT PORN

Addiction.com Staff. (2011, November 20). *Pornography At Work.* Retrieved from Addiction.com: https://www.addiction.com/7819/pornography-at-work/

Al-Kaheel, A. (n.d.). *The dangerous psychological effects of Pornography.* Retrieved April 14, 2019, from Secrets of Quran Miracles: http://www.kaheel7.com/eng/index.php/health-a-medicine/826-the-dangerous-psychological-effects-of-pornography

American Public Health Association. (2010, November 9). *Prevention and Control of Sexually Transmitted Infections and HIV in the Adult Film Industry.* Retrieved from American Public Health Association: https://www.apha.org/policies-and-advocacy/public-health-policy-statements/policy-database/2014/07/28/15/23/

prevention-and-control-of-sexually-transmitted-infections-and-hiv-in-the-adult-film-industry

AntiDopamine. (n.d.). *27 NoFap Benefits to Supercharge Your Manliness*. Retrieved May 12, 2019, from AntiDopamine: https://www.antidopamine.com/nofap/list-of-benefits/

Archebelle, C. (n.d.). *5 Ways Pornography Will Ruin Your Life… and How to Break Free*. Retrieved May 9, 2019, from Conquer Series: https://conquerseries.com/5-ways-pornography-will-ruin-life/

Bacter, P. (n.d.). *10 ADVANTAGES OF QUITTING PORN*. Retrieved May 12, 2019, from Steemit: https://steemit.com/steemit/@paulobacter/10-reasons-why-you-should-quit-porn

Baesler, A. J. (2017, June 19). *Effects of Pornography in the Workplace*. Retrieved from Slideshare: https://www.slideshare.net/AdamBaesler1/effects-of-pornography-in-the-workplace

Barrett, D. (2015, March 17). *Judges dismissed after watching pornography on court computers*. Retrieved from The Telegraph: https://www.telegraph.co.uk/news/uknews/law-and-order/11476880/Judges-dismissed-after-watching-pornography-on-court-computers.html

Baxter, A. (2018, January 9). *How Pornography Harms Children: The Advocate's Role*. Retrieved from American Bar Association: https://www.americanbar.org/groups/child_law/resources/child_law_practiceonline/child_law_practice/vol-33/may-2014/how-pornography-harms-children--the-advocate-s-role/

Becca. (2019, March 20). *How Pornography Affects Marriage*. Retrieved from The Dating Divas: https://www.thedatingdivas.com/pornography-affects-marriage/

Beck, J. (n.d.). *How Pornography Affects Teenagers [and Children]*. Retrieved March 22, 2019, from Ever Accountable: https://everaccountable.com/blog/how-pornography-affects-teenagers-and-children/

Brenner, G. (2018, March 5). *4 Ways Porn Use Causes Problems*. Retrieved from Psychology Today: https://www.psychologytoday.com/intl/blog/experimentations/201803/4-ways-porn-use-causes-problems

Brenner, G. (2017, July 17). *Pornography and Broken Relationships*. Retrieved from Psychology Today: https://www.psychologytoday.com/us/blog/experimentations/201707/pornography-and-broken-relationships

Calonzo, A., & Heijmans, P. (2019, May 12). *The Philippines' Midterm Election Will Test Duterte's Presidency*. Retrieved from Bloomberg: https://www.bloomberg.com/news/articles/2019-05-11/duterte-set-to-gain-allies-shut-out-critics-in-midterm-vote

Chang, M. (2014, August 3). *Why Having Only ONE Orgasm a Month Leads to Success*. Retrieved from Next Shark: https://nextshark.com/this-is-why-the-key-to-productivity-and-success-is-having-only-one-orgasm-a-month/

Covenant Eyes. (2015). *Pornography Statistics*. Owosso: Covenant Eyes.

Craig, C. (2014, January 27). *5 Things You MUST Do To Quit Porn – and it's NOT about Porn*. Retrieved from Feed the Right Wolf: http://www.feedtherightwolf.org/2014/01/5-things-you-must-do-to-quit-porn-and-its-not-about-porn/

References

Culture Reframed. (2017, June 27). *Extensive Research into the Harms of Pornography on Children and Young People*. Retrieved from Culture Reframed: https://www.culturereframed.org/researched-harms/

Cushing, J. (2018, November 1). *Employee Watching Porn At Work Infected US Government Agency's Network*. Retrieved from TechDirt: https://www.techdirt.com/articles/20181031/11124040951/employee-watching-porn-work-infected-us-government-agencys-network.shtml

Darbyshire, M. (2017, December 14). *The consequences of looking at pornography at work*. Retrieved from Financial Times: https://www.ft.com/content/ead0956e-de96-11e7-a0d4-0944c5f49e46

Daubney, M. (2017, March 29). *Men's lives are being ruined by pornography. So why aren't we angry about it?* Retrieved from The Telegraph: https://www.telegraph.co.uk/men/thinking-man/mens-lives-ruined-pornography-arent-angry/

De Robien, M. (2018, April 4). *A family therapist reveals the worst effects of adult content on children*. Retrieved from Aleteia: https://aleteia.org/2018/04/04/a-family-therapist-reveals-the-worst-affects-of-porn-on-children/

Digital Kids Initiative. (2014, August). *Children and Pornography*. Retrieved from Digital Kids Initative: https://digitalkidsinitiative.com/wp-content/uploads/2014/08/Children_and_Pornography_Factsheet-Revised-August-2014.pdf

Douglas, Z. (2015, May 18). *5 Ways Porn Ruins Relationships*. Retrieved from Relevant Magazine: https://relevantmagazine.com/life5/relationships/5-ways-porn-ruins-relationships/

Doyel, J. (2012, June 4). *How Do I Keep My Husband from Looking at Pornography*. Retrieved from Covenant Eyes: https://www.covenanteyes.com/2012/06/04/how-do-i-keep-my-husband-from-looking-at-pornography/

Emezi, J. (n.d.). *How Pornography Erodes Your Masculinity*. Retrieved May 10, 2019, from Steven Aitchison: https://www.stevenaitchison.co.uk/pornography-erodes-masculinity/

Fight the New Drug. (2017, February 3). *3 Reasons Why Relationships And Porn Don't Mix*. Retrieved from Fight the New Drug: https://fightthenewdrug.org/3-reasons-why-relationships-and-porn-dont-mix/

Fight the New Drug. (2017, April 11). *3 Ways Porn Damaged Our Relationship & Killed Our Sex Life*. Retrieved from Fight the New Drug: https://fightthenewdrug.org/3-ways-porn-damaged-our-relationship-killed-our-sex-life/

Fight the New Drug. (2017, April 2). *4 Hidden Problems With Watching Porn That You Might Not Know*. Retrieved from Fight the New Drug: https://fightthenewdrug.org/hidden-problems-with-watching-porn/

Fight the New Drug. (2018, March 16). *4 Studies That Show How Porn-Obsessed Brains Can Heal Over Time*. Retrieved from Fight the New Drug: https://fightthenewdrug.org/4-studies-that-prove-porn-addicted-brains-can-return-to-normal/

Fight the New Drug. (2018, August 19). *How My Obsession With Extreme Porn Impacts My Ability To Be Naturally Aroused.* Retrieved from Fight the New Drug: https://fightthenewdrug.org/true-story-how-porn-twisted-my-sexuality/

Fight the New Drug. (2017, July 27). *Kids Who Find Hardcore Porn Want To Repeat What They've Seen, Study Shows.* Retrieved from Fight the New Drug: https://fightthenewdrug.org/massive-study-reveals-what-kids-are-watching-learning-from-online-porn/

Fight the New Drug. (2018, June 20). *Let's Talk About Porn. Is It As Harmless As Society Says It Is?* Retrieved from Fight the New Drug: https://fightthenewdrug.org/3-reasons-why-watching-porn-is-harmful/

Fight the New Drug. (2017, October 25). *Why You Feel Anxious And Disconnected After Watching Porn.* Retrieved from Fight the New Drug: https://fightthenewdrug.org/the-serious-mental-costs-of-watching-porn/

Frank. (2018, April 9). *5 Life-Changing Health Benefits of Nofap.* Retrieved from My Wealth Shop: https://www.mywealthshop.com/health-benefits-of-nofap/

Frank. (2018, May 11). *Nofap and Social Anxiety: Can porn watching be affecting your social life?* Retrieved from My Wealth Shop: https://www.mywealthshop.com/nofap-and-social-anxiety/

Garner, D. (2016, September 15). *Counselor Shares 5 Strategies to Keep Kids from Porn Addiction.* Retrieved from Protect Young Minds: https://protectyoungminds.org/2016/09/15/counselor-strategies-porn-addiction/

Gholiphour, B. (2014, July 7). *Hypersexuality in Women Linked to High Porn Use.* Retrieved from Live Science: https://www.livescience.com/46687-hypersexuality-women.html

Goulston, M. (2010, January 7). *Why Men Use Porn (and How to Get Yours to Stop).* Retrieved from Psychology Today: https://www.psychologytoday.com/us/blog/just-listen/201001/why-men-use-porn-and-how-get-yours-stop

Gregoire, S. W. (2014, March 18). *Top 10 Effects of Porn on Your Brain, Your Marriage, and Your Sex Life.* Retrieved from To Love, Honor, & Vacuum: https://tolovehonorandvacuum.com/2014/03/effects-of-porn-on-your-marriage/

Hambrick, B. (2018, September 16). *6 Ways Watching Pornography Affects Your Mental Health.* Retrieved from Church Leaders: https://churchleaders.com/outreach-missions/outreach-missions-articles/333466-6-ways-watching-pornography-affects-your-mental-health-brad-hambrick.html

Huerta, D. (n.d.). *Seven Strategies to Combat Teen Porn Use.* Retrieved March 23, 2019, from Focus on the Family: https://www.focusonthefamily.com/parenting/sexuality/kids-and-pornography/seven-strategies-to-combat-teen-porn-use

Jacobs, T. (2017, June 14). *PORN VIEWING IMPACTS ATTITUDES ON WOMEN IN WORKPLACE.* Retrieved from Pacific Standard: https://psmag.com/social-justice/porn-viewing-impacts-attitudes-women-workplace-66280

References

Ketcham, J. (2012, November 11). *Pornography Does Lasting Harm to Performers.* Retrieved from The New York Times: https://www.nytimes.com/roomfordebate/2012/11/11/does-pornography-deserve-its-bad-rap/pornography-does-lasting-harm-to-performers

Los Angeles Daily News. (2012, November 2). *STDs In Porn Industry Higher Than Reported.* Retrieved from HuffPost: https://www.huffpost.com/entry/stds-porn-industry_n_2064639

MacLaughlin, K. (2017, December 19). *The Detrimental Effects of Pornography on Small Children.* Retrieved from Net Nanny: https://www.netnanny.com/blog/the-detrimental-effects-of-pornography-on-small-children/

Marripedia. (n.d.). *Effects of Pornography on Adolescents.* Retrieved March 22, 2019, from Marripedia: http://marripedia.org/effects_of_pornography_on_adolescents

McKay, B., & McKay, K. (2009, May 11). *The Problem With Porn.* Retrieved from Art of Manliness: https://www.artofmanliness.com/articles/the-problem-with-porn/

Moore, A. (2018, June 26). *Does My Child Need Counseling? Reassuring Advice from a Porn Addiction Therapist.* Retrieved from Protect Young Minds: https://protectyoungminds.org/2018/06/26/does-child-need-counseling-advice-porn-addiction-therapist/

Morris, C. (2018, April 18). *Adult Entertainment Industry Remains Shut Down After Positive HIV Test.* Retrieved from Fortune: http://fortune.com/2018/04/18/adult-entertainment-industry-shut-down-positive-hiv-test-porn/

Mosel, S. (n.d.). *12-STEP BEHAVIORAL ADDICTION SUPPORT GROUPS.* Retrieved April 18, 2019, from Project Know: https://www.projectknow.com/support-groups/

Muresan, R. (2016, September 20). *One in 10 visitors of porn sites is under 10 years old.* Retrieved from Hot for Security: https://hotforsecurity.bitdefender.com/blog/one-in-10-visitors-of-porn-sites-is-under-10-years-old-16675.html

National Society for the Prevention of Cruelty to Children. (2016, April 6). *50% of children admit to seeing sexual and violent material online.* Retrieved from National Society for the Prevention of Cruelty to Children: https://www.nspcc.org.uk/what-we-do/news-opinion/net-aware-reveals-risky-social-media-sites/

National Society for the Prevention of Cruelty to Children. (2018, August 30). *New survey reveals risks children and young people face online.* Retrieved from National Society for the Prevention of Cruelty to Children: https://www.nspcc.org.uk/what-we-do/news-opinion/new-survey-online-risks-wild-west-web/

News.com.au. (2016, March 26). *Former porn star Bree Olson goes public: 'I'm shunned by society'.* Retrieved from News.com.au: https://www.news.com.au/entertainment/celebrity-life/former-porn-star-bree-olsen-goes-public-im-shunned-by-society/news-story/106695d7e5eec3e050538697cfac7d28

Park, J. S. (2016, December 1). *4 Unexpected Things That Happen When You Quit Porn.* Retrieved from XXX Church: https://www.xxxchurch.com/men/4-unexpected-things-that-happen-when-you-quit-porn.html

Park, J. S. (2016, December 10). *4 Unexpected Things That Happen When You Quit Porn*. Retrieved from Christian Post: https://www.christianpost.com/news/4-unexpected-things-that-happen-when-you-quit-porn.html

Perry, L. (2016, June). *The Impact of Pornography on Children*. Retrieved from American College of Pediatricians: https://www.acpeds.org/the-college-speaks/position-statements/the-impact-of-pornography-on-children

Pornhub. (2018, December 11). *2018 Year in Review*. Retrieved from Pornhub: https://www.pornhub.com/insights/2018-year-in-review

Quadarra, A., El-Murr, A., & Latham, J. (2017, December). *The effects of pornography on children and young people*. Retrieved from Australian Institute of Family Studies: https://aifs.gov.au/publications/effects-pornography-children-and-young-people-snapshot

Rausch, J. (2017, July 27). *Porn Addiction Therapy: What You Need to Know*. Retrieved from TalkSpace: https://www.talkspace.com/blog/porn-addiction-therapy-need-know/

Renaud-Komiya, N. (2013, SEptember 4). *Parliament's porn habit revealed as 300,000 attempts made to access 'adult' websites from work computers in last year*. Retrieved from Independent: https://www.independent.co.uk/news/parliaments-porn-habit-revealed-as-300000-attempts-made-to-access-adult-websites-from-work-computers-8797386.html

Ross, C. C. (2012, August 13). *Overexposed and Under-Prepared: The Effects of Early Exposure to Sexual Content*. Retrieved from Psychology Today: https://www.psychologytoday.com/us/blog/real-healing/201208/overexposed-and-under-prepared-the-effects-early-exposure-sexual-content

Scott, C. (2013, November 20). *10 Reasons Why You Should Quit Watching Porn*. Retrieved from GQ: https://www.gq.com/story/10-reasons-why-you-should-quit-watching-porn

Skinner, K. B. (2011, November 22). *Daily Porn May Not Be Good for Your Mental Health*. Retrieved from Psychology Today: https://www.psychologytoday.com/us/blog/inside-porn-addiction/201111/daily-porn-may-not-be-good-your-mental-health

Stritof, S. (2018, September 27). *What to Do When Your Husband Won't Stop Watching Pornography*. Retrieved from Very Well Mind: https://www.verywellmind.com/husband-wont-stop-watching-pornography-2303586

Tackett, B. (n.d.). *ARE YOU ADDICTED TO PORN?* Retrieved April 18, 2019, from Project Know: https://www.projectknow.com/porn-addiction/test/?utm_term=p_addiction

The Edge. (2018, August 29). *Can Porn Addiction Lead to Viagra Addiction?* Retrieved from The Edge Rehab: https://www.theedgerehab.com/blog/can-porn-addiction-lead-to-viagra-addiction/

The Fortify Team. (2017, September 18). *How Self-Esteem Issues May Be Fueling Your Struggle With Porn*. Retrieved from Fortify: http://blog.joinfortify.com/self-esteem-pornography/

Thompson, D. (2017, May 12). *Study Sees Link Between Porn and Sexual Dysfunction*. Retrieved from WebMD: https://www.webmd.com/sex/news/20170512/study-sees-link-between-porn-and-sexual-dysfunction#1

References

Tuell, C. (2016, SeptembeR 30). *Mental illness, Addiction and Digital Infidelity.* Retrieved from Lindner Center of Hope: https://lindnercenterofhope.org/blog/mental-illness-addiction-and-digital-infidelity/

Villines, Z. (2018, July 30). *How can porn induce erectile dysfunction?* Retrieved from Medical News Today: https://www.medicalnewstoday.com/articles/317117.php

WebRoot. (n.d.). *Internet Pornography by the Numbers; A Significant Threat to Society.* Retrieved April 10, 2019, from WebRoot: https://www.webroot.com/us/en/resources/tips-articles/internet-pornography-by-the-numbers

WebRoot. (n.d.). *Internet Pornography by the Numbers; A Significant Threat to Society.* Retrieved 12 2019, May, from WebRoot: https://www.webroot.com/us/en/resources/tips-articles/internet-pornography-by-the-numbers

Weiss, R. (2019, January 30). *3 Ways Porn Is Affecting Your Relationship (And What You Can Do About It).* Retrieved from Mind Body Green: https://www.mindbodygreen.com/0-27470/3-ways-porn-is-affecting-your-relationship-and-what-you-can-do-about-it.html

Weiss, R. (2014, January 20). *Is Male Porn Use Ruining Sex?* Retrieved from Psychology Today: https://www.psychologytoday.com/us/blog/love-and-sex-in-the-digital-age/201401/is-male-porn-use-ruining-sex

Wiley, W. (n.d.). *9 Reasons Why Porn Will Ruin Your Marriage.* Retrieved April 1, 2019, from Debt to Life: http://www.debttolife.com/9-reasons-why-porn-will-ruin-your-marriage

Ybarra, M. L., & Thompson, R. (2017, July 7). *Predicting the Emergence of Sexual Violence in Adolescence.* Retrieved from John Hopkins University: https://jhu.pure.elsevier.com/en/publications/predicting-the-emergence-of-sexual-violence-in-adolescence

Your Brain on Porn. (n.d.). *6 Habits That Will (Indirectly) Help You Quit Porn.* Retrieved April 11, 2019, from Your Brain on Porn: https://www.yourbrainonporn.com/blogs-vlogs-by-friends-of-ybop/reboot-blueprints-blog/6-habits-that-will-indirectly-help-you-quit-porn/

Your Brain on Porn. (n.d.). *How long will it take to recover from Porn-Induced Sexual Dysfunction?* Retrieved April 6, 2019, from Your Brain on Porn: https://www.yourbrainonporn.com/porn-induced-sexual-dysfunctions/how-long-will-it-take-to-recover-from-porn-induced-sexual-dysfunction/

Your Greatest Version. (2017, April 1). *10 Amazing Benefits of NoFap.* Retrieved from Your Greatest Version: https://www.yourgreatestversion.com/benefits-of-nofap/

Your Internet on Porn. (n.d.). *Can porn use affect memory and concentration?* Retrieved April 10, 2019, from Your Internet on Porn: https://www.yourbrainonporn.com/rebooting-porn-use-faqs/can-porn-use-affect-memory-and-concentration/

CHAPTER 9: YOUR BRAIN WITHOUT PORN

Addiction.com Staff. (2011, November 20). *Pornography At Work*. Retrieved from Addiction.com: https://www.addiction.com/7819/pornography-at-work/

Al-Kaheel, A. (n.d.). *The dangerous psychological effects of Pornography*. Retrieved April 14, 2019, from Secrets of Quran Miracles: http://www.kaheel7.com/eng/index.php/health-a-medicine/826-the-dangerous-psychological-effects-of-pornography

American Public Health Association. (2010, November 9). *Prevention and Control of Sexually Transmitted Infections and HIV in the Adult Film Industry*. Retrieved from American Public Health Association: https://www.apha.org/policies-and-advocacy/public-health-policy-statements/policy-database/2014/07/28/15/23/prevention-and-control-of-sexually-transmitted-infections-and-hiv-in-the-adult-film-industry

AntiDopamine. (n.d.). *27 NoFap Benefits to Supercharge Your Manliness*. Retrieved May 12, 2019, from AntiDopamine: https://www.antidopamine.com/nofap/list-of-benefits/

Archebelle, C. (n.d.). *5 Ways Pornography Will Ruin Your Life... and How to Break Free*. Retrieved May 9, 2019, from Conquer Series: https://conquerseries.com/5-ways-pornography-will-ruin-life/

Archebelle, C. (n.d.). *5 Ways Pornography Will Ruin Your Life... and How to Break Free*. Retrieved May 26, 2019, from Conquer Series: https://conquerseries.com/5-ways-pornography-will-ruin-life/

Bacter, P. (n.d.). *10 ADVANTAGES OF QUITTING PORN*. Retrieved May 12, 2019, from Steemit: https://steemit.com/steemit/@paulobacter/10-reasons-why-you-should-quit-porn

Baesler, A. J. (2017, June 19). *Effects of Pornography in the Workplace*. Retrieved from Slideshare: https://www.slideshare.net/AdamBaesler1/effects-of-pornography-in-the-workplace

Barrett, D. (2015, March 17). *Judges dismissed after watching pornography on court computers*. Retrieved from The Telegraph: https://www.telegraph.co.uk/news/uknews/law-and-order/11476880/Judges-dismissed-after-watching-pornography-on-court-computers.html

Baxter, A. (2018, January 9). *How Pornography Harms Children: The Advocate's Role*. Retrieved from American Bar Association: https://www.americanbar.org/groups/child_law/resources/child_law_practiceonline/child_law_practice/vol-33/may-2014/how-pornography-harms-children--the-advocate-s-role/

Becca. (2019, March 20). *How Pornography Affects Marriage*. Retrieved from The Dating Divas: https://www.thedatingdivas.com/pornography-affects-marriage/

Beck, J. (n.d.). *How Pornography Affects Teenagers [and Children]*. Retrieved March 22, 2019, from Ever Accountable: https://everaccountable.com/blog/how-pornography-affects-teenagers-and-children/

Brenner, G. (2018, March 5). *4 Ways Porn Use Causes Problems*. Retrieved from Psychology Today: https://www.psychologytoday.com/intl/blog/experimentations/201803/4-ways-porn-use-causes-problems

References

Brenner, G. (2017, July 17). *Pornography and Broken Relationships*. Retrieved from Psychology Today: https://www.psychologytoday.com/us/blog/experimentations/201707/pornography-and-broken-relationships

Calonzo, A., & Heijmans, P. (2019, May 12). *The Philippines' Midterm Election Will Test Duterte's Presidency*. Retrieved from Bloomberg: https://www.bloomberg.com/news/articles/2019-05-11/duterte-set-to-gain-allies-shut-out-critics-in-midterm-vote

Chang, M. (2014, August 3). *Why Having Only ONE Orgasm a Month Leads to Success*. Retrieved from Next Shark: https://nextshark.com/this-is-why-the-key-to-productivity-and-success-is-having-only-one-orgasm-a-month/

Covenant Eyes. (n.d.). *Pornography Statistics*. Retrieved May 29, 2019, from Covenant Eyes: https://www.covenanteyes.com/pornstats/

Covenant Eyes. (2015). *Pornography Statistics*. Owosso: Covenant Eyes.

Craig, C. (2014, January 27). *5 Things You MUST Do To Quit Porn – and it's NOT about Porn*. Retrieved from Feed the Right Wolf: http://www.feedtherightwolf.org/2014/01/5-things-you-must-do-to-quit-porn-and-its-not-about-porn/

Culture Reframed. (2017, June 27). *Extensive Research into the Harms of Pornography on Children and Young People*. Retrieved from Culture Reframed: https://www.culturereframed.org/researched-harms/

Cushing, J. (2018, November 1). *Employee Watching Porn At Work Infected US Government Agency's Network*. Retrieved from TechDirt: https://www.techdirt.com/articles/20181031/11124040951/employee-watching-porn-work-infected-us-government-agencys-network.shtml

Darbyshire, M. (2017, December 14). *The consequences of looking at pornography at work*. Retrieved from Financial Times: https://www.ft.com/content/ead0956e-de96-11e7-a0d4-0944c5f49e46

Daubney, M. (2017, March 29). *Men's lives are being ruined by pornography. So why aren't we angry about it?* Retrieved from The Telegraph: https://www.telegraph.co.uk/men/thinking-man/mens-lives-ruined-pornography-arent-angry/

De Robien, M. (2018, April 4). *A family therapist reveals the worst effects of adult content on children*. Retrieved from Aleteia: https://aleteia.org/2018/04/04/a-family-therapist-reveals-the-worst-affects-of-porn-on-children/

Dias, B. (2018, October 1). *The Brain on Porn*. Retrieved from Grey Matters Journal: http://greymattersjournal.com/the-brain-on-porn/

Digital Kids Initiative. (2014, August). *Children and Pornography*. Retrieved from Digital Kids Initative: https://digitalkidsinitiative.com/wp-content/uploads/2014/08/Children_and_Pornography_Factsheet-Revised-August-2014.pdf

Douglas, Z. (2015, May 18). *5 Ways Porn Ruins Relationships*. Retrieved from Relevant Magazine: https://relevantmagazine.com/life5/relationships/5-ways-porn-ruins-relationships/

Doyel, J. (2012, June 4). *How Do I Keep My Husband from Looking at Pornography*. Retrieved from Covenant Eyes: https://www.covenanteyes.com/2012/06/04/how-do-i-keep-my-husband-from-looking-at-pornography/

Emezi, J. (n.d.). *How Pornography Erodes Your Masculinity*. Retrieved May 10, 2019, from Steven Aitchison: https://www.stevenaitchison.co.uk/pornography-erodes-masculinity/

Fight the New Drug. (2017, February 3). *3 Reasons Why Relationships And Porn Don't Mix*. Retrieved from Fight the New Drug: https://fightthenewdrug.org/3-reasons-why-relationships-and-porn-dont-mix/

Fight the New Drug. (2017, April 11). *3 Ways Porn Damaged Our Relationship & Killed Our Sex Life*. Retrieved from Fight the New Drug: https://fightthenewdrug.org/3-ways-porn-damaged-our-relationship-killed-our-sex-life/

Fight the New Drug. (2017, April 2). *4 Hidden Problems With Watching Porn That You Might Not Know*. Retrieved from Fight the New Drug: https://fightthenewdrug.org/hidden-problems-with-watching-porn/

Fight the New Drug. (2018, March 16). *4 Studies That Show How Porn-Obsessed Brains Can Heal Over Time*. Retrieved from Fight the New Drug: https://fightthenewdrug.org/4-studies-that-prove-porn-addicted-brains-can-return-to-normal/

Fight the New Drug. (2018, August 19). *How My Obsession With Extreme Porn Impacts My Ability To Be Naturally Aroused*. Retrieved from Fight the New Drug: https://fightthenewdrug.org/true-story-how-porn-twisted-my-sexuality/

Fight the New Drug. (2017, July 27). *Kids Who Find Hardcore Porn Want To Repeat What They've Seen, Study Shows*. Retrieved from Fight the New Drug: https://fightthenewdrug.org/massive-study-reveals-what-kids-are-watching-learning-from-online-porn/

Fight the New Drug. (2018, June 20). *Let's Talk About Porn. Is It As Harmless As Society Says It Is?* Retrieved from Fight the New Drug: https://fightthenewdrug.org/3-reasons-why-watching-porn-is-harmful/

Fight the New Drug. (2018, June 20). *Let's Talk About Porn. Is It As Harmless As Society Says It Is?* Retrieved from Fight the New Drug: https://fightthenewdrug.org/3-reasons-why-watching-porn-is-harmful/

Fight the New Drug. (2017, October 25). *Why You Feel Anxious And Disconnected After Watching Porn*. Retrieved from Fight the New Drug: https://fightthenewdrug.org/the-serious-mental-costs-of-watching-porn/

Frank. (2018, April 9). *5 Life-Changing Health Benefits of Nofap*. Retrieved from My Wealth Shop: https://www.mywealthshop.com/health-benefits-of-nofap/

Frank. (2018, May 11). *Nofap and Social Anxiety: Can porn watching be affecting your social life?* Retrieved from My Wealth Shop: https://www.mywealthshop.com/nofap-and-social-anxiety/

Garner, D. (2016, September 15). *Counselor Shares 5 Strategies to Keep Kids from Porn Addiction*. Retrieved from Protect Young Minds: https://protectyoungminds.org/2016/09/15/counselor-strategies-porn-addiction/

References

Gholiphour, B. (2014, July 7). *Hypersexuality in Women Linked to High Porn Use*. Retrieved from Live Science: https://www.livescience.com/46687-hypersexuality-women.html

Ghose, T. (2015, October 13). *Bye, Bye, Playboy Bunnies: 5 Ways Porn Affects the Brain*. Retrieved from Live Science: https://www.livescience.com/52469-how-porn-affects-brains.html

Goulston, M. (2010, January 7). *Why Men Use Porn (and How to Get Yours to Stop)*. Retrieved from Psychology Today: https://www.psychologytoday.com/us/blog/just-listen/201001/why-men-use-porn-and-how-get-yours-stop

Gregoire, S. W. (2014, March 18). *Top 10 Effects of Porn on Your Brain, Your Marriage, and Your Sex Life*. Retrieved from To Love, Honor, & Vacuum: https://tolovehonorandvacuum.com/2014/03/effects-of-porn-on-your-marriage/

Hambrick, B. (2018, September 16). *6 Ways Watching Pornography Affects Your Mental Health*. Retrieved from Church Leaders: https://churchleaders.com/outreach-missions/outreach-missions-articles/333466-6-ways-watching-pornography-affects-your-mental-health-brad-hambrick.html

Huerta, D. (n.d.). *Seven Strategies to Combat Teen Porn Use*. Retrieved March 23, 2019, from Focus on the Family: https://www.focusonthefamily.com/parenting/sexuality/kids-and-pornography/seven-strategies-to-combat-teen-porn-use

Jacobs, T. (2017, June 14). *PORN VIEWING IMPACTS ATTITUDES ON WOMEN IN WORKPLACE*. Retrieved from Pacific Standard: https://psmag.com/social-justice/porn-viewing-impacts-attitudes-women-workplace-66280

Ketcham, J. (2012, November 11). *Pornography Does Lasting Harm to Performers*. Retrieved from The New York Times: https://www.nytimes.com/roomfordebate/2012/11/11/does-pornography-deserve-its-bad-rap/pornography-does-lasting-harm-to-performers

Loosemore, P. (2017, February 5). *What Effects Does Porn Have on My Brain?* Retrieved from Addiction Hope: https://www.addictionhope.com/blog/effects-porn-brain/

Los Angeles Daily News. (2012, November 2). *STDs In Porn Industry Higher Than Reported*. Retrieved from HuffPost: https://www.huffpost.com/entry/stds-porn-industry_n_2064639

MacLaughlin, K. (2017, December 19). *The Detrimental Effects of Pornography on Small Children*. Retrieved from Net Nanny: https://www.netnanny.com/blog/the-detrimental-effects-of-pornography-on-small-children/

Marripedia. (n.d.). *Effects of Pornography on Adolescents*. Retrieved March 22, 2019, from Marripedia: http://marripedia.org/effects_of_pornography_on_adolescents

McKay, B., & McKay, K. (2009, May 11). *The Problem With Porn*. Retrieved from Art of Manliness: https://www.artofmanliness.com/articles/the-problem-with-porn/

Moore, A. (2018, June 26). *Does My Child Need Counseling? Reassuring Advice from a Porn Addiction Therapist*. Retrieved from Protect Young Minds: https://protectyoungminds.org/2018/06/26/does-child-need-counseling-advice-porn-addiction-therapist/

Morris, C. (2018, April 18). *Adult Entertainment Industry Remains Shut Down After Positive HIV Test*. Retrieved from Fortune: http://fortune.com/2018/04/18/adult-entertainment-industry-shut-down-positive-hiv-test-porn/

Mosel, S. (n.d.). *12-STEP BEHAVIORAL ADDICTION SUPPORT GROUPS*. Retrieved April 18, 2019, from Project Know: https://www.projectknow.com/support-groups/

Muresan, R. (2016, September 20). *One in 10 visitors of porn sites is under 10 years old*. Retrieved from Hot for Security: https://hotforsecurity.bitdefender.com/blog/one-in-10-visitors-of-porn-sites-is-under-10-years-old-16675.html

National Society for the Prevention of Cruelty to Children. (2016, April 6). *50% of children admit to seeing sexual and violent material online*. Retrieved from National Society for the Prevention of Cruelty to Children: https://www.nspcc.org.uk/what-we-do/news-opinion/net-aware-reveals-risky-social-media-sites/

National Society for the Prevention of Cruelty to Children. (2018, August 30). *New survey reveals risks children and young people face online*. Retrieved from National Society for the Prevention of Cruelty to Children: https://www.nspcc.org.uk/what-we-do/news-opinion/new-survey-online-risks-wild-west-web/

News.com.au. (2016, March 26). *Former porn star Bree Olson goes public: 'I'm shunned by society'*. Retrieved from News.com.au: https://www.news.com.au/entertainment/celebrity-life/former-porn-star-bree-olsen-goes-public-im-shunned-by-society/news-story/106695d7e5eec3e050538697cfac7d28

Park, J. S. (2016, December 1). *4 Unexpected Things That Happen When You Quit Porn*. Retrieved from XXX Church: https://www.xxxchurch.com/men/4-unexpected-things-that-happen-when-you-quit-porn.html

Park, J. S. (2016, December 10). *4 Unexpected Things That Happen When You Quit Porn*. Retrieved from Christian Post: https://www.christianpost.com/news/4-unexpected-things-that-happen-when-you-quit-porn.html

Perry, L. (2016, June). *The Impact of Pornography on Children*. Retrieved from American College of Pediatricians: https://www.acpeds.org/the-college-speaks/position-statements/the-impact-of-pornography-on-children

Pornhub. (2018, December 11). *2018 Year in Review*. Retrieved from Pornhub: https://www.pornhub.com/insights/2018-year-in-review

PornHub. (2018, December 11). *2018 Year in Review*. Retrieved from PornHub: https://www.pornhub.com/insights/2018-year-in-review

Quadarra, A., El-Murr, A., & Latham, J. (2017, December). *The effects of pornography on children and young people*. Retrieved from Australian Institute of Family Studies: https://aifs.gov.au/publications/effects-pornography-children-and-young-people-snapshot

Rausch, J. (2017, July 27). *Porn Addiction Therapy: What You Need to Know*. Retrieved from TalkSpace: https://www.talkspace.com/blog/porn-addiction-therapy-need-know/

References

Renaud-Komiya, N. (2013, SEptember 4). *Parliament's porn habit revealed as 300,000 attempts made to access 'adult' websites from work computers in last year.* Retrieved from Independent: https://www.independent.co.uk/news/parliaments-porn-habit-revealed-as-300000-attempts-made-to-access-adult-websites-from-work-computers-8797386.html

Ross, C. C. (2012, August 13). *Overexposed and Under-Prepared: The Effects of Early Exposure to Sexual Content.* Retrieved from Psychology Today: https://www.psychologytoday.com/us/blog/real-healing/201208/overexposed-and-under-prepared-the-effects-early-exposure-sexual-content

Scott, C. (2013, November 20). *10 Reasons Why You Should Quit Watching Porn.* Retrieved from GQ: https://www.gq.com/story/10-reasons-why-you-should-quit-watching-porn

Skinner, K. B. (2011, November 22). *Daily Porn May Not Be Good for Your Mental Health.* Retrieved from Psychology Today: https://www.psychologytoday.com/us/blog/inside-porn-addiction/201111/daily-porn-may-not-be-good-your-mental-health

Stritof, S. (2018, September 27). *What to Do When Your Husband Won't Stop Watching Pornography.* Retrieved from Very Well Mind: https://www.verywellmind.com/husband-wont-stop-watching-pornography-2303586

Tackett, B. (n.d.). *ARE YOU ADDICTED TO PORN?* Retrieved April 18, 2019, from Project Know: https://www.projectknow.com/porn-addiction/test/?utm_term=p_addiction

The Edge. (2018, August 29). *Can Porn Addiction Lead to Viagra Addiction?* Retrieved from The Edge Rehab: https://www.theedgerehab.com/blog/can-porn-addiction-lead-to-viagra-addiction/

The Fortify Team. (2017, September 18). *How Self-Esteem Issues May Be Fueling Your Struggle With Porn.* Retrieved from Fortify: http://blog.joinfortify.com/self-esteem-pornography/

Thompson, D. (2017, May 12). *Study Sees Link Between Porn and Sexual Dysfunction.* Retrieved from WebMD: https://www.webmd.com/sex/news/20170512/study-sees-link-between-porn-and-sexual-dysfunction#1

Tuell, C. (2016, SeptembeR 30). *Mental illness, Addiction and Digital Infidelity.* Retrieved from Lindner Center of Hope: https://lindnercenterofhope.org/blog/mental-illness-addiction-and-digital-infidelity/

Villines, Z. (2018, July 30). *How can porn induce erectile dysfunction?* Retrieved from Medical News Today: https://www.medicalnewstoday.com/articles/317117.php

WebRoot. (n.d.). *Internet Pornography by the Numbers; A Significant Threat to Society.* Retrieved April 10, 2019, from WebRoot: https://www.webroot.com/us/en/resources/tips-articles/internet-pornography-by-the-numbers

WebRoot. (n.d.). *Internet Pornography by the Numbers; A Significant Threat to Society.* Retrieved 12 2019, May, from WebRoot: https://www.webroot.com/us/en/resources/tips-articles/internet-pornography-by-the-numbers

Weiss, R. (2019, January 30). *3 Ways Porn Is Affecting Your Relationship (And What You Can Do About It).* Retrieved from Mind Body Green: https://www.mindbodygreen.com/0-27470/3-ways-porn-is-affecting-your-relationship-and-what-you-can-do-about-it.html

Weiss, R. (2014, January 20). *Is Male Porn Use Ruining Sex?* Retrieved from Psychology Today: https://www.psychologytoday.com/us/blog/love-and-sex-in-the-digital-age/201401/is-male-porn-use-ruining-sex

Wiley, W. (n.d.). *9 Reasons Why Porn Will Ruin Your Marriage.* Retrieved April 1, 2019, from Debt to Life: http://www.debttolife.com/9-reasons-why-porn-will-ruin-your-marriage

Ybarra, M. L., & Thompson, R. (2017, July 7). *Predicting the Emergence of Sexual Violence in Adolescence.* Retrieved from John Hopkins University: https://jhu.pure.elsevier.com/en/publications/predicting-the-emergence-of-sexual-violence-in-adolescence

Your Brain on Porn. (n.d.). *6 Habits That Will (Indirectly) Help You Quit Porn.* Retrieved April 11, 2019, from Your Brain on Porn: https://www.yourbrainonporn.com/blogs-vlogs-by-friends-of-ybop/reboot-blueprints-blog/6-habits-that-will-indirectly-help-you-quit-porn/

Your Brain on Porn. (n.d.). *How long will it take to recover from Porn-Induced Sexual Dysfunction?* Retrieved April 6, 2019, from Your Brain on Porn: https://www.yourbrainonporn.com/porn-induced-sexual-dysfunctions/how-long-will-it-take-to-recover-from-porn-induced-sexual-dysfunction/

Your Greatest Version. (2017, April 1). *10 Amazing Benefits of NoFap.* Retrieved from Your Greatest Version: https://www.yourgreatestversion.com/benefits-of-nofap/

Your Internet on Porn. (n.d.). *Can porn use affect memory and concentration?* Retrieved April 10, 2019, from Your Internet on Porn: https://www.yourbrainonporn.com/rebooting-porn-use-faqs/can-porn-use-affect-memory-and-concentration/

CHAPTER 10: MEN WITHOUT PORN

Addiction.com Staff. (2011, November 20). *Pornography At Work.* Retrieved from Addiction.com: https://www.addiction.com/7819/pornography-at-work/

Al-Kaheel, A. (n.d.). *The dangerous psychological effects of Pornography.* Retrieved April 14, 2019, from Secrets of Quran Miracles: http://www.kaheel7.com/eng/index.php/health-a-medicine/826-the-dangerous-psychological-effects-of-pornography

American Public Health Association. (2010, November 9). *Prevention and Control of Sexually Transmitted Infections and HIV in the Adult Film Industry.* Retrieved from American Public Health Association: https://www.apha.org/policies-and-advocacy/public-health-policy-statements/policy-database/2014/07/28/15/23/prevention-and-control-of-sexually-transmitted-infections-and-hiv-in-the-adult-film-industry

Andrews, C. (n.d.). *8 Harmful Effects of Pornography on Individuals.* Retrieved June 14, 2019, from Educate Empower Kids: https://educateempowerkids.org/8-harmful-effects-of-pornography-on-individuals/

AntiDopamine. (n.d.). *27 NoFap Benefits to Supercharge Your Manliness.* Retrieved May 12, 2019, from AntiDopamine: https://www.antidopamine.com/nofap/list-of-benefits/

Archebelle, C. (n.d.). *5 Ways Pornography Will Ruin Your Life… and How to Break Free.* Retrieved May 9, 2019, from Conquer Series: https://conquerseries.com/5-ways-pornography-will-ruin-life/

References

Archebelle, C. (n.d.). *5 Ways Pornography Will Ruin Your Life... and How to Break Free.* Retrieved May 26, 2019, from Conquer Series: https://conquerseries.com/5-ways-pornography-will-ruin-life/

Bacter, P. (n.d.). *10 ADVANTAGES OF QUITTING PORN.* Retrieved May 12, 2019, from Steemit: https://steemit.com/steemit/@paulobacter/10-reasons-why-you-should-quit-porn

Baesler, A. J. (2017, June 19). *Effects of Pornography in the Workplace.* Retrieved from Slideshare: https://www.slideshare.net/AdamBaesler1/effects-of-pornography-in-the-workplace

Barrett, D. (2015, March 17). *Judges dismissed after watching pornography on court computers.* Retrieved from The Telegraph: https://www.telegraph.co.uk/news/uknews/law-and-order/11476880/Judges-dismissed-after-watching-pornography-on-court-computers.html

Baxter, A. (2018, January 9). *How Pornography Harms Children: The Advocate's Role.* Retrieved from American Bar Association: https://www.americanbar.org/groups/child_law/resources/child_law_practiceonline/child_law_practice/vol-33/may-2014/how-pornography-harms-children--the-advocate-s-role/

Becca. (2019, March 20). *How Pornography Affects Marriage.* Retrieved from The Dating Divas: https://www.thedatingdivas.com/pornography-affects-marriage/

Beck, J. (n.d.). *How Pornography Affects Teenagers [and Children].* Retrieved March 22, 2019, from Ever Accountable: https://everaccountable.com/blog/how-pornography-affects-teenagers-and-children/

Brenner, G. (2018, March 5). *4 Ways Porn Use Causes Problems.* Retrieved from Psychology Today: https://www.psychologytoday.com/intl/blog/experimentations/201803/4-ways-porn-use-causes-problems

Brenner, G. (2017, July 17). *Pornography and Broken Relationships.* Retrieved from Psychology Today: https://www.psychologytoday.com/us/blog/experimentations/201707/pornography-and-broken-relationships

Brenner, G. (2017, July 17). *Pornography and Broken Relationships.* Retrieved from Psychology Today: https://www.psychologytoday.com/intl/blog/experimentations/201707/pornography-and-broken-relationships

Brock, M. (2017, January 30). *The Real Effect of Porn on Women.* Retrieved from Relevant Magazine: https://relevantmagazine.com/current/the-real-effect-of-porn-on-women/

Calonzo, A., & Heijmans, P. (2019, May 12). *The Philippines' Midterm Election Will Test Duterte's Presidency.* Retrieved from Bloomberg: https://www.bloomberg.com/news/articles/2019-05-11/duterte-set-to-gain-allies-shut-out-critics-in-midterm-vote

Chang, M. (2014, August 3). *Why Having Only ONE Orgasm a Month Leads to Success.* Retrieved from Next Shark: https://nextshark.com/this-is-why-the-key-to-productivity-and-success-is-having-only-one-orgasm-a-month/

Covenant Eyes. (n.d.). *Pornography Statistics.* Retrieved May 29, 2019, from Covenant Eyes: https://www.covenanteyes.com/pornstats/

Covenant Eyes. (2015). *Pornography Statistics.* Owosso: Covenant Eyes.

Craig, C. (2014, January 27). *5 Things You MUST Do To Quit Porn – and it's NOT about Porn*. Retrieved from Feed the Right Wolf: http://www.feedtherightwolf.org/2014/01/5-things-you-must-do-to-quit-porn-and-its-not-about-porn/

Culture Reframed. (2017, June 27). *Extensive Research into the Harms of Pornography on Children and Young People*. Retrieved from Culture Reframed: https://www.culturereframed.org/researched-harms/

Cushing, J. (2018, November 1). *Employee Watching Porn At Work Infected US Government Agency's Network*. Retrieved from TechDirt: https://www.techdirt.com/articles/20181031/11124040951/employee-watching-porn-work-infected-us-government-agencys-network.shtml

Darbyshire, M. (2017, December 14). *The consequences of looking at pornography at work*. Retrieved from Financial Times: https://www.ft.com/content/ead0956e-de96-11e7-a0d4-0944c5f49e46

Daubney, M. (2017, March 29). *Men's lives are being ruined by pornography. So why aren't we angry about it?* Retrieved from The Telegraph: https://www.telegraph.co.uk/men/thinking-man/mens-lives-ruined-pornography-arent-angry/

De Robien, M. (2018, April 4). *A family therapist reveals the worst effects of adult content on children*. Retrieved from Aleteia: https://aleteia.org/2018/04/04/a-family-therapist-reveals-the-worst-affects-of-porn-on-children/

Dias, B. (2018, October 1). *The Brain on Porn*. Retrieved from Grey Matters Journal: http://greymattersjournal.com/the-brain-on-porn/

Digital Kids Initiative. (2014, August). *Children and Pornography*. Retrieved from Digital Kids Initative: https://digitalkidsinitiative.com/wp-content/uploads/2014/08/Children_and_Pornography_Factsheet-Revised-August-2014.pdf

Douglas, Z. (2015, May 18). *5 Ways Porn Ruins Relationships*. Retrieved from Relevant Magazine: https://relevantmagazine.com/life5/relationships/5-ways-porn-ruins-relationships/

Doyel, J. (2012, June 4). *How Do I Keep My Husband from Looking at Pornography*. Retrieved from Covenant Eyes: https://www.covenanteyes.com/2012/06/04/how-do-i-keep-my-husband-from-looking-at-pornography/

Emezi, J. (n.d.). *How Pornography Erodes Your Masculinity*. Retrieved May 10, 2019, from Steven Aitchison: https://www.stevenaitchison.co.uk/pornography-erodes-masculinity/

Erickson, M. (2012, May 11). *Braingasm: How Porn "Shuts Down" Women's Brains*. Retrieved from Big Think: https://bigthink.com/think-tank/porn-shuts-down-womens-brains

Fight the New Drug. (2017, February 3). *3 Reasons Why Relationships And Porn Don't Mix*. Retrieved from Fight the New Drug: https://fightthenewdrug.org/3-reasons-why-relationships-and-porn-dont-mix/

Fight the New Drug. (2017, April 11). *3 Ways Porn Damaged Our Relationship & Killed Our Sex Life*. Retrieved from Fight the New Drug: https://fightthenewdrug.org/3-ways-porn-damaged-our-relationship-killed-our-sex-life/

References

Fight the New Drug. (2017, April 2). *4 Hidden Problems With Watching Porn That You Might Not Know*. Retrieved from Fight the New Drug: https://fightthenewdrug.org/hidden-problems-with-watching-porn/

Fight the New Drug. (2018, March 16). *4 Studies That Show How Porn-Obsessed Brains Can Heal Over Time*. Retrieved from Fight the New Drug: https://fightthenewdrug.org/4-studies-that-prove-porn-addicted-brains-can-return-to-normal/

Fight the New Drug. (2018, December 18). *5 Legit Reasons To Stop Watching Porn For Good, Starting Today*. Retrieved from Fight the New Drug: https://fightthenewdrug.org/legit-reasons-stop-watching-porn/

Fight the New Drug. (2019, June 5). *50 Reasons To Add Quitting Porn To Your 2019 Summer Goal List*. Retrieved from Fight the New Drug: https://fightthenewdrug.org/40-reasons-you-should-quit-watching-porn-today/

Fight the New Drug. (2018, August 19). *How My Obsession With Extreme Porn Impacts My Ability To Be Naturally Aroused*. Retrieved from Fight the New Drug: https://fightthenewdrug.org/true-story-how-porn-twisted-my-sexuality/

Fight the New Drug. (2017, July 27). *Kids Who Find Hardcore Porn Want To Repeat What They've Seen, Study Shows*. Retrieved from Fight the New Drug: https://fightthenewdrug.org/massive-study-reveals-what-kids-are-watching-learning-from-online-porn/

Fight the New Drug. (2018, June 20). *Let's Talk About Porn. Is It As Harmless As Society Says It Is?* Retrieved from Fight the New Drug: https://fightthenewdrug.org/3-reasons-why-watching-porn-is-harmful/

Fight the New Drug. (2018, June 20). *Let's Talk About Porn. Is It As Harmless As Society Says It Is?* Retrieved from Fight the New Drug: https://fightthenewdrug.org/3-reasons-why-watching-porn-is-harmful/

Fight the New Drug. (n.d.). *Who Watches More Porn: Guys or Girls? (Infographic)*. Retrieved June 16, 2019, from Fight the New Drug: https://fightthenewdrug.org/media/gender-of-online-pornography-viewers/

Fight the New Drug. (2017, October 25). *Why You Feel Anxious And Disconnected After Watching Porn*. Retrieved from Fight the New Drug: https://fightthenewdrug.org/the-serious-mental-costs-of-watching-porn/

Frank. (2018, April 9). *5 Life-Changing Health Benefits of Nofap*. Retrieved from My Wealth Shop: https://www.mywealthshop.com/health-benefits-of-nofap/

Frank. (2018, May 11). *Nofap and Social Anxiety: Can porn watching be affecting your social life?* Retrieved from My Wealth Shop: https://www.mywealthshop.com/nofap-and-social-anxiety/

Garner, D. (2016, September 15). *Counselor Shares 5 Strategies to Keep Kids from Porn Addiction*. Retrieved from Protect Young Minds: https://protectyoungminds.org/2016/09/15/counselor-strategies-porn-addiction/

Gholiphour, B. (2014, July 7). *Hypersexuality in Women Linked to High Porn Use*. Retrieved from Live Science: https://www.livescience.com/46687-hypersexuality-women.html

Ghose, T. (2015, October 13). *Bye, Bye, Playboy Bunnies: 5 Ways Porn Affects the Brain*. Retrieved from Live Science: https://www.livescience.com/52469-how-porn-affects-brains.html

Gil, N. (2016, August 15). *Women Get Addicted To Porn Too – And It's Equally Damaging*. Retrieved from Refinery 29: https://www.refinery29.com/en-gb/2016/08/120058/porn-womens-health

Gilkerson, L. (2010, December 17). *The Impact of Pornography on Women*. Retrieved from Covenant Eyes: https://www.covenanteyes.com/2010/12/17/the-impact-of-pornography-on-women/

Goulston, M. (2010, January 7). *Why Men Use Porn (and How to Get Yours to Stop)*. Retrieved from Psychology Today: https://www.psychologytoday.com/us/blog/just-listen/201001/why-men-use-porn-and-how-get-yours-stop

Gregoire, S. W. (2014, March 18). *Top 10 Effects of Porn on Your Brain, Your Marriage, and Your Sex Life*. Retrieved from To Love, Honor, & Vacuum: https://tolovehonorandvacuum.com/2014/03/effects-of-porn-on-your-marriage/

Hambrick, B. (2018, September 16). *6 Ways Watching Pornography Affects Your Mental Health*. Retrieved from Church Leaders: https://churchleaders.com/outreach-missions/outreach-missions-articles/333466-6-ways-watching-pornography-affects-your-mental-health-brad-hambrick.html

Huerta, D. (n.d.). *Seven Strategies to Combat Teen Porn Use*. Retrieved March 23, 2019, from Focus on the Family: https://www.focusonthefamily.com/parenting/sexuality/kids-and-pornography/seven-strategies-to-combat-teen-porn-use

Indy 100 Staff. (2018, January 10). *Women watched a lot more porn in 2017*. Retrieved from Indy 100: https://www.indy100.com/article/pornhub-year-in-review-report-2017-women-porn-porography-data-map-infographic-8151131

Jacobs, T. (2017, June 14). *PORN VIEWING IMPACTS ATTITUDES ON WOMEN IN WORKPLACE*. Retrieved from Pacific Standard: https://psmag.com/social-justice/porn-viewing-impacts-attitudes-women-workplace-66280

Ketcham, J. (2012, November 11). *Pornography Does Lasting Harm to Performers*. Retrieved from The New York Times: https://www.nytimes.com/roomfordebate/2012/11/11/does-pornography-deserve-its-bad-rap/pornography-does-lasting-harm-to-performers

Loosemore, P. (2017, February 5). *What Effects Does Porn Have on My Brain?* Retrieved from Addiction Hope: https://www.addictionhope.com/blog/effects-porn-brain/

Los Angeles Daily News. (2012, November 2). *STDs In Porn Industry Higher Than Reported*. Retrieved from HuffPost: https://www.huffpost.com/entry/stds-porn-industry_n_2064639

MacLaughlin, K. (2017, December 19). *The Detrimental Effects of Pornography on Small Children*. Retrieved from Net Nanny: https://www.netnanny.com/blog/the-detrimental-effects-of-pornography-on-small-children/

References

Marripedia. (n.d.). *Effects of Pornography on Adolescents*. Retrieved March 22, 2019, from Marripedia: http://marripedia.org/effects_of_pornography_on_adolescents

McKay, B. (2009, May 11). *The Problem With Porn*. Retrieved from The Art of Maniliness: https://www.artofmanliness.com/articles/the-problem-with-porn/

McKay, B., & McKay, K. (2009, May 11). *The Problem With Porn*. Retrieved from Art of Manliness: https://www.artofmanliness.com/articles/the-problem-with-porn/

Moore, A. (2018, June 26). *Does My Child Need Counseling? Reassuring Advice from a Porn Addiction Therapist*. Retrieved from Protect Young Minds: https://protectyoungminds.org/2018/06/26/does-child-need-counseling-advice-porn-addiction-therapist/

Morris, C. (2018, April 18). *Adult Entertainment Industry Remains Shut Down After Positive HIV Test*. Retrieved from Fortune: http://fortune.com/2018/04/18/adult-entertainment-industry-shut-down-positive-hiv-test-porn/

Mosel, S. (n.d.). *12-STEP BEHAVIORAL ADDICTION SUPPORT GROUPS*. Retrieved April 18, 2019, from Project Know: https://www.projectknow.com/support-groups/

Muresan, R. (2016, September 20). *One in 10 visitors of porn sites is under 10 years old*. Retrieved from Hot for Security: https://hotforsecurity.bitdefender.com/blog/one-in-10-visitors-of-porn-sites-is-under-10-years-old-16675.html

Murray, S. H. (2018, JunE 30). *4 Revelations About Women and Porn*. Retrieved from Psychology Today: https://www.psychologytoday.com/us/blog/myths-desire/201806/4-revelations-about-women-and-porn

National Society for the Prevention of Cruelty to Children. (2016, April 6). *50% of children admit to seeing sexual and violent material online*. Retrieved from National Society for the Prevention of Cruelty to Children: https://www.nspcc.org.uk/what-we-do/news-opinion/net-aware-reveals-risky-social-media-sites/

National Society for the Prevention of Cruelty to Children. (2018, August 30). *New survey reveals risks children and young people face online*. Retrieved from National Society for the Prevention of Cruelty to Children: https://www.nspcc.org.uk/what-we-do/news-opinion/new-survey-online-risks-wild-west-web/

News.com.au. (2016, March 26). *Former porn star Bree Olson goes public: 'I'm shunned by society'*. Retrieved from News.com.au: https://www.news.com.au/entertainment/celebrity-life/former-porn-star-bree-olsen-goes-public-im-shunned-by-society/news-story/106695d7e5eec3e050538697cfac7d28

Park, J. S. (2016, December 1). *4 Unexpected Things That Happen When You Quit Porn*. Retrieved from XXX Church: https://www.xxxchurch.com/men/4-unexpected-things-that-happen-when-you-quit-porn.html

Park, J. S. (2016, December 10). *4 Unexpected Things That Happen When You Quit Porn*. Retrieved from Christian Post: https://www.christianpost.com/news/4-unexpected-things-that-happen-when-you-quit-porn.html

Pattison, M. (2014, May 21). *Research details pornography's harmful effects to women, society*. Retrieved from National Catholic Reporter: https://www.ncronline.org/news/accountability/research-details-pornographys-harmful-effects-women-society

Perry, L. (2016, June). *The Impact of Pornography on Children*. Retrieved from American College of Pediatricians: https://www.acpeds.org/the-college-speaks/position-statements/the-impact-of-pornography-on-children

Pornhub. (2018, December 11). *2018 Year in Review*. Retrieved from Pornhub: https://www.pornhub.com/insights/2018-year-in-review

PornHub. (2018, December 11). *2018 Year in Review*. Retrieved from PornHub: https://www.pornhub.com/insights/2018-year-in-review

Pornhub Insights. (2018, December 11). *2018 Year in Review*. Retrieved from Pornhub: https://www.pornhub.com/insights/2018-year-in-review#gender

Quadarra, A., El-Murr, A., & Latham, J. (2017, December). *The effects of pornography on children and young people*. Retrieved from Australian Institute of Family Studies: https://aifs.gov.au/publications/effects-pornography-children-and-young-people-snapshot

Rausch, J. (2017, July 27). *Porn Addiction Therapy: What You Need to Know*. Retrieved from TalkSpace: https://www.talkspace.com/blog/porn-addiction-therapy-need-know/

Reeves, B. (2015, November 29). *6 Reasons Why Men Who Don't Watch Porn Are Better Lovers*. Retrieved from Thought Catalog: https://thoughtcatalog.com/bryan-reeves/2015/11/6-reasons-why-men-who-dont-watch-porn-are-better-lovers/

Renaud-Komiya, N. (2013, SEptember 4). *Parliament's porn habit revealed as 300,000 attempts made to access 'adult' websites from work computers in last year*. Retrieved from Independent: https://www.independent.co.uk/news/parliaments-porn-habit-revealed-as-300000-attempts-made-to-access-adult-websites-from-work-computers-8797386.html

Ross, C. C. (2012, August 13). *Overexposed and Under-Prepared: The Effects of Early Exposure to Sexual Content*. Retrieved from Psychology Today: https://www.psychologytoday.com/us/blog/real-healing/201208/overexposed-and-under-prepared-the-effects-early-exposure-sexual-content

Scott, C. (2013, November 20). *10 Reasons Why You Should Quit Watching Porn*. Retrieved from GQ: https://www.gq.com/story/10-reasons-why-you-should-quit-watching-porn

Skinner, K. B. (2011, November 22). *Daily Porn May Not Be Good for Your Mental Health*. Retrieved from Psychology Today: https://www.psychologytoday.com/us/blog/inside-porn-addiction/201111/daily-porn-may-not-be-good-your-mental-health

Stritof, S. (2018, September 27). *What to Do When Your Husband Won't Stop Watching Pornography*. Retrieved from Very Well Mind: https://www.verywellmind.com/husband-wont-stop-watching-pornography-2303586

Tackett, B. (n.d.). *ARE YOU ADDICTED TO PORN?* Retrieved April 18, 2019, from Project Know: https://www.projectknow.com/porn-addiction/test/?utm_term=p_addiction

References

The Edge. (2018, August 29). *Can Porn Addiction Lead to Viagra Addiction?* Retrieved from The Edge Rehab: https://www.theedgerehab.com/blog/can-porn-addiction-lead-to-viagra-addiction/

The Fortify Team. (2017, September 18). *How Self-Esteem Issues May Be Fueling Your Struggle With Porn.* Retrieved from Fortify: http://blog.joinfortify.com/self-esteem-pornography/

Thompson, D. (2017, May 12). *Study Sees Link Between Porn and Sexual Dysfunction.* Retrieved from WebMD: https://www.webmd.com/sex/news/20170512/study-sees-link-between-porn-and-sexual-dysfunction#1

Tuell, C. (2016, SeptembeR 30). *Mental illness, Addiction and Digital Infidelity.* Retrieved from Lindner Center of Hope: https://lindnercenterofhope.org/blog/mental-illness-addiction-and-digital-infidelity/

Villines, Z. (2018, July 30). *How can porn induce erectile dysfunction?* Retrieved from Medical News Today: https://www.medicalnewstoday.com/articles/317117.php

WebRoot. (n.d.). *Internet Pornography by the Numbers; A Significant Threat to Society.* Retrieved April 10, 2019, from WebRoot: https://www.webroot.com/us/en/resources/tips-articles/internet-pornography-by-the-numbers

WebRoot. (n.d.). *Internet Pornography by the Numbers; A Significant Threat to Society.* Retrieved 12 2019, May, from WebRoot: https://www.webroot.com/us/en/resources/tips-articles/internet-pornography-by-the-numbers

Weiss, R. (2019, January 30). *3 Ways Porn Is Affecting Your Relationship (And What You Can Do About It).* Retrieved from Mind Body Green: https://www.mindbodygreen.com/0-27470/3-ways-porn-is-affecting-your-relationship-and-what-you-can-do-about-it.html

Weiss, R. (2014, January 20). *Is Male Porn Use Ruining Sex?* Retrieved from Psychology Today: https://www.psychologytoday.com/us/blog/love-and-sex-in-the-digital-age/201401/is-male-porn-use-ruining-sex

Wiley, W. (n.d.). *9 Reasons Why Porn Will Ruin Your Marriage.* Retrieved April 1, 2019, from Debt to Life: http://www.debttolife.com/9-reasons-why-porn-will-ruin-your-marriage

Ybarra, M. L., & Thompson, R. (2017, July 7). *Predicting the Emergence of Sexual Violence in Adolescence.* Retrieved from John Hopkins University: https://jhu.pure.elsevier.com/en/publications/predicting-the-emergence-of-sexual-violence-in-adolescence

Your Brain on Porn. (n.d.). *6 Habits That Will (Indirectly) Help You Quit Porn.* Retrieved April 11, 2019, from Your Brain on Porn: https://www.yourbrainonporn.com/blogs-vlogs-by-friends-of-ybop/reboot-blueprints-blog/6-habits-that-will-indirectly-help-you-quit-porn/

Your Brain on Porn. (n.d.). *How long will it take to recover from Porn-Induced Sexual Dysfunction?* Retrieved April 6, 2019, from Your Brain on Porn: https://www.yourbrainonporn.com/porn-induced-sexual-dysfunctions/how-long-will-it-take-to-recover-from-porn-induced-sexual-dysfunction/

Your Greatest Version. (2017, April 1). *10 Amazing Benefits of NoFap.* Retrieved from Your Greatest Version: https://www.yourgreatestversion.com/benefits-of-nofap/

Your Internet on Porn. (n.d.). *Can porn use affect memory and concentration?* Retrieved April 10, 2019, from Your Internet on Porn: https://www.yourbrainonporn.com/rebooting-porn-use-faqs/can-porn-use-affect-memory-and-concentration/

CHAPTER 11: WOMEN WITHOUT PORN

Addiction.com Staff. (2011, November 20). *Pornography At Work*. Retrieved from Addiction.com: https://www.addiction.com/7819/pornography-at-work/

Al-Kaheel, A. (n.d.). *The dangerous psychological effects of Pornography*. Retrieved April 14, 2019, from Secrets of Quran Miracles: http://www.kaheel7.com/eng/index.php/health-a-medicine/826-the-dangerous-psychological-effects-of-pornography

American Public Health Association. (2010, November 9). *Prevention and Control of Sexually Transmitted Infections and HIV in the Adult Film Industry*. Retrieved from American Public Health Association: https://www.apha.org/policies-and-advocacy/public-health-policy-statements/policy-database/2014/07/28/15/23/prevention-and-control-of-sexually-transmitted-infections-and-hiv-in-the-adult-film-industry

Andrews, C. (n.d.). *8 Harmful Effects of Pornography on Individuals*. Retrieved June 14, 2019, from Educate Empower Kids: https://educateempowerkids.org/8-harmful-effects-of-pornography-on-individuals/

AntiDopamine. (n.d.). *27 NoFap Benefits to Supercharge Your Manliness*. Retrieved May 12, 2019, from AntiDopamine: https://www.antidopamine.com/nofap/list-of-benefits/

Archebelle, C. (n.d.). *5 Ways Pornography Will Ruin Your Life... and How to Break Free*. Retrieved May 9, 2019, from Conquer Series: https://conquerseries.com/5-ways-pornography-will-ruin-life/

Archebelle, C. (n.d.). *5 Ways Pornography Will Ruin Your Life... and How to Break Free*. Retrieved May 26, 2019, from Conquer Series: https://conquerseries.com/5-ways-pornography-will-ruin-life/

Bacter, P. (n.d.). *10 ADVANTAGES OF QUITTING PORN*. Retrieved May 12, 2019, from Steemit: https://steemit.com/steemit/@paulobacter/10-reasons-why-you-should-quit-porn

Baesler, A. J. (2017, June 19). *Effects of Pornography in the Workplace*. Retrieved from Slideshare: https://www.slideshare.net/AdamBaesler1/effects-of-pornography-in-the-workplace

Barrett, D. (2015, March 17). *Judges dismissed after watching pornography on court computers*. Retrieved from The Telegraph: https://www.telegraph.co.uk/news/uknews/law-and-order/11476880/Judges-dismissed-after-watching-pornography-on-court-computers.html

Baxter, A. (2018, January 9). *How Pornography Harms Children: The Advocate's Role*. Retrieved from American Bar Association: https://www.americanbar.org/groups/child_law/resources/child_law_practiceonline/child_law_practice/vol-33/may-2014/how-pornography-harms-children--the-advocate-s-role/

Becca. (2019, March 20). *How Pornography Affects Marriage*. Retrieved from The Dating Divas: https://www.thedatingdivas.com/pornography-affects-marriage/

References

Beck, J. (n.d.). *How Pornography Affects Teenagers [and Children]*. Retrieved March 22, 2019, from Ever Accountable: https://everaccountable.com/blog/how-pornography-affects-teenagers-and-children/

Brenner, G. (2018, March 5). *4 Ways Porn Use Causes Problems*. Retrieved from Psychology Today: https://www.psychologytoday.com/intl/blog/experimentations/201803/4-ways-porn-use-causes-problems

Brenner, G. (2017, July 17). *Pornography and Broken Relationships*. Retrieved from Psychology Today: https://www.psychologytoday.com/us/blog/experimentations/201707/pornography-and-broken-relationships

Brenner, G. (2017, July 17). *Pornography and Broken Relationships*. Retrieved from Psychology Today: https://www.psychologytoday.com/intl/blog/experimentations/201707/pornography-and-broken-relationships

Brock, M. (2017, January 30). *The Real Effect of Porn on Women*. Retrieved from Relevant Magazine: https://relevantmagazine.com/current/the-real-effect-of-porn-on-women/

Calonzo, A., & Heijmans, P. (2019, May 12). *The Philippines' Midterm Election Will Test Duterte's Presidency*. Retrieved from Bloomberg: https://www.bloomberg.com/news/articles/2019-05-11/duterte-set-to-gain-allies-shut-out-critics-in-midterm-vote

Chang, M. (2014, August 3). *Why Having Only ONE Orgasm a Month Leads to Success*. Retrieved from Next Shark: https://nextshark.com/this-is-why-the-key-to-productivity-and-success-is-having-only-one-orgasm-a-month/

Covenant Eyes. (n.d.). *Pornography Statistics*. Retrieved May 29, 2019, from Covenant Eyes: https://www.covenanteyes.com/pornstats/

Covenant Eyes. (2015). *Pornography Statistics*. Owosso: Covenant Eyes.

Craig, C. (2014, January 27). *5 Things You MUST Do To Quit Porn – and it's NOT about Porn*. Retrieved from Feed the Right Wolf: http://www.feedtherightwolf.org/2014/01/5-things-you-must-do-to-quit-porn-and-its-not-about-porn/

Culture Reframed. (2017, June 27). *Extensive Research into the Harms of Pornography on Children and Young People*. Retrieved from Culture Reframed: https://www.culturereframed.org/researched-harms/

Cushing, J. (2018, November 1). *Employee Watching Porn At Work Infected US Government Agency's Network*. Retrieved from TechDirt: https://www.techdirt.com/articles/20181031/11124040951/employee-watching-porn-work-infected-us-government-agencys-network.shtml

Darbyshire, M. (2017, December 14). *The consequences of looking at pornography at work*. Retrieved from Financial Times: https://www.ft.com/content/ead0956e-de96-11e7-a0d4-0944c5f49e46

Daubney, M. (2017, March 29). *Men's lives are being ruined by pornography. So why aren't we angry about it?* Retrieved from The Telegraph: https://www.telegraph.co.uk/men/thinking-man/mens-lives-ruined-pornography-arent-angry/

De Robien, M. (2018, April 4). *A family therapist reveals the worst effects of adult content on children.* Retrieved from Aleteia: https://aleteia.org/2018/04/04/a-family-therapist-reveals-the-worst-affects-of-porn-on-children/

Dias, B. (2018, October 1). *The Brain on Porn.* Retrieved from Grey Matters Journal: http://greymattersjournal.com/the-brain-on-porn/

Digital Kids Initiative. (2014, August). *Children and Pornography.* Retrieved from Digital Kids Initative: https://digitalkidsinitiative.com/wp-content/uploads/2014/08/Children_and_Pornography_Factsheet-Revised-August-2014.pdf

Douglas, Z. (2015, May 18). *5 Ways Porn Ruins Relationships.* Retrieved from Relevant Magazine: https://relevantmagazine.com/life5/relationships/5-ways-porn-ruins-relationships/

Doyel, J. (2012, June 4). *How Do I Keep My Husband from Looking at Pornography.* Retrieved from Covenant Eyes: https://www.covenanteyes.com/2012/06/04/how-do-i-keep-my-husband-from-looking-at-pornography/

Emezi, J. (n.d.). *How Pornography Erodes Your Masculinity.* Retrieved May 10, 2019, from Steven Aitchison: https://www.stevenaitchison.co.uk/pornography-erodes-masculinity/

Erickson, M. (2012, May 11). *Braingasm: How Porn "Shuts Down" Women's Brains.* Retrieved from Big Think: https://bigthink.com/think-tank/porn-shuts-down-womens-brains

Fight the New Drug. (2017, February 3). *3 Reasons Why Relationships And Porn Don't Mix.* Retrieved from Fight the New Drug: https://fightthenewdrug.org/3-reasons-why-relationships-and-porn-dont-mix/

Fight the New Drug. (2017, April 11). *3 Ways Porn Damaged Our Relationship & Killed Our Sex Life.* Retrieved from Fight the New Drug: https://fightthenewdrug.org/3-ways-porn-damaged-our-relationship-killed-our-sex-life/

Fight the New Drug. (2017, April 2). *4 Hidden Problems With Watching Porn That You Might Not Know.* Retrieved from Fight the New Drug: https://fightthenewdrug.org/hidden-problems-with-watching-porn/

Fight the New Drug. (2018, March 16). *4 Studies That Show How Porn-Obsessed Brains Can Heal Over Time.* Retrieved from Fight the New Drug: https://fightthenewdrug.org/4-studies-that-prove-porn-addicted-brains-can-return-to-normal/

Fight the New Drug. (2018, December 18). *5 Legit Reasons To Stop Watching Porn For Good, Starting Today.* Retrieved from Fight the New Drug: https://fightthenewdrug.org/legit-reasons-stop-watching-porn/

Fight the New Drug. (2018, August 19). *How My Obsession With Extreme Porn Impacts My Ability To Be Naturally Aroused.* Retrieved from Fight the New Drug: https://fightthenewdrug.org/true-story-how-porn-twisted-my-sexuality/

Fight the New Drug. (2017, July 27). *Kids Who Find Hardcore Porn Want To Repeat What They've Seen, Study Shows.* Retrieved from Fight the New Drug: https://fightthenewdrug.org/massive-study-reveals-what-kids-are-watching-learning-from-online-porn/

References

Fight the New Drug. (2018, June 20). *Let's Talk About Porn. Is It As Harmless As Society Says It Is?* Retrieved from Fight the New Drug: https://fightthenewdrug.org/3-reasons-why-watching-porn-is-harmful/

Fight the New Drug. (2018, June 20). *Let's Talk About Porn. Is It As Harmless As Society Says It Is?* Retrieved from Fight the New Drug: https://fightthenewdrug.org/3-reasons-why-watching-porn-is-harmful/

Fight the New Drug. (n.d.). *Who Watches More Porn: Guys or Girls? (Infographic).* Retrieved June 16, 2019, from Fight the New Drug: https://fightthenewdrug.org/media/gender-of-online-pornography-viewers/

Fight the New Drug. (2017, October 25). *Why You Feel Anxious And Disconnected After Watching Porn.* Retrieved from Fight the New Drug: https://fightthenewdrug.org/the-serious-mental-costs-of-watching-porn/

Frank. (2018, April 9). *5 Life-Changing Health Benefits of Nofap.* Retrieved from My Wealth Shop: https://www.mywealthshop.com/health-benefits-of-nofap/

Frank. (2018, May 11). *Nofap and Social Anxiety: Can porn watching be affecting your social life?* Retrieved from My Wealth Shop: https://www.mywealthshop.com/nofap-and-social-anxiety/

Garner, D. (2016, September 15). *Counselor Shares 5 Strategies to Keep Kids from Porn Addiction.* Retrieved from Protect Young Minds: https://protectyoungminds.org/2016/09/15/counselor-strategies-porn-addiction/

Gholiphour, B. (2014, July 7). *Hypersexuality in Women Linked to High Porn Use.* Retrieved from Live Science: https://www.livescience.com/46687-hypersexuality-women.html

Ghose, T. (2015, October 13). *Bye, Bye, Playboy Bunnies: 5 Ways Porn Affects the Brain.* Retrieved from Live Science: https://www.livescience.com/52469-how-porn-affects-brains.html

Gil, N. (2016, August 15). *Women Get Addicted To Porn Too – And It's Equally Damaging.* Retrieved from Refinery 29: https://www.refinery29.com/en-gb/2016/08/120058/porn-womens-health

Gilkerson, L. (2010, December 17). *The Impact of Pornography on Women.* Retrieved from Covenant Eyes: https://www.covenanteyes.com/2010/12/17/the-impact-of-pornography-on-women/

Goulston, M. (2010, January 7). *Why Men Use Porn (and How to Get Yours to Stop).* Retrieved from Psychology Today: https://www.psychologytoday.com/us/blog/just-listen/201001/why-men-use-porn-and-how-get-yours-stop

Gregoire, S. W. (2014, March 18). *Top 10 Effects of Porn on Your Brain, Your Marriage, and Your Sex Life.* Retrieved from To Love, Honor, & Vacuum: https://tolovehonorandvacuum.com/2014/03/effects-of-porn-on-your-marriage/

Hambrick, B. (2018, September 16). *6 Ways Watching Pornography Affects Your Mental Health.* Retrieved from Church Leaders: https://churchleaders.com/outreach-missions/outreach-missions-articles/333466-6-ways-watching-pornography-affects-your-mental-health-brad-hambrick.html

Huerta, D. (n.d.). *Seven Strategies to Combat Teen Porn Use*. Retrieved March 23, 2019, from Focus on the Family: https://www.focusonthefamily.com/parenting/sexuality/kids-and-pornography/seven-strategies-to-combat-teen-porn-use

Indy 100 Staff. (2018, January 10). *Women watched a lot more porn in 2017*. Retrieved from Indy 100: https://www.indy100.com/article/pornhub-year-in-review-report-2017-women-porn-porography-data-map-infographic-8151131

Jacobs, T. (2017, June 14). *PORN VIEWING IMPACTS ATTITUDES ON WOMEN IN WORKPLACE*. Retrieved from Pacific Standard: https://psmag.com/social-justice/porn-viewing-impacts-attitudes-women-workplace-66280

Ketcham, J. (2012, November 11). *Pornography Does Lasting Harm to Performers*. Retrieved from The New York Times: https://www.nytimes.com/roomfordebate/2012/11/11/does-pornography-deserve-its-bad-rap/pornography-does-lasting-harm-to-performers

Loosemore, P. (2017, February 5). *What Effects Does Porn Have on My Brain?* Retrieved from Addiction Hope: https://www.addictionhope.com/blog/effects-porn-brain/

Los Angeles Daily News. (2012, November 2). *STDs In Porn Industry Higher Than Reported*. Retrieved from HuffPost: https://www.huffpost.com/entry/stds-porn-industry_n_2064639

MacLaughlin, K. (2017, December 19). *The Detrimental Effects of Pornography on Small Children*. Retrieved from Net Nanny: https://www.netnanny.com/blog/the-detrimental-effects-of-pornography-on-small-children/

Marripedia. (n.d.). *Effects of Pornography on Adolescents*. Retrieved March 22, 2019, from Marripedia: http://marripedia.org/effects_of_pornography_on_adolescents

McKay, B., & McKay, K. (2009, May 11). *The Problem With Porn*. Retrieved from Art of Manliness: https://www.artofmanliness.com/articles/the-problem-with-porn/

Moore, A. (2018, June 26). *Does My Child Need Counseling? Reassuring Advice from a Porn Addiction Therapist*. Retrieved from Protect Young Minds: https://protectyoungminds.org/2018/06/26/does-child-need-counseling-advice-porn-addiction-therapist/

Morris, C. (2018, April 18). *Adult Entertainment Industry Remains Shut Down After Positive HIV Test*. Retrieved from Fortune: http://fortune.com/2018/04/18/adult-entertainment-industry-shut-down-positive-hiv-test-porn/

Mosel, S. (n.d.). *12-STEP BEHAVIORAL ADDICTION SUPPORT GROUPS*. Retrieved April 18, 2019, from Project Know: https://www.projectknow.com/support-groups/

Muresan, R. (2016, September 20). *One in 10 visitors of porn sites is under 10 years old*. Retrieved from Hot for Security: https://hotforsecurity.bitdefender.com/blog/one-in-10-visitors-of-porn-sites-is-under-10-years-old-16675.html

Murray, S. H. (2018, JunE 30). *4 Revelations About Women and Porn*. Retrieved from Psychology Today: https://www.psychologytoday.com/us/blog/myths-desire/201806/4-revelations-about-women-and-porn

References

National Society for the Prevention of Cruelty to Children. (2016, April 6). *50% of children admit to seeing sexual and violent material online*. Retrieved from National Society for the Prevention of Cruelty to Children: https://www.nspcc.org.uk/what-we-do/news-opinion/net-aware-reveals-risky-social-media-sites/

National Society for the Prevention of Cruelty to Children. (2018, August 30). *New survey reveals risks children and young people face online*. Retrieved from National Society for the Prevention of Cruelty to Children: https://www.nspcc.org.uk/what-we-do/news-opinion/new-survey-online-risks-wild-west-web/

News.com.au. (2016, March 26). *Former porn star Bree Olson goes public: 'I'm shunned by society'*. Retrieved from News.com.au: https://www.news.com.au/entertainment/celebrity-life/former-porn-star-bree-olsen-goes-public-im-shunned-by-society/news-story/106695d7e5eec3e050538697cfac7d28

Park, J. S. (2016, December 1). *4 Unexpected Things That Happen When You Quit Porn*. Retrieved from XXX Church: https://www.xxxchurch.com/men/4-unexpected-things-that-happen-when-you-quit-porn.html

Park, J. S. (2016, December 10). *4 Unexpected Things That Happen When You Quit Porn*. Retrieved from Christian Post: https://www.christianpost.com/news/4-unexpected-things-that-happen-when-you-quit-porn.html

Pattison, M. (2014, May 21). *Research details pornography's harmful effects to women, society*. Retrieved from National Catholic Reporter: https://www.ncronline.org/news/accountability/research-details-pornographys-harmful-effects-women-society

Perry, L. (2016, June). *The Impact of Pornography on Children*. Retrieved from American College of Pediatricians: https://www.acpeds.org/the-college-speaks/position-statements/the-impact-of-pornography-on-children

Pornhub. (2018, December 11). *2018 Year in Review*. Retrieved from Pornhub: https://www.pornhub.com/insights/2018-year-in-review

PornHub. (2018, December 11). *2018 Year in Review*. Retrieved from PornHub: https://www.pornhub.com/insights/2018-year-in-review

Quadarra, A., El-Murr, A., & Latham, J. (2017, December). *The effects of pornography on children and young people*. Retrieved from Australian Institute of Family Studies: https://aifs.gov.au/publications/effects-pornography-children-and-young-people-snapshot

Rausch, J. (2017, July 27). *Porn Addiction Therapy: What You Need to Know*. Retrieved from TalkSpace: https://www.talkspace.com/blog/porn-addiction-therapy-need-know/

Renaud-Komiya, N. (2013, SEptember 4). *Parliament's porn habit revealed as 300,000 attempts made to access 'adult' websites from work computers in last year*. Retrieved from Independent: https://www.independent.co.uk/news/parliaments-porn-habit-revealed-as-300000-attempts-made-to-access-adult-websites-from-work-computers-8797386.html

Ross, C. C. (2012, August 13). *Overexposed and Under-Prepared: The Effects of Early Exposure to Sexual Content*. Retrieved from Psychology Today: https://www.psychologytoday.com/us/blog/real-healing/201208/overexposed-and-under-prepared-the-effects-early-exposure-sexual-content

Scott, C. (2013, November 20). *10 Reasons Why You Should Quit Watching Porn*. Retrieved from GQ: https://www.gq.com/story/10-reasons-why-you-should-quit-watching-porn

Skinner, K. B. (2011, November 22). *Daily Porn May Not Be Good for Your Mental Health*. Retrieved from Psychology Today: https://www.psychologytoday.com/us/blog/inside-porn-addiction/201111/daily-porn-may-not-be-good-your-mental-health

Stritof, S. (2018, September 27). *What to Do When Your Husband Won't Stop Watching Pornography*. Retrieved from Very Well Mind: https://www.verywellmind.com/husband-wont-stop-watching-pornography-2303586

Tackett, B. (n.d.). *ARE YOU ADDICTED TO PORN?* Retrieved April 18, 2019, from Project Know: https://www.projectknow.com/porn-addiction/test/?utm_term=p_addiction

The Edge. (2018, August 29). *Can Porn Addiction Lead to Viagra Addiction?* Retrieved from The Edge Rehab: https://www.theedgerehab.com/blog/can-porn-addiction-lead-to-viagra-addiction/

The Fortify Team. (2017, September 18). *How Self-Esteem Issues May Be Fueling Your Struggle With Porn*. Retrieved from Fortify: http://blog.joinfortify.com/self-esteem-pornography/

Thompson, D. (2017, May 12). *Study Sees Link Between Porn and Sexual Dysfunction*. Retrieved from WebMD: https://www.webmd.com/sex/news/20170512/study-sees-link-between-porn-and-sexual-dysfunction#1

Tuell, C. (2016, SeptembeR 30). *Mental illness, Addiction and Digital Infidelity*. Retrieved from Lindner Center of Hope: https://lindnercenterofhope.org/blog/mental-illness-addiction-and-digital-infidelity/

Villines, Z. (2018, July 30). *How can porn induce erectile dysfunction?* Retrieved from Medical News Today: https://www.medicalnewstoday.com/articles/317117.php

WebRoot. (n.d.). *Internet Pornography by the Numbers; A Significant Threat to Society*. Retrieved April 10, 2019, from WebRoot: https://www.webroot.com/us/en/resources/tips-articles/internet-pornography-by-the-numbers

WebRoot. (n.d.). *Internet Pornography by the Numbers; A Significant Threat to Society*. Retrieved 12 2019, May, from WebRoot: https://www.webroot.com/us/en/resources/tips-articles/internet-pornography-by-the-numbers

Weiss, R. (2019, January 30). *3 Ways Porn Is Affecting Your Relationship (And What You Can Do About It)*. Retrieved from Mind Body Green: https://www.mindbodygreen.com/0-27470/3-ways-porn-is-affecting-your-relationship-and-what-you-can-do-about-it.html

Weiss, R. (2014, January 20). *Is Male Porn Use Ruining Sex?* Retrieved from Psychology Today: https://www.psychologytoday.com/us/blog/love-and-sex-in-the-digital-age/201401/is-male-porn-use-ruining-sex

Wiley, W. (n.d.). *9 Reasons Why Porn Will Ruin Your Marriage*. Retrieved April 1, 2019, from Debt to Life: http://www.debttolife.com/9-reasons-why-porn-will-ruin-your-marriage

References

Ybarra, M. L., & Thompson, R. (2017, July 7). *Predicting the Emergence of Sexual Violence in Adolescence*. Retrieved from John Hopkins University: https://jhu.pure.elsevier.com/en/publications/predicting-the-emergence-of-sexual-violence-in-adolescence

Your Brain on Porn. (n.d.). *6 Habits That Will (Indirectly) Help You Quit Porn*. Retrieved April 11, 2019, from Your Brain on Porn: https://www.yourbrainonporn.com/blogs-vlogs-by-friends-of-ybop/reboot-blueprints-blog/6-habits-that-will-indirectly-help-you-quit-porn/

Your Brain on Porn. (n.d.). *How long will it take to recover from Porn-Induced Sexual Dysfunction?* Retrieved April 6, 2019, from Your Brain on Porn: https://www.yourbrainonporn.com/porn-induced-sexual-dysfunctions/how-long-will-it-take-to-recover-from-porn-induced-sexual-dysfunction/

Your Greatest Version. (2017, April 1). *10 Amazing Benefits of NoFap*. Retrieved from Your Greatest Version: https://www.yourgreatestversion.com/benefits-of-nofap/

Your Internet on Porn. (n.d.). *Can porn use affect memory and concentration?* Retrieved April 10, 2019, from Your Internet on Porn: https://www.yourbrainonporn.com/rebooting-porn-use-faqs/can-porn-use-affect-memory-and-concentration/

CHAPTER 12: FAITH WITHOUT PORN

Addiction.com Staff. (2011, November 20). *Pornography At Work*. Retrieved from Addiction.com: https://www.addiction.com/7819/pornography-at-work/

Al-Kaheel, A. (n.d.). *The dangerous psychological effects of Pornography*. Retrieved April 14, 2019, from Secrets of Quran Miracles: http://www.kaheel7.com/eng/index.php/health-a-medicine/826-the-dangerous-psychological-effects-of-pornography

American Public Health Association. (2010, November 9). *Prevention and Control of Sexually Transmitted Infections and HIV in the Adult Film Industry*. Retrieved from American Public Health Association: https://www.apha.org/policies-and-advocacy/public-health-policy-statements/policy-database/2014/07/28/15/23/prevention-and-control-of-sexually-transmitted-infections-and-hiv-in-the-adult-film-industry

Andrews, C. (n.d.). *8 Harmful Effects of Pornography on Individuals*. Retrieved June 14, 2019, from Educate Empower Kids: https://educateempowerkids.org/8-harmful-effects-of-pornography-on-individuals/

AntiDopamine. (n.d.). *27 NoFap Benefits to Supercharge Your Manliness*. Retrieved May 12, 2019, from AntiDopamine: https://www.antidopamine.com/nofap/list-of-benefits/

Archebelle, C. (n.d.). *5 Ways Pornography Will Ruin Your Life... and How to Break Free*. Retrieved May 9, 2019, from Conquer Series: https://conquerseries.com/5-ways-pornography-will-ruin-life/

Archebelle, C. (n.d.). *5 Ways Pornography Will Ruin Your Life... and How to Break Free*. Retrieved May 26, 2019, from Conquer Series: https://conquerseries.com/5-ways-pornography-will-ruin-life/

Bacter, P. (n.d.). *10 ADVANTAGES OF QUITTING PORN*. Retrieved May 12, 2019, from Steemit: https://steemit.com/steemit/@paulobacter/10-reasons-why-you-should-quit-porn

Baesler, A. J. (2017, June 19). *Effects of Pornography in the Workplace.* Retrieved from Slideshare: https://www.slideshare.net/AdamBaesler1/effects-of-pornography-in-the-workplace

Barrett, D. (2015, March 17). *Judges dismissed after watching pornography on court computers.* Retrieved from The Telegraph: https://www.telegraph.co.uk/news/uknews/law-and-order/11476880/Judges-dismissed-after-watching-pornography-on-court-computers.html

Baxter, A. (2018, January 9). *How Pornography Harms Children: The Advocate's Role.* Retrieved from American Bar Association: https://www.americanbar.org/groups/child_law/resources/child_law_practiceonline/child_law_practice/vol-33/may-2014/how-pornography-harms-children--the-advocate-s-role/

Becca. (2019, March 20). *How Pornography Affects Marriage.* Retrieved from The Dating Divas: https://www.thedatingdivas.com/pornography-affects-marriage/

Beck, J. (n.d.). *How Pornography Affects Teenagers [and Children].* Retrieved March 22, 2019, from Ever Accountable: https://everaccountable.com/blog/how-pornography-affects-teenagers-and-children/

Brenner, G. (2018, March 5). *4 Ways Porn Use Causes Problems.* Retrieved from Psychology Today: https://www.psychologytoday.com/intl/blog/experimentations/201803/4-ways-porn-use-causes-problems

Brenner, G. (2017, July 17). *Pornography and Broken Relationships.* Retrieved from Psychology Today: https://www.psychologytoday.com/us/blog/experimentations/201707/pornography-and-broken-relationships

Brenner, G. (2017, July 17). *Pornography and Broken Relationships.* Retrieved from Psychology Today: https://www.psychologytoday.com/intl/blog/experimentations/201707/pornography-and-broken-relationships

Brock, M. (2017, January 30). *The Real Effect of Porn on Women.* Retrieved from Relevant Magazine: https://relevantmagazine.com/current/the-real-effect-of-porn-on-women/

Calonzo, A., & Heijmans, P. (2019, May 12). *The Philippines' Midterm Election Will Test Duterte's Presidency.* Retrieved from Bloomberg: https://www.bloomberg.com/news/articles/2019-05-11/duterte-set-to-gain-allies-shut-out-critics-in-midterm-vote

Challies, T. (2017, April 25). *8 Sins You Commit Whenever You Look at Porn.* Retrieved from Challies: https://www.challies.com/articles/8-sins-you-commit-whenever-you-look-at-porn/

Chang, M. (2014, August 3). *Why Having Only ONE Orgasm a Month Leads to Success.* Retrieved from Next Shark: https://nextshark.com/this-is-why-the-key-to-productivity-and-success-is-having-only-one-orgasm-a-month/

Covenant Eyes. (n.d.). *Pornography Statistics.* Retrieved May 29, 2019, from Covenant Eyes: https://www.covenanteyes.com/pornstats/

Covenant Eyes. (2015). *Pornography Statistics.* Owosso: Covenant Eyes.

Craig, C. (2014, January 27). *5 Things You MUST Do To Quit Porn – and it's NOT about Porn.* Retrieved from Feed the Right Wolf: http://www.feedtherightwolf.org/2014/01/5-things-you-must-do-to-quit-porn-and-its-not-about-porn/

References

Culture Reframed. (2017, June 27). *Extensive Research into the Harms of Pornography on Children and Young People*. Retrieved from Culture Reframed: https://www.culturereframed.org/researched-harms/

Cushing, J. (2018, November 1). *Employee Watching Porn At Work Infected US Government Agency's Network*. Retrieved from TechDirt: https://www.techdirt.com/articles/20181031/11124040951/employee-watching-porn-work-infected-us-government-agencys-network.shtml

CWALAC Staff. (2014, August 5). *Spiritual and Physical Harms of Pornography*. Retrieved from Concerned Women for America: https://concernedwomen.org/spiritual-and-physical-harms-of-pornography/

Darbyshire, M. (2017, December 14). *The consequences of looking at pornography at work*. Retrieved from Financial Times: https://www.ft.com/content/ead0956e-de96-11e7-a0d4-0944c5f49e46

Daubney, M. (2017, March 29). *Men's lives are being ruined by pornography. So why aren't we angry about it?* Retrieved from The Telegraph: https://www.telegraph.co.uk/men/thinking-man/mens-lives-ruined-pornography-arent-angry/

De Robien, M. (2018, April 4). *A family therapist reveals the worst effects of adult content on children*. Retrieved from Aleteia: https://aleteia.org/2018/04/04/a-family-therapist-reveals-the-worst-affects-of-porn-on-children/

Dias, B. (2018, October 1). *The Brain on Porn*. Retrieved from Grey Matters Journal: http://greymattersjournal.com/the-brain-on-porn/

Digital Kids Initiative. (2014, August). *Children and Pornography*. Retrieved from Digital Kids Initative: https://digitalkidsinitiative.com/wp-content/uploads/2014/08/Children_and_Pornography_Factsheet-Revised-August-2014.pdf

Douglas, Z. (2015, May 18). *5 Ways Porn Ruins Relationships*. Retrieved from Relevant Magazine: https://relevantmagazine.com/life5/relationships/5-ways-porn-ruins-relationships/

Doyel, J. (2012, June 4). *How Do I Keep My Husband from Looking at Pornography*. Retrieved from Covenant Eyes: https://www.covenanteyes.com/2012/06/04/how-do-i-keep-my-husband-from-looking-at-pornography/

Emezi, J. (n.d.). *How Pornography Erodes Your Masculinity*. Retrieved May 10, 2019, from Steven Aitchison: https://www.stevenaitchison.co.uk/pornography-erodes-masculinity/

Erickson, M. (2012, May 11). *Braingasm: How Porn "Shuts Down" Women's Brains*. Retrieved from Big Think: https://bigthink.com/think-tank/porn-shuts-down-womens-brains

Fight the New Drug. (2017, February 3). *3 Reasons Why Relationships And Porn Don't Mix*. Retrieved from Fight the New Drug: https://fightthenewdrug.org/3-reasons-why-relationships-and-porn-dont-mix/

Fight the New Drug. (2017, April 11). *3 Ways Porn Damaged Our Relationship & Killed Our Sex Life*. Retrieved from Fight the New Drug: https://fightthenewdrug.org/3-ways-porn-damaged-our-relationship-killed-our-sex-life/

Fight the New Drug. (2017, April 2). *4 Hidden Problems With Watching Porn That You Might Not Know*. Retrieved from Fight the New Drug: https://fightthenewdrug.org/hidden-problems-with-watching-porn/

Fight the New Drug. (2018, March 16). *4 Studies That Show How Porn-Obsessed Brains Can Heal Over Time*. Retrieved from Fight the New Drug: https://fightthenewdrug.org/4-studies-that-prove-porn-addicted-brains-can-return-to-normal/

Fight the New Drug. (2018, December 18). *5 Legit Reasons To Stop Watching Porn For Good, Starting Today*. Retrieved from Fight the New Drug: https://fightthenewdrug.org/legit-reasons-stop-watching-porn/

Fight the New Drug. (2019, June 5). *50 Reasons To Add Quitting Porn To Your 2019 Summer Goal List*. Retrieved from Fight the New Drug: https://fightthenewdrug.org/40-reasons-you-should-quit-watching-porn-today/

Fight the New Drug. (2018, August 19). *How My Obsession With Extreme Porn Impacts My Ability To Be Naturally Aroused*. Retrieved from Fight the New Drug: https://fightthenewdrug.org/true-story-how-porn-twisted-my-sexuality/

Fight the New Drug. (2017, July 27). *Kids Who Find Hardcore Porn Want To Repeat What They've Seen, Study Shows*. Retrieved from Fight the New Drug: https://fightthenewdrug.org/massive-study-reveals-what-kids-are-watching-learning-from-online-porn/

Fight the New Drug. (2018, June 20). *Let's Talk About Porn. Is It As Harmless As Society Says It Is?* Retrieved from Fight the New Drug: https://fightthenewdrug.org/3-reasons-why-watching-porn-is-harmful/

Fight the New Drug. (2018, June 20). *Let's Talk About Porn. Is It As Harmless As Society Says It Is?* Retrieved from Fight the New Drug: https://fightthenewdrug.org/3-reasons-why-watching-porn-is-harmful/

Fight the New Drug. (n.d.). *Who Watches More Porn: Guys or Girls? (Infographic)*. Retrieved June 16, 2019, from Fight the New Drug: https://fightthenewdrug.org/media/gender-of-online-pornography-viewers/

Fight the New Drug. (2017, October 25). *Why You Feel Anxious And Disconnected After Watching Porn*. Retrieved from Fight the New Drug: https://fightthenewdrug.org/the-serious-mental-costs-of-watching-porn/

Frank. (2018, April 9). *5 Life-Changing Health Benefits of Nofap*. Retrieved from My Wealth Shop: https://www.mywealthshop.com/health-benefits-of-nofap/

Frank. (2018, May 11). *Nofap and Social Anxiety: Can porn watching be affecting your social life?* Retrieved from My Wealth Shop: https://www.mywealthshop.com/nofap-and-social-anxiety/

Garner, D. (2016, September 15). *Counselor Shares 5 Strategies to Keep Kids from Porn Addiction*. Retrieved from Protect Young Minds: https://protectyoungminds.org/2016/09/15/counselor-strategies-porn-addiction/

Gholiphour, B. (2014, July 7). *Hypersexuality in Women Linked to High Porn Use*. Retrieved from Live Science: https://www.livescience.com/46687-hypersexuality-women.html

References

Ghose, T. (2015, October 13). *Bye, Bye, Playboy Bunnies: 5 Ways Porn Affects the Brain*. Retrieved from Live Science: https://www.livescience.com/52469-how-porn-affects-brains.html

Gibbons, L. (2018, September 18). *15 Statistics About the Church and Pornography That Will Blow Your Mind*. Retrieved from Charisma News: https://www.charismanews.com/us/73208-15-statistics-about-the-church-and-pornography-that-will-blow-your-mind

Gil, N. (2016, August 15). *Women Get Addicted To Porn Too – And It's Equally Damaging*. Retrieved from Refinery 29: https://www.refinery29.com/en-gb/2016/08/120058/porn-womens-health

Gilkerson, L. (2010, December 17). *The Impact of Pornography on Women*. Retrieved from Covenant Eyes: https://www.covenanteyes.com/2010/12/17/the-impact-of-pornography-on-women/

Goulston, M. (2010, January 7). *Why Men Use Porn (and How to Get Yours to Stop)*. Retrieved from Psychology Today: https://www.psychologytoday.com/us/blog/just-listen/201001/why-men-use-porn-and-how-get-yours-stop

Gregoire, S. W. (2014, March 18). *Top 10 Effects of Porn on Your Brain, Your Marriage, and Your Sex Life*. Retrieved from To Love, Honor, & Vacuum: https://tolovehonorandvacuum.com/2014/03/effects-of-porn-on-your-marriage/

Hambrick, B. (2018, September 16). *6 Ways Watching Pornography Affects Your Mental Health*. Retrieved from Church Leaders: https://churchleaders.com/outreach-missions/outreach-missions-articles/333466-6-ways-watching-pornography-affects-your-mental-health-brad-hambrick.html

Huerta, D. (n.d.). *Seven Strategies to Combat Teen Porn Use*. Retrieved March 23, 2019, from Focus on the Family: https://www.focusonthefamily.com/parenting/sexuality/kids-and-pornography/seven-strategies-to-combat-teen-porn-use

Indy 100 Staff. (2018, January 10). *Women watched a lot more porn in 2017*. Retrieved from Indy 100: https://www.indy100.com/article/pornhub-year-in-review-report-2017-women-porn-porography-data-map-infographic-8151131

Jacobs, T. (2017, June 14). *PORN VIEWING IMPACTS ATTITUDES ON WOMEN IN WORKPLACE*. Retrieved from Pacific Standard: https://psmag.com/social-justice/porn-viewing-impacts-attitudes-women-workplace-66280

Ketcham, J. (2012, November 11). *Pornography Does Lasting Harm to Performers*. Retrieved from The New York Times: https://www.nytimes.com/roomfordebate/2012/11/11/does-pornography-deserve-its-bad-rap/pornography-does-lasting-harm-to-performers

Ley, D. J. (2016, June 8). *Porn vs. Religion*. Retrieved from Psychology Today: https://www.psychologytoday.com/us/blog/women-who-stray/201606/porn-vs-religion

Loosemore, P. (2017, February 5). *What Effects Does Porn Have on My Brain?* Retrieved from Addiction Hope: https://www.addictionhope.com/blog/effects-porn-brain/

Los Angeles Daily News. (2012, November 2). *STDs In Porn Industry Higher Than Reported*. Retrieved from HuffPost: https://www.huffpost.com/entry/stds-porn-industry_n_2064639

MacLaughlin, K. (2017, December 19). *The Detrimental Effects of Pornography on Small Children*. Retrieved from Net Nanny: https://www.netnanny.com/blog/the-detrimental-effects-of-pornography-on-small-children/

Marripedia. (n.d.). *Effects of Pornography on Adolescents*. Retrieved March 22, 2019, from Marripedia: http://marripedia.org/effects_of_pornography_on_adolescents

McKay, B. (2009, May 11). *The Problem With Porn*. Retrieved from The Art of Maniliness: https://www.artofmanliness.com/articles/the-problem-with-porn/

McKay, B., & McKay, K. (2009, May 11). *The Problem With Porn*. Retrieved from Art of Manliness: https://www.artofmanliness.com/articles/the-problem-with-porn/

Moore, A. (2018, June 26). *Does My Child Need Counseling? Reassuring Advice from a Porn Addiction Therapist*. Retrieved from Protect Young Minds: https://protectyoungminds.org/2018/06/26/does-child-need-counseling-advice-porn-addiction-therapist/

Morris, C. (2018, April 18). *Adult Entertainment Industry Remains Shut Down After Positive HIV Test*. Retrieved from Fortune: http://fortune.com/2018/04/18/adult-entertainment-industry-shut-down-positive-hiv-test-porn/

Mosel, S. (n.d.). *12-STEP BEHAVIORAL ADDICTION SUPPORT GROUPS*. Retrieved April 18, 2019, from Project Know: https://www.projectknow.com/support-groups/

Muresan, R. (2016, September 20). *One in 10 visitors of porn sites is under 10 years old*. Retrieved from Hot for Security: https://hotforsecurity.bitdefender.com/blog/one-in-10-visitors-of-porn-sites-is-under-10-years-old-16675.html

Murray, S. H. (2018, JunE 30). *4 Revelations About Women and Porn*. Retrieved from Psychology Today: https://www.psychologytoday.com/us/blog/myths-desire/201806/4-revelations-about-women-and-porn

Naselli, A. (2016, December). Seven Reasons You Should Not Indulge in Pornography. *Themelios, 41* (3).

National Society for the Prevention of Cruelty to Children. (2016, April 6). *50% of children admit to seeing sexual and violent material online*. Retrieved from National Society for the Prevention of Cruelty to Children: https://www.nspcc.org.uk/what-we-do/news-opinion/net-aware-reveals-risky-social-media-sites/

National Society for the Prevention of Cruelty to Children. (2018, August 30). *New survey reveals risks children and young people face online*. Retrieved from National Society for the Prevention of Cruelty to Children: https://www.nspcc.org.uk/what-we-do/news-opinion/new-survey-online-risks-wild-west-web/

News.com.au. (2016, March 26). *Former porn star Bree Olson goes public: 'I'm shunned by society'*. Retrieved from News.com.au: https://www.news.com.au/entertainment/celebrity-life/former-porn-star-bree-olsen-goes-public-im-shunned-by-society/news-story/106695d7e5eec3e050538697cfac7d28

Park, J. S. (2016, December 1). *4 Unexpected Things That Happen When You Quit Porn*. Retrieved from XXX Church: https://www.xxxchurch.com/men/4-unexpected-things-that-happen-when-you-quit-porn.html

References

Park, J. S. (2016, December 10). *4 Unexpected Things That Happen When You Quit Porn*. Retrieved from Christian Post: https://www.christianpost.com/news/4-unexpected-things-that-happen-when-you-quit-porn.html

Pattison, M. (2014, May 21). *Research details pornography's harmful effects to women, society*. Retrieved from National Catholic Reporter: https://www.ncronline.org/news/accountability/research-details-pornographys-harmful-effects-women-society

Perry, L. (2016, June). *The Impact of Pornography on Children*. Retrieved from American College of Pediatricians: https://www.acpeds.org/the-college-speaks/position-statements/the-impact-of-pornography-on-children

Pornhub. (2018, December 11). *2018 Year in Review*. Retrieved from Pornhub: https://www.pornhub.com/insights/2018-year-in-review

PornHub. (2018, December 11). *2018 Year in Review*. Retrieved from PornHub: https://www.pornhub.com/insights/2018-year-in-review

Pornhub Insights. (2018, December 11). *2018 Year in Review*. Retrieved from Pornhub: https://www.pornhub.com/insights/2018-year-in-review#gender

Proven Men. (2016, March 1). *3 WAYS PORNOGRAPHY AFFECTS YOUR RELATIONSHIP WITH GOD*. Retrieved from Proven Men: https://www.provenmen.org/pornography-affect-relationship-god/

Quadarra, A., El-Murr, A., & Latham, J. (2017, December). *The effects of pornography on children and young people*. Retrieved from Australian Institute of Family Studies: https://aifs.gov.au/publications/effects-pornography-children-and-young-people-snapshot

Rausch, J. (2017, July 27). *Porn Addiction Therapy: What You Need to Know*. Retrieved from TalkSpace: https://www.talkspace.com/blog/porn-addiction-therapy-need-know/

Ray, S. (2014, September 2). *Stunning Statistics on Christian Men and Porn*. Retrieved from Catholic Convert: https://www.catholicconvert.com/blog/2014/09/02/stunning-statistics-on-christian-men-and-porn/

Reeves, B. (2015, November 29). *6 Reasons Why Men Who Don't Watch Porn Are Better Lovers*. Retrieved from Thought Catalog: https://thoughtcatalog.com/bryan-reeves/2015/11/6-reasons-why-men-who-dont-watch-porn-are-better-lovers/

Renaud-Komiya, N. (2013, SEptember 4). *Parliament's porn habit revealed as 300,000 attempts made to access 'adult' websites from work computers in last year*. Retrieved from Independent: https://www.independent.co.uk/news/parliaments-porn-habit-revealed-as-300000-attempts-made-to-access-adult-websites-from-work-computers-8797386.html

Ross, C. C. (2012, August 13). *Overexposed and Under-Prepared: The Effects of Early Exposure to Sexual Content*. Retrieved from Psychology Today: https://www.psychologytoday.com/us/blog/real-healing/201208/overexposed-and-under-prepared-the-effects-early-exposure-sexual-content

Scott, C. (2013, November 20). *10 Reasons Why You Should Quit Watching Porn*. Retrieved from GQ: https://www.gq.com/story/10-reasons-why-you-should-quit-watching-porn

Skinner, K. B. (2011, November 22). *Daily Porn May Not Be Good for Your Mental Health*. Retrieved from Psychology Today: https://www.psychologytoday.com/us/blog/inside-porn-addiction/201111/daily-porn-may-not-be-good-your-mental-health

Stritof, S. (2018, September 27). *What to Do When Your Husband Won't Stop Watching Pornography*. Retrieved from Very Well Mind: https://www.verywellmind.com/husband-wont-stop-watching-pornography-2303586

Tackett, B. (n.d.). *ARE YOU ADDICTED TO PORN?* Retrieved April 18, 2019, from Project Know: https://www.projectknow.com/porn-addiction/test/?utm_term=p_addiction

The Edge. (2018, August 29). *Can Porn Addiction Lead to Viagra Addiction?* Retrieved from The Edge Rehab: https://www.theedgerehab.com/blog/can-porn-addiction-lead-to-viagra-addiction/

The Fortify Team. (2017, September 18). *How Self-Esteem Issues May Be Fueling Your Struggle With Porn*. Retrieved from Fortify: http://blog.joinfortify.com/self-esteem-pornography/

Thompson, D. (2017, May 12). *Study Sees Link Between Porn and Sexual Dysfunction*. Retrieved from WebMD: https://www.webmd.com/sex/news/20170512/study-sees-link-between-porn-and-sexual-dysfunction#1

Tuell, C. (2016, SeptembeR 30). *Mental illness, Addiction and Digital Infidelity*. Retrieved from Lindner Center of Hope: https://lindnercenterofhope.org/blog/mental-illness-addiction-and-digital-infidelity/

Villines, Z. (2018, July 30). *How can porn induce erectile dysfunction?* Retrieved from Medical News Today: https://www.medicalnewstoday.com/articles/317117.php

WebRoot. (n.d.). *Internet Pornography by the Numbers; A Significant Threat to Society*. Retrieved April 10, 2019, from WebRoot: https://www.webroot.com/us/en/resources/tips-articles/internet-pornography-by-the-numbers

WebRoot. (n.d.). *Internet Pornography by the Numbers; A Significant Threat to Society*. Retrieved 12 2019, May, from WebRoot: https://www.webroot.com/us/en/resources/tips-articles/internet-pornography-by-the-numbers

Weiss, R. (2019, January 30). *3 Ways Porn Is Affecting Your Relationship (And What You Can Do About It)*. Retrieved from Mind Body Green: https://www.mindbodygreen.com/0-27470/3-ways-porn-is-affecting-your-relationship-and-what-you-can-do-about-it.html

Weiss, R. (2014, January 20). *Is Male Porn Use Ruining Sex?* Retrieved from Psychology Today: https://www.psychologytoday.com/us/blog/love-and-sex-in-the-digital-age/201401/is-male-porn-use-ruining-sex

Wiley, W. (n.d.). *9 Reasons Why Porn Will Ruin Your Marriage*. Retrieved April 1, 2019, from Debt to Life: http://www.debttolife.com/9-reasons-why-porn-will-ruin-your-marriage

Ybarra, M. L., & Thompson, R. (2017, July 7). *Predicting the Emergence of Sexual Violence in Adolescence*. Retrieved from John Hopkins University: https://jhu.pure.elsevier.com/en/publications/predicting-the-emergence-of-sexual-violence-in-adolescence

References

Your Brain on Porn. (n.d.). *6 Habits That Will (Indirectly) Help You Quit Porn*. Retrieved April 11, 2019, from Your Brain on Porn: https://www.yourbrainonporn.com/blogs-vlogs-by-friends-of-ybop/reboot-blueprints-blog/6-habits-that-will-indirectly-help-you-quit-porn/

Your Brain on Porn. (n.d.). *How long will it take to recover from Porn-Induced Sexual Dysfunction?* Retrieved April 6, 2019, from Your Brain on Porn: https://www.yourbrainonporn.com/porn-induced-sexual-dysfunctions/how-long-will-it-take-to-recover-from-porn-induced-sexual-dysfunction/

Your Greatest Version. (2017, April 1). *10 Amazing Benefits of NoFap*. Retrieved from Your Greatest Version: https://www.yourgreatestversion.com/benefits-of-nofap/

Your Internet on Porn. (n.d.). *Can porn use affect memory and concentration?* Retrieved April 10, 2019, from Your Internet on Porn: https://www.yourbrainonporn.com/rebooting-porn-use-faqs/can-porn-use-affect-memory-and-concentration/

Notes

Aware

Notes

www.ingramcontent.com/pod-product-compliance
Lightning Source LLC
Chambersburg PA
CBHW021832110526
R18278200001B/R182782PG44588CBX00007B/9